The Executioner's Knife

Or, Joan of Arc

Eugène Sue

Alpha Editions

This edition published in 2021

ISBN : 9789355340726

Design and Setting By
Alpha Editions
www.alphaedis.com
Email - info@alphaedis.com

As per information held with us this book is in Public Domain.
This book is a reproduction of an important historical work. Alpha Editions uses the best technology to reproduce historical work in the same manner it was first published to preserve its original nature. Any marks or number seen are left intentionally to preserve its true form.

Contents

TRANSLATOR'S PREFACE.	- 1 -
PART I. DOMREMY	- 3 -
CHAPTER I. JEANNETTE.	- 5 -
CHAPTER II. GILLON THE FURTIVE.	- 7 -
CHAPTER III. AT THE FOUNTAIN OF THE FAIRIES.	- 10 -
CHAPTER IV. THE HARP OF MERLIN.	- 14 -
CHAPTER V. THE PROPHECY OF MERLIN.	- 20 -
CHAPTER VI. THE LEGEND OF HENA.	- 25 -
CHAPTER VII. GERMINATION.	- 29 -
CHAPTER VIII. THE ENGLISH!	- 31 -
CHAPTER IX. THE FLIGHT.	- 36 -
CHAPTER X. "BURGUNDY!"—"FRANCE!"	- 38 -
CHAPTER XI. THE VISION.	- 45 -
CHAPTER XII. RETURNING VISIONS.	- 48 -
CHAPTER XIII. WRESTLING WITH THE ANGELS.	- 51 -
CHAPTER XIV. "THE TIME HAS ARRIVED."	- 54 -
CHAPTER XV. CAPTAIN ROBERT OF BAUDRICOURT.	- 57 -

CHAPTER XVI. AT THE CASTLE OF VAUCOULEURS.	- 60 -
CHAPTER XVII. JOHN OF NOVELPONT.	- 65 -
CHAPTER XVIII. "GOOD LUCK, JOAN!"	- 68 -
PART II. CHINON.	- 73 -
CHAPTER I. THE COUNCIL OF CHARLES VII.	- 75 -
CHAPTER II. ALOYSE OF CASTELNAU.	- 81 -
CHAPTER III. THE TEST.	- 85 -
CHAPTER IV. THE HALL OF RABATEAU.	- 88 -
PART III. ORLEANS.	- 97 -
CHAPTER I. FRIDAY, APRIL 29, 1429.	- 99 -
CHAPTER II. SATURDAY, APRIL 30, 1429.	- 105 -
CHAPTER III. SUNDAY, MAY 1, 1429.	- 110 -
CHAPTER IV. MONDAY, MAY 2, 1429.	- 112 -
CHAPTER V. TUESDAY, MAY 3, 1429.	- 113 -
CHAPTER VI. WEDNESDAY, MAY 4, 1429.	- 114 -
CHAPTER VII. THURSDAY, MAY 5, 1429.	- 124 -
CHAPTER VIII. FRIDAY, MAY 6, 1429.	- 130 -
CHAPTER IX. SATURDAY, MAY 7, 1429.	- 141 -
CHAPTER X. THE KING CROWNED.	- 148 -
PART IV. ROUEN; OR, THE MYSTERY OF THE PASSION OF JOAN DARC	- 157 -

CHAPTER I. BISHOP AND CANON.	- 159 -
CHAPTER II. IN THE DUNGEON.	- 179 -
CHAPTER III. THE INQUISITION.	- 189 -
CHAPTER IV. THE TEMPTATION.	- 207 -
CHAPTER V. THE SENTENCE.	- 214 -
CHAPTER VI. PHYSICAL COLLAPSE.	- 223 -
CHAPTER VII. REMORSE.	- 237 -
CHAPTER VIII. THE RELAPSE.	- 241 -
CHAPTER IX. THE WORM TURNS.	- 243 -
CHAPTER X. TO THE FLAMES!	- 246 -
CHAPTER XI. THE PYRE.	- 250 -
EPILOGUE.	- 259 -
FOOTNOTES:	- 262 -

TRANSLATOR'S PREFACE.

Whether one will be satisfied with nothing but a scientific diagnosis in psychology, or a less ponderous and infinitely more lyric presentation of certain mental phenomena will do for him; whether the student of history insist on strict chronology, or whether he prize at its true value the meat and coloring of history; whether a reader prefer in matters canonical the rigid presentation of dogma, or whether the tragic fruits of theocracy offer a more attractive starting point for his contemplation;—whichever the case might be, *The Executioner's Knife; or, Joan of Arc* will gratify his intellectual cravings on all the three heads.

This, the fifteenth story of the series of Eugene Sue's matchless historic novels entitled *The Mysteries of the People; or, History of a Proletarian Family Across the Ages*, presents the picture of the Fifteenth Century—a historic elevation climbed up to from the hills of the era sketched in the preceding story, *The Iron Trevet; or Jocelyn the Champion*, and from which, in turn, the outlines become vaguely visible of the critically historic era that forms the subject of the next story, *The Pocket Bible; or, Christian the Printer*.

As in all the stories of this stupendous series bestowed by the genius of Sue upon posterity, the leading characters are historic, the leading events are historic, and the coloring is true to history. How true to the facts are the historic revelations made by the author in this series, and how historically true are the conclusions he draws, as they rise in relief on the canvas of these novels, appears with peculiar conspicuousness in *The Executioner's Knife; or, Joan of Arc*, above all in this century, when the science of history has remodeled its theory, and, instead of, as in former days, basing man's acts upon impulse, has learned to plant impulse upon material facts.

In the pages of this story the central figure is the charming one generally known to history as the Maid of Orleans. If ever there was in the annals of man a figure that superstitious mysticism combined with grovelling interests to annihilate, it was the figure of the pure-minded, self-sacrificing, intrepid shepherdess of Domremy. Even the genius of a Voltaire succumbed. In righteous revolt against man-degrading superstition, his satire "La Pucelle" in fact contributed, by the slur it placed upon Joan, to vindicate the very lay and prelatical interests he fought, and whose predecessors dragged her name through the ditch and had consigned her body to the flames. Harried by the political interests whom her integrity of purpose menaced and actually thwarted; insulted and put to death by the allies of these, ambushed behind religion; the successors of both elements perpetuating the wrong with false history; and even the enlightened contributing their sneers out of just repugnance for supernaturalism;—all this notwithstanding, the figure of Joan triumphed. Even the head of the prelatic political machine, which had presumed to speak in the name of the Deity with Anathema over Joan's head, has felt constrained to fall in line with the awakened popular knowledge. The Papal beatification of Joan of Arc in this century is a public retraction and apology to the heroine born from the lowly.

Of the many works of art—poetic, dramatic, pictorial—that have contributed to this conspicuous "reversal of judgment" Sue's *The Executioner's Knife; or, Joan of Arc* has been the most powerful. The pathetic story cleanses Joan of the miraculous, uncovers the grovelling influences she had to contend against, exposes the sordid ambitions she had to overcome and that finally slaked their vengeance in her blood. The master's hand weaves together and draws, in the garb of fiction, a picture that is monumental—at once as a work of science, of history and of art.

DANIEL DE LEON.

Milford, Conn., October, 1909.

PART I.

DOMREMY

CHAPTER I.

JEANNETTE.

Domremy is a frontier village of Lorraine that cosily nestles on the slope of a fertile valley whose pasture grounds are watered by the Meuse. An oak forest, that still preserves some mementoes of druid tradition, reaches out almost to the village church. This church is the handsomest of all in the valley, which begins at Vaucouleurs and ends at Domremy. St. Catherine and St. Marguerite, superbly painted and gilded, ornament the sanctuary. St. Michael, the Archangel, with his sword in one hand and the scales in the other, glistens from the depths of a dark recess in the chapel. Happy is the valley that begins at Vaucouleurs and ends at Domremy! A royal seigniory, lost on the confines of Gaul, it has not yet suffered from the disasters of war that for more than a half century have been desolating the center of the country. Its inhabitants, profiting by the civil broils of their sovereign and his distance from them, being separated from his main domains by Champagne, which had fallen into the power of the English, had emancipated themselves from serfdom.

James Darc, a member of a family that had long been serfs of the Abbey of St. Remy, and subsequently of the Sire of Joinville before the fief of Vaucouleurs was consolidated with the royal domain, an honest laborer, stern head of his household and rather rude of manners, lived by the cultivation of the fields. His wife was called Isabelle Romée; his eldest son, Peter; the second, John; and his daughter, born on "the day of Kings" in 1412, was named Jeannette. At the time when this narrative commences, Jeannette was a little over thirteen years of age. She was of pleasant appearance, a sweet and pious child and endowed with precocious intelligence. Her disposition was serious for her age. This notwithstanding, she joined in the games of other girls, her friends, and never gloried in her own superior agility when, as usually happened, she won in the races. She could neither read nor write. Active and industrious, she helped her mother in the household, led the sheep to pasture and was skilful with the needle and at the distaff. Often pensive, when alone in secluded spots of the woods she watched over her flock, she found an inexpressible delight in listening to the distant sound of the church bells, to the point that at times she made little presents of fruits or skeins of wool to the parish clerk of Domremy, joining to the gifts the gentle request that he prolong a little the chimes of the vespers or of the Angelus.[1] Jeannette also took delight in leading her sheep in the ancient forest of oaks, known as the "Bois Chesnu",[2] towards a limpid spring shaded by a beech tree that was between two and three hundred years old and which was known in the region as the "Fairies' Tree". The legend had it that the priests of the old gods of Gaul sometimes appeared, dressed in their long white robes, under the dark vaults of the oaks of this forest, and that often little fairies approached the fountain by moonlight to see their reflection in its waters.

Jeannette did not fear the fairies, knowing that a single sign of the cross would put any malignant sprite to flight. She entertained a special spirit of devotion for St. Marguerite and St. Catherine, the two beautiful saints of the parish. When, on feast days, she accompanied her venerated parents to divine service, she was never tired of contemplating and admiring the good saints, who were at once smiling and majestic under their golden crowns. Likewise did St. Michael attract her attention. But the severity of the archangel's face and his flaming sword somewhat intimidated the young shepherdess, while, on the contrary, her dear saints inspired her with ineffable confidence.

Jeannette's god-mother was Sybille, an old woman, originally from Brittany, and a washerwoman by occupation. Sybille knew a mass of marvelous legends; and she spoke familiarly about the fairies, genii and other supernatural beings. Some people took her for a witch;[3] but her good heart, her piety and upright life in no way justified the suspicion. Jeannette, of whom her god-mother was very fond, drank in with avidity the legends narrated by the latter when they met on the way to the "Fountain of the Fairies" whither the former frequently took her sheep to water while her god-mother spun her hemp on the banks of a nearby stream. The narratives of her god-mother of the miraculous doings of the fairies and genii impressed themselves profoundly on the imaginative spirit of Jeannette, who grew ever more serious and pensive as she approached her fourteenth year. She was frequently subject to a vague sense of sadness. Often, when alone in the woods or on the meadows, the distant sounds of the church bells, that she so much loved to hear, struck her ears, and she would weep without knowing why. The involuntary tears comforted her. But her nights grew restless. She no longer slept peacefully as is the wont of rustic children after their wholesome labors. She dreamed much; and her visions would raise before her the spirits of the legends of her god-mother or present to her St. Marguerite and St. Catherine smiling tenderly upon her.

CHAPTER II.

GILLON THE FURTIVE.

On a brilliant summer day the sun was westering behind the Castle of Ile, a small fortress raised between the two arms of the Meuse at a considerable distance from Domremy. James Darc inhabited a house near the church, the garden of which bordered on that of his own habitation. The laborer's family, gathered before the door of their lodging, were enjoying the coolness of the evening; some were seated on a bench and others on the floor. James Darc, a robust man of severe countenance, spare of face and grey of hair, was in the group resting from his day's labor; his wife, Isabelle, spun; Jeannette was sewing. Large and strong for her age, lissom and well proportioned, her hair was black, as were also her large brilliant eyes. The ensemble of her features made promise of a virile and yet tender beauty.[4] She wore, after the fashion of Lorraine, a skirt of coarse scarlet fabric, with a corsage that, looped over her shoulders, allowed the short sleeves of her skirt to escape at her upper arms, the rest of which remained bare and were well built and slightly tanned by the sun.

Darc's family were listening to the account of a stranger dressed in a brown coat, shod in tall and spurred boots, holding a whip in his hands and carrying on his shoulder a tin box held by a leather strap. The stranger, Gillon the Furtive, was in the habit of traversing long distances on horseback in the capacity of "flying messenger", carrying the correspondence of important personages. He had just returned from one of these errands to the Duke of Lorraine and was going back to Charles VII, who then resided at Bourges. While crossing Domremy, Gillon the Furtive had asked James Darc to direct him to some inn where he could sup and feed his horse.

"Share my meal; my sons will take your horse to the stable," the hospitable laborer answered the messenger. The offer being accepted, supper was taken and the stranger, desirous to pay his reckoning in his own way by giving the latest news of France to the family of Darc, reported how the English, masters of Paris and of almost all the provinces, governed despotically, terrorizing the inhabitants by their continuous acts of violence and rapine; how the King of England, still a boy and under the guardianship of the Duke of Bedford, had inherited the crown of France; while poor Charles VII, the King by right, deserted by almost all his seigneurs and relegated to Touraine, the last shred of his domains, did not even entertain the hope of ever being able to redeem those provinces from the domination of the English. Being a court messenger and therefore, naturally, a royalist of the Armagnac party, Gillon the Furtive professed, after the fashion of inferior courtiers, a sort of stupid, false, blind and grovelling adoration for Charles VII. That young prince, unnerved by his early debaucheries, selfish, greedy, envious and, above all, cowardly, never appeared at the head of the troops still left to him; and consoled himself for their defeats and his disgrace by drinking deep and singing with his mistresses. In his royalist fervor, however, Gillon the Furtive forgot his master's vices and saw only his misfortunes.

"Poor young King! It is a pity to see what he has to endure!" said the messenger at the close of his report. "His accursed mother, Isabelle of Bavaria, is the cause of it all. Her misconduct with the Duke of Orleans and her hatred for the Duke of Burgundy have brought on the frightful feud between the Burgundians and the Armagnacs. The English, already masters of several of our provinces since the battle of Poitiers, easily took possession of almost all France, torn in factions as the country was. They now impose upon the country an intolerable yoke, sack and burn it right and left and butcher its people. Finally, the Duke of Bedford, tutor of a king in his cradle, reigns in the place of our gentle Dauphin! A curse upon Isabelle of Bavaria! That woman was the ruin of the kingdom. We are no longer French. We are English!"

"God be praised! We, at least," said James Darc, "still remain French, all of us in this valley. We have not experienced the disasters that you describe, friend messenger. You say that Charles VII, our young prince, is a worthy sire?"

"Just heaven!" cried Gillon the Furtive, a flatterer and liar, like all court valets, "Charles VII is an angel! All who approach him admire him, revere and bless him! He has the meekness of a lamb, the beauty of a swan and the courage of a lion!"

"The courage of a lion!" exclaimed James Darc with admiration. "Then our young Sire has fought bravely?"

"If he had had his will he would by this time have been killed at the head of the troops that have remained faithful," promptly answered Gillon the Furtive, puffing out his cheeks. "But the life of our august master is so precious that the seigneurs of his family and council were bound to oppose his risking his precious days in a fashion that I shall be bold to call—uselessly heroic. The soldiers who still follow the royal banners are completely discouraged by the defeats that they have sustained. The larger number of bishops and seigneurs have declared themselves for the party of the Burgundians and the English; everybody is deserting our young Sire; and soon perhaps, forced to abandon France, he will not find in the whole kingdom of his fathers a place to rest his head! Oh, accursed, triply accursed be his wicked mother, Isabella of Bavaria!"

With nightfall Gillon the Furtive thanked the laborer of Domremy for his hospitality, mounted his horse and pursued his route. After mutually expressing their sorrow at the fate of the young King, the family of Darc joined in evening prayer and its members retired to sleep.

CHAPTER III.

AT THE FOUNTAIN OF THE FAIRIES.

That night Jeannette slept late and little. Silent and attentive during the messenger's narrative, she had then for the first time heard imprecations uttered at the ravages of the English, and about the misfortunes of the gentle Dauphin of France.

James Darc, his wife and sons continued long after the departure of Gillon the Furtive to lament the public calamities. Vassals of the King, they loved him; and they served him all the more seeing they knew him less and in no wise felt his feudal overlordship, having emancipated themselves with the aid of the distance that separated them from him and from the troubles that had fallen upon him. They were worthy but credulous people.

Children usually are the echoes of their parents. Accordingly, following the example of her father and mother, Jeannette, in her naïve and tender credulity, pitied with all her heart the young prince who was so beautiful, so brave and yet so unfortunate only through the fault of his wicked mother. "Oh," thought she, "he is almost without a place to rest his head, deserted by everybody, and soon will be forced to flee from the kingdom of his ancestors!" So the messenger had said.

Jeannette, who lately was subject to causeless spells of weeping, now wept over the misfortunes of the King; and fell asleep praying to her dear saints Marguerite and Catherine and to the archangel Michael to intercede with the Lord in behalf of the poor young prince. These thoughts followed the little shepherdess even in her dreams, bizarre dreams, in which she now would see the Dauphin of France, beautiful as an angel, smiling upon her with sadness and kindness; and then again hordes of armed Englishmen, armed with torches and swords, marching, marching and leaving behind them a long trail of blood and flames.

Jeannette awoke, but her imagination being strongly affected by the remembrance of her dreams, she could not keep her mind from ever returning to the gentle Dauphin and being greatly moved with pity for him. At early daylight she gathered her lambs, that every morning she took to pasture, and led them towards the oak forest where the shade was cool and the grass dotted with flowers. While her sheep were pasturing Jeannette sat down near the Fountain of the Fairies, shaded by the centennarian beech tree; and mechanically she plied her distaff.

Jeannette had not been long absorbed in her revery when she was joined by her god-mother, Sybille, who arrived carrying on her shoulder a large bundle of hemp that she wished to lay in the streamlet, formed by the overflow of the spring, in order to have it retted. Although simple minded people took Sybille for a witch, nothing in her features recalled those usually ascribed to old women possessed of the evil spirit—hooked nose and chin, cavernous eyes and an owlish aspect. No, far from it, nothing could be more venerable than Sybille's pale face framed in her white hair. Her eyes shone with concentrated fire when she narrated the legends of the olden times or recited the heroic chants of Armorica, as her native Brittany was once called. Without at all believing in magic, Sybille had a profound faith in certain prophecies made by the ancient Gallic bards. Faithful to the druidic creed of her fathers, Jeannette's god-mother held that man never dies, but continues to live eternally, body and soul, in the stars, new and mysterious worlds. Nevertheless, respecting her god-daughter's religious views, Sybille never sought to throw doubt upon the faith of the child. She loved the child tenderly and was ever ready to tell her some legend that Jeannette would listen to in rapt attention. Thus there was developed in the young shepherdess a contemplative and reflecting spirit that was unusual in one of her years, and that was no less striking than the precociousness of her intellect. She was prepared for a mystic role.

Jeannette continued, mechanically, to ply her distaff while her eyes, with an absent minded look in them, followed her sheep. She neither saw nor heard Sybille approach. The latter, after having laid her hemp in the streamlet and placed a stone on it to keep it in place, approached Jeannette slowly and impressed a kiss upon the bowed neck of the young girl, who uttered a startled cry and said smilingly, "Oh god-mother, you frightened me so!"

"And yet you are not timid! You were braver the other day than I should have been when you stoned the large viper to death. What were you thinking about just now?"

"Oh, I was thinking that the Dauphin, our dear Sire, who is so gentle, so beautiful, so brave and yet so unfortunate through the fault of his mother, may, perhaps, be forced to leave France!"

"Who told you that?"

"A messenger, who stopped yesterday at our house. He told us of the harm the English are doing the country whence he came; and also of the troubles of our young Sire. Oh, god-mother, I felt as grieved for him as if he were my own brother. I could not help crying before falling asleep. Oh, the messenger repeated it over and over again that the mother of the young prince is to blame for all of his sufferings; and that that bad woman had lost Gaul."

"Did the messenger say all that?" asked Sybille, thrilling at a sudden recollection, "did he say that a woman had lost Gaul?"

"Yes, he did. And he told how, through her fault, the English are heaping sorrows upon the country people. They pillage them, kill them and burn down their houses. They have no mercy for women or children. They drive away the peasants' cattle"—and Jeannette cast an uneasy glance upon her woolly flock. "Oh, god-mother, my heart bled at the messenger's report of our young King's sufferings and at the trials of the poor folks of those regions. To think that one bad woman could cause so much harm!"

"A woman caused the harm," said Sybille, raising her head with a faraway look in her eyes, "a woman will redress it."

"How can that be?"

"A woman lost Gaul," resumed Sybille, more and more dreamily, with her eyes resting on space, "a young girl shall save Gaul. Is the prophecy about to be fulfilled? Praise be to God!"

"What prophecy, god-mother?"

"The prophecy of Merlin, the famous enchanter. Merlin, the bard of Brittany."

"And when did he make the prophecy?"

"More than a thousand years ago."

"More than a thousand years! Was Merlin then a saint, god-mother? He must have been a great saint!"

Absorbed in her own thoughts, Sybille did not seem to hear the young shepherdess's question. With her eyes still gazing afar, she murmured slowly the old chant of Armorica:

> "Merlin, Merlin, whither this morning with your black dog?
> 'I come here to look for the egg that is red and laid by the serpent that lives in the sea.
> I come here to look for the cress that is green and the herb that is golden which grow in the valley,
> And the branch of the oak that is stately, in the woods on the banks of the fountain.'"[5]

"The branch of the oak that is stately—in the woods—on the banks of the fountain?" repeated Jeannette, questioningly, looking above and around her, as though struck both by the words and the significant expression on Sybille's face. "It looks like this spot, god-mother, it looks like this spot!" But noticing that the old Breton woman did not listen to her and was seemingly lost in contemplation, she laid her hand upon her arm and said, insistently, "God-mother, who is that Merlin of whom you speak? Answer me, dear god-mother!"

"He was a Gallic bard whose chants are still sung in my country," answered Sybille, awaking from her revery; "he is spoken of in our oldest legends."

"Oh, god-mother, tell me one of them, if you please. I love so much to hear your beautiful legends. I often dream of them!"

"Very well, you shall be pleased, dear child. I shall tell you the legend of a peasant who wed the daughter of the King of Brittany."

"Is it possible! A peasant wed a king's daughter?"

"Yes, and thanks to Merlin's harp and ring."

CHAPTER IV.

THE HARP OF MERLIN.

Sybille seemed to be in a trance. "The legend," she said, "that I shall tell you is called *The Harp of Merlin*;" and she proceeded to recite in a rythmic cadence:

> "'My poor grandmother, Oh, I wish to attend
> The feast that the King doth give.'
> 'No, Alain, to this feast shall you not go:
> Last night you wept in your dream.'
> 'Dear little mother, if truly you love me,
> Let me this feast attend.'
> 'No, you will sing when you go;
> When you come back you'll weep.'
> But despite his grandmother, Alain did go."

"It was wrong in him to disobey," Jeannette could not help saying, while she listened with avidity to her god-mother's recital; "it was wrong in him to disobey!"

Sybille kissed Jeannette on the forehead and proceeded:

> "Alain equipped his black colt,
> Shod it well with polished steel,
> Placed a ring on its neck, a bow on its tail,
> And arrived at the feast.
> Upon his arrival the trumpets were sounded:
> 'Whoever shall clear at one bound,
> Clear and free, the barrier around the fair grounds,
> His shall the King's daughter be.'"

"The King's daughter! Can it be!" repeated the little shepherdess wonderingly, and, dropping her distaff, she pressed her hands together in ecstasy.

Sybille proceeded:

> "Hearing these words of the crier,
> The black colt of Alain neighed loud and long;
> He leaped and ran, his nostrils shot fire,
> His eyes emitted flashes of lightning; he distanced all other horses,
> And cleared the barrier with a leap neat and

clean.
'Sire,' said Alain, addressing the King,
'You swore it; your daughter, Linor, must now be mine.'
'Not thine, nor of such as you can ever she be—
Yours is not our race.'"

"The King had promised and sworn," cried Jeannette, "did he fail in his word? Oh, the lovely Dauphin, our Sire, he would never break his word! Would he, god-mother?"

Sybille shook her head sadly and continued:

"'An old man stood by the King,
An old man with long white beard,
Whiter than is the wool on the bush of the heather;
His robe was laced with gold from top to bottom.
He spoke to the King in a low voice;
And the latter, after he had heard what the old man said,
Struck three times on the ground with his scepter
To order silence,
And said to Alain:

"'If you bring me the harp of Merlin,
That hangs at the head of his bed from three chains of gold;
Yes, if you can loosen that harp and bring it to me,
You shall have my daughter,
Perhaps.'"

"And where was that harp, god-mother?" asked Jeannette, more and more interested in the legend. "What must he do to get it?"

"'My poor grandmother,'
Said Alain when he returned to the house,
'If truly you love me you'll help and advise me.
My heart is broken! My heart is broken!'
'Bad boy, had you but listened to me,
Had you not gone to that feast,
Your heart would not be broken.

> But come, do not cry. The harp shall be
> loosened.
> Here's a hammer of gold;
> Now go.'

"Alain returned to the King's palace, saying:
'Good luck and joy! Here am I,
And I bring the harp of Merlin'—"

"Then he succeeded in getting the harp?" Jeannette asked in amazement. "But where and how did he do it, god-mother?"

Sybille, with a mysterious look, placed her finger to her lips in token of silence:

> "'I bring here the harp of Merlin,' said Alain to
> the King;
> 'Sire, your daughter, Linor, must now be mine.
> You promised me so.'
> When the King's son heard this, he made a wry
> face
> And spoke to his father, the King, in a low
> voice.
> The King, having listened, then said to Alain:
> 'If you fetch me the ring
> From the finger of Merlin's right hand,
> Then you shall have my daughter, Linor.'"

"Oh, god-mother, twice to fail in his promise! Oh, that was wrong on the part of the King! What is to become of poor Alain?"

> "Alain returns all in tears,
> And seeks his grandmother in great haste.
> 'Oh, grandmother, the King had said—
> And now he gainsays himself!'
> 'Do not grieve so, dear child!
> Take a twiglet you'll find in my chest,
> On which twelve leaves you'll see—
> Twelve leaves as yellow as gold,
> And that I looked for se'en nights
> In se'en woods, now se'en years agone.'"

"What were those gold leaves, god-mother? Did the angels or the saints give them to the grandmother?"

Sybille shook her head negatively and proceeded:

> "When at midnight the chanticleer crowed,
> The black colt of Alain awaited his master
> Just outside the door.
> 'Fear not, my dear little grandson,
> Merlin will not awake;
> You have my twelve leaves of gold.
> Go quickly.'
> The chanticleer had not yet done with his chant
> When the black colt was galloping swiftly over the road.
> The chanticleer had not yet done with his chant
> When the ring of Merlin was taken away—"

"And this time Alain married the King's daughter, did he not, godmother?"

> "At break of dawn was Alain at the King's palace,
> Presenting him with Merlin's ring.
> Stupefied the King did stand;
> And all who stood near him declared:
> 'Lo, how, after all, this young peasant
> Won the daughter of our Sire!'
> 'It is true,' the King to Alain did say,
> 'But still there is one thing I now ask of you,
> And it will be the last. Do you that,
> And my daughter you'll have,
> And with her the glorious kingdom of Leon.'
> 'What must I do, Sire?'
> 'To my court bring Merlin,
> Your wedding to sing with my daughter Linor.'"

"My God!" interrupted the little shepherdess, more and more carried away with the marvelousness of the story, "how will it end?"

> "While Alain was at the King's palace,
> His grandmother saw Merlin go by;
> Merlin the Enchanter went by her house.
> 'Whence, Merlin, come you with your clothes all in rags
> Whither thus bare-headed and bare-footed go you?
> Whither, old Merlin, with your holly staff go you?'
> 'Alack! Alack! I'm looking for my harp,

My heart's only solace in all this broad world.
I'm looking for my harp and also for my ring,
Which both I lost, or they have been stolen
from me.'

"'Merlin, Merlin, do not grieve!
Your harp is not lost, and neither is your ring.
Walk in, Merlin, walk in,
Take rest and food.'
'I shall neither eat nor rest in this world
Till I've recovered my harp and my ring.
They have not been stolen, I've lost them, the two.'
'Merlin, walk in, your harp will be found.—
Merlin, walk in, your ring will be found.'
So hard the grandmother begged
That Merlin entered her hut.

"When in the evening Alain returned to his house,
He trembled with a great fear when,
On casting his eyes towards the hearth,
He there saw Merlin the Enchanter,
Who was seated, his head on his breast reclining.
Alain knew not whither to flee.

"'Fear not, my lad, fear not.
Merlin sleeps a slumber profound.
He has eaten three apples, three red ones,
Which I in the embers have baked.
Now he'll follow wherever we go.
We'll lead him towards the palace
Of our Sire, the King!'"

"And did Merlin go, god-mother?"

"'What has happened in town, that I hear such a noise?'
Said the next day the Queen to the servant;
'What has happened at court, that the crowd
Are cheering so joyfully?'
'Madam, the whole town is having a feast.
Merlin is entering the town with an old,

A very old woman, dressed in white,
The grandmother she of the lad who is your daughter to marry.
Aye, Madam the Queen.'

"And the wedding took place.
Alain espoused Linor. Merlin chanted the nuptials.
There were a hundred white robes for the priests,
A hundred gold chains for the knights,
A hundred festal blue mantles for the dames,
And eight hundred hose for the poor.
And all left satisfied.
Alain left for the country of Leon
With his wife, his grandmother, and a numerous suite.—
But Merlin alone disappeared. Merlin was lost.
No one knows what of him is become.
No one knows when Merlin will return."[6]

CHAPTER V.

THE PROPHECY OF MERLIN.

Jeannette had listened to Sybille in rapt attention, struck above all by the singular circumstance of a peasant marrying the daughter of a king. From that moment Jeannette pardoned herself for having so often, since the previous evening, permitted her thoughts to turn to that young Sire, so sweet, so beautiful, so brave and yet so unfortunate through his mother's misconduct and the cruelty of the English.

When Sybille's recital was ended, a short silence ensued which was broken by Jeannette:

"Oh, god-mother, what a beautiful legend! It would be still more beautiful if, the Sire of Leon having to fight so cruel an enemy as the English, Alain, the peasant, had saved the King before wedding his daughter! But what did become of Merlin, the great enchanter Merlin?"

"It is said that he must sleep a thousand years. But before he fell asleep he prophesied that the harm a woman would do to Gaul would be redressed by a young girl, a young girl of this region—"

"This region in which we live, god-mother?"

"Yes, of the borders of Lorraine; and that she would be born near a large oak forest."

Jeannette clasped her hands in astonishment and she looked at Sybille in silence, revolving in her mind the prophecy of Merlin that France was to be saved by a young girl of Lorraine, perchance of Domremy! Was not the emancipatrix to come from an old oak forest? Was not the village of Domremy situated close to a forest of centennarian oaks?[7]

"What! God-mother," Jeannette inquired, "can that be true—did Merlin make that prophecy?"

"Yes," answered Sybille, thinking that surely the time had come when the prophecy of the Gallic bard was to be fulfilled, "yes, more than a thousand years ago Merlin so prophesied."

"How did he do it, god-mother?"

Sybille leaned her forehead on her hand, collected herself, and in a low voice, speaking slowly, she imparted to her god-daughter the mysterious prophecy in the following words, to which the child listened with religious absorption:

"When down goes the sun and the moon shines, I sing.
Young, I sang—become old still I sing.
People look for me, but they find me not.
People will cease looking for, and then will they find me.
It matters little what may happen—
What must be shall be!

"I see Gaul lost by a woman. I see Gaul saved by a virgin
From the borders of Lorraine and a forest of oaks.
I see at the borders of Lorraine a thick forest of oaks
Where, near a clear fountain, grows the divine druid herb,
Which the druid cuts with a sickle of gold.
I see an angel with wings of azure and dazzling with light.
He holds in his hands a royal crown.
I see a steed of battle as white as snow—
I see an armor of battle as brilliant as silver.—
For whom is that crown, that steed, that armor?
Gaul, lost by a woman, will be saved by a virgin
From the borders of Lorraine and a forest of oaks.—
For whom that crown, that steed, that armor?
Oh, how much blood!
It spouts up, it flows in torrents!
It steams; its vapor rises—rises like an autumn mist to heaven,
Where the thunder peals and where the lightning flashes.
Athwart those peals of thunder, those flashes of lightning,
That crimson mist, I see a martial virgin.
She battles, she battles—she battles still in a forest of lances!
She seems to be riding on the backs of the archers.[8]
The white steed, as white as snow, was for the martial virgin!

For her was the armor of battle as brilliant as silver.
She is surrounded by an escort.
But for whom the royal crown?
Gaul, lost by a woman, will be saved by a virgin
From the borders of Lorraine and a forest of oaks.
For the martial maid the steed and the armor!
But for whom the royal crown?
The angel with wings of azure holds it in his hands.
The blood has ceased to run in torrents,
The thunder to peal, and the lightning to flash.
The warriors are at rest.
I see a serene sky. The banners float;
The clarions sound; the bells ring.
Cries of joy! Chants of victory!
The martial virgin receives the crown
From the hands of the angel of light.
A man on his knees, wearing a long mantle of ermine,
Is crowned by the warrior virgin.
Who is the virgin's elect?

"It matters little what may happen.
What must be shall be!
Gaul, lost by a woman,
Is saved by a virgin
From the borders of Lorraine and a forest of oaks.
The prophecy is in the Book of Destiny."

Hanging upon the lips of Sybille, Jeannette never once interrupted her as she listened to the mysterious prophecy with waxing emotion. Her active, impressionable imagination pictured to her mind's eye the virgin of Lorraine clad in her white armor, mounted on her white courser, battling in the midst of a forest of lances, and, in the words of the prophetic chant, "riding on the backs of the archers." And after that, the war being ended and the foreigner vanquished, the angel of light—no doubt St. Michael, thought the little shepherdess—passed the crown to the warrior maid; who, amidst the blare of trumpets, the ringing of bells and the chants of victory, rendered his crown back to the king. And that king, who else could he be but the lovely Dauphin whose mother had brought on the misfortunes of France? It never yet occurred to the little shepherdess that she, herself, might be the martial virgin prophesied of in the legend. But the heart of the naïve child beat with joy at the thought that the virgin who was to emancipate Gaul was to be a Lorrainian.

"Oh, thanks, god-mother, for having recited this beautiful legend to me!" said Jeannette, throwing herself, with tears in her eyes, on the neck of Sybille. "Morning and noon shall I pray to God and St. Michael soon to fulfil the prophecy of Merlin. The English will then finally be driven from France and our young Sire crowned, thanks to the courage of the young Lorrainian maid from the forest of old oaks! May God grant our prayers!"

"'It matters little what may happen. What must be shall be.' The prophecy will be fulfilled."

"And yet," replied the little shepherdess, after reflecting a moment, "think of a young maid riding to battle and commanding armed men like a captain! Is such a thing possible? But God will give her courage!"

"My father knew one time, in my country of Brittany, the wife of the Count of Montfort, who was vanquished and taken prisoner by the King of France. Her name was Jeannette, like yours. Long did she fight valiantly, both on land and on sea, with casque and cuirass. She wished to save the heritage of her son, a three-year-old boy. The sword weighed no more to the arm of the Countess Jeannette than does the distaff to the hands of a girl that spins."

"What a woman, god-mother! What a woman!"

"And there were a good many other martial women, hundreds and hundreds of years ago! They came in vessels from the countries of the North; and they were daring enough to row up the Seine as far even as Paris. They were called the Buckler Maidens. They did not fear the bravest soldier. And who wished to wed them had first to overcome them by force of arms."[9]

"You do not say so! What furious women they must have been!"

"And in still older days, the Breton women of Gaul followed their husbands, sons, fathers and brothers to battle. They assisted at the councils of war; and often fought unto death."

"God-mother, is not the story of Hena that you once told me, a legend of those days?"[10]

"Yes, my child."

"Oh, god-mother," replied the enraptured little shepherdess, caressingly, "tell me that legend once more. Hena proved herself as courageous as will be the young Lorrainian maid whose advent Merlin predicts."

"Very well," said Sybille, smiling, "I shall tell you this legend also and shall then return home. My hemp is retting. I shall return for it before evening."

CHAPTER VI.

THE LEGEND OF HENA.

With the enchanted Jeannette for her audience, Sybille proceeded to recite the legend of Hena:

"She was young, she was fair,
And holy was she.
To Hesus her blood gave
For Gaul to be free.
Hena her name!
Hena, the Maid of the Island of Sen!

"'Blessed be the gods, my sweet daughter,'
Said her father Joel,
The brenn of the tribe of Karnak.
'Blessed be the gods, my sweet daughter,
Since you are home this night
To celebrate the day of your birth!'

"'Blessed be the gods, my sweet girl,'
Said Margarid, her mother.
'Blessed be your coming!
But why is your face so sad?'

"'My face is sad, my good mother,
My face is sad, my good father,
Because Hena your daughter
Comes to bid you Adieu,
Till we meet again.'

"'And where are you going, my sweet daughter?
Will your journey, then, be long?
Whither thus are you going?'

"'I go to those worlds
So mysterious, above,
That no one yet knows,
But that all will yet know.
Where living ne'er traveled,
Where all will yet travel,

> To live there again
> With those we have loved.'"

"And those worlds," asked Jeannette, "are they the paradise where the angels and the saints of the good God are? Are they, god-mother?"

Sybille shook her head doubtfully, without answering, and continued the recital of her legend:

> "Hearing Hena speak these words,
> Sadly gazed upon her her father,
> And her mother, aye, all the family,
> Even the little children,
> For Hena loved them very dearly.
>
> "'But why, dear daughter,
> Why now quit this world,
> And travel away beyond
> Without the Angel of Death having called you?'
>
> "'Good father, good mother,
> Hesus is angry.
> The stranger now threatens our Gaul, so beloved.
> The innocent blood of a virgin
> Offered by her to the gods
> May their anger well soften.
> Adieu then, till we meet again,
> Good father, good mother.
>
> "'Adieu till we meet again,
> All, my dear ones and friends.
> These collars preserve, and these rings,
> As mementoes of me.
> Let me kiss for the last time your blonde heads,
> Dear little ones. Good-bye till we meet.
> Remember your Hena, she waits for you yonder,
> In the worlds yet unknown.'
>
> "Bright is the moon, high is the pyre
> Which rises near the sacred stones of Karnak;
> Vast is the gathering of the tribes
> Which presses 'round the funeral pile.

"Behold her, it is she, it is Hena!
She mounts the pyre, her golden harp in hand,
And singeth thus:

"'Take my blood, O Hesus,
And deliver my land from the stranger.
Take my blood, O Hesus.
Pity for Gaul! Victory to our arms!'

"So it flowed, the blood of Hena.
O, holy Virgin, in vain 'twill not have been,
The shedding of your innocent and generous
blood.
To arms! To arms!
Let us chase away the stranger!
Victory to our arms!"

The eyes of Jeannette filled anew with tears; and she said to Sybille, when the latter had finished her recital:

"Oh, god-mother, if the good God, his saints and his archangels should ask me: 'Jeannette, which would you prefer to be, Hena or the martial maid of Lorraine who is to drive the wicked English from France and restore his crown to our gentle Dauphin?'—"

"Which would you prefer?"

"I would prefer to be Hena, who, in order to deliver her country, offered her blood to the good God without shedding the blood of any other people! To be obliged to kill so many people before vanquishing the enemy and before crowning our poor young Sire! Oh, god-mother," added Jeannette, shivering, "Merlin said that he saw blood flowing in torrents and steaming like a fog!"

Jeannette broke off and rose precipitately upon hearing, a few steps off in the copse, a great noise mixed with plaintive bleatings. Just then one of her lambs leaped madly out of the bush pursued silently by a large black dog which was snapping viciously at its legs. To drop her distaff, pick up two stones that she armed herself with and throw herself upon the dog was the work of an instant for the child, thoroughly aroused by the danger to one of her pets, while Sybille cried in frightened tones:

"Take care! Take care! The dog that does not bark is mad!"

But the little shepherdess, with eyes afire and face animated, and paying no heed to her god-mother's warning, instead of throwing her stones at the dog from a safe distance, attacked him with them in her hands, striking him with one and the other alternately until he dropped his prey and fled, howling with pain and with great tufts of wool hanging from his jaws, while Jeannette pursued him, picking up more stones and throwing them with unerring aim until the dog had disappeared in the thicket.

When Jeannette returned to Sybille the latter was struck by the intrepid mien of the child. The ribbons on her head having become untied, her hair was left free to tumble down upon her shoulders in long black tresses. Still out of breath from running, she leaned for a moment against the moss-grown rocks near the fountain with her arms hanging down upon her scarlet skirt, when, noticing the lamb that lay bleeding on the ground, still palpitating with fear, the little shepherdess fell to crying. Her anger gave place to intense pity. She dipped up some water at the spring in the hollow of her hands, knelt down beside the lamb, washed its wounds and said in a low voice:

"Our gentle Dauphin is innocent as you, poor lambkin; and those wicked English dogs seek to tear him up."

In the distance the bells of the church of Domremy began their measured chimes. At the sound, of which she was so passionately fond, the little shepherdess cried delightedly:

"Oh, god-mother, the bells, the bells!"

And in a sort of ecstasy, with her lamb pressed to her breast, Jeannette listened to the sonorous vibrations that the morning breeze wafted to the forest of oaks.

CHAPTER VII.

GERMINATION.

Several weeks went by. The prophecy of Merlin, the remembrance of the King's misfortunes and of the disasters of France, ravaged by the English, obstinately crowded upon Jeannette's mind, before whom her parents frequently conversed upon the sad plight of the country. Thus, often during the hours she spent in solitary musings with her flock in the fields or the woods, she repeated in a low voice the passage from the prophecy of the Gallic bard:

> "Gaul, lost by a woman, shall be saved by a virgin
> From the borders of Lorraine and a forest of old oaks."

Or that other:

> "Oh, how much blood!
> It spouts up, it flows in torrents!
> It steams and, like a mist, it rises heavenward
> Where the thunder peals, where the lightning flashes!
> Athwart those peals of thunder, those flashes of lightning,
> I see a martial virgin.
> White is her steed, white is her armor;
> She battles, she battles still in the midst of a forest of lances,
> And seems to be riding on the backs of the archers."

Whereupon the angel of dazzling light would place the royal crown in the hands of the martial virgin, who crowned her King in the midst of shouts of joy and chants of victory!

Every day, looking with her mind's eyes towards the borders of Lorraine and failing to see the emancipating virgin, Jeannette beseeched her two good saints—St. Marguerite and St. Catherine—to intercede with the Lord in behalf of the safety of the gentle Dauphin, who had been deprived of his throne. Vainly did she beseech them to obtain the deliverance of poor France, for so many years a prey to the English; and she also fervently implored heaven for the fulfilment of the prophecy of Merlin, a prophecy that seemed plausible to Jeannette's mind after Sybille had told her of the exploits of the martial virgins who came in their ships from the distant seas of the North and besieged Paris; or the prowess of Jeannette of Montfort, battling like a lioness defending her whelps; or, finally, the heroic deeds of the Gallic women of olden days who accompanied their husbands, their brothers and their fathers to battle.

Jeannette was approaching her fourteenth year, an age at which robust and healthy natures, well developed by the invigorating labors of a rustic life, ordinarily enter their period of puberty. In that period of their lives, on the point, so grave for their sex, of becoming maids, they are assailed by unaccountable fears, by a vague sense of sadness, by an imperious demand for solitude where to give a loose rein to languorous reveries, novel sensations at which their chaste instincts take alarm, symptoms of the awakening of the virginal heart, first and shadowy aspirations of the maid for the sweet pleasures and austere duties of the wife and mother—the sacred destinies of woman.

It was not thus with Jeannette. She experienced these mysterious symptoms; but her simplicity misled her as to their cause. Her imagination filled with the marvelous legends of her god-mother, whom she continued to meet almost daily at the Fountain of the Fairies, her spirit ever more impressed by the prophecies of Merlin, although she never identified herself with them, Jeannette imputed, in the chaste ignorance of her soul, the vague sense of sadness that assailed her, her involuntary tears, her confused aspirations—all precursory symptoms of puberty—to the painful and tender compassion that the misfortunes of Gaul and of her young King inspired her with.

Jeannette Darc was to know but one love, the sacred love of her motherland.

CHAPTER VIII.

THE ENGLISH!

"Isabelle," one evening James Darc said to his wife, with a severe air, she and he being left alone near the hearth, "I am not at all satisfied with Jeannette. In a few months she will be fourteen; large and strong though she is for her age, she is becoming lazy. Yesterday I ordered her to draw water from the well to water the vegetables in the garden and I saw her stop a score of times with her hands on the rope and her nose in the air gaping at the eaves of the house. I shall have to shake her rudely out of the sin of laziness."

"James, listen to me. Have you not noticed that for some time our Jeannette is rather pale, has hardly any appetite, is often absent minded; and, moreover, she is more reserved than formerly?"

"I do not complain of her talking little. I do not love gabblers. I complain of her laziness. I wish her to become again industrious as she once was, and active as of old."

"The change that we notice in the girl does not, my friend, proceed from bad will."

"Whence then?"

"Only yesterday, feeling truly alarmed for her health, I questioned Jeannette. She suffered, she said, with violent headaches for some time; her limbs grew stiff without her having done hardly any walking; she could hardly sleep and was at times so dizzy that everything turned around her.

"This morning, as I went to Neufchateau with butter and poultry, I consulted Brother Arsene, the surgeon, on Jeannette's condition."

"And what did Brother Arsene say?"

"Having been told what her ailments were, he asked her age. 'Thirteen and a half, near fourteen,' I answered him. 'Is she strong and otherwise of good health?' 'Yes, brother, she is strong and was always well until these changes came that so much alarm me.' 'Be easy,' was Brother Arsene's final remark, 'be easy, good woman, your "little" daughter will surely soon be a "big" daughter. In a word, she will have "developed." At the approach of that crisis, always grave, young girls grow languishing and dreamy. They experience aches. They become taciturn and seek solitude. Even the most robust become feeble, the most industrious indolent, the gayest sad. That lasts a few months and then they become themselves again. But,' added Brother Arsene, 'you must be careful, under pain of provoking serious accidents, not to cross or scold your daughter at such a period of her life. Strong emotions have been known to check and suppress forever the salutary crisis that nature brings on. In such cases serious, often irreparable harm may follow. There are young girls who, in that manner, have gone wholly insane.' So you see, James, how we shall have to humor Jeannette."

"You have done wisely in consulting Brother Arsene; and I would blame myself for having thought so severely of the child's laziness and absent mindedness were it not that this evening, when she embraced me as usual before retiring, she showed that she no longer minded my words."

"Oh, mercy! On the contrary, I noticed that she was as affectionate toward you as ever—"

Isabelle was suddenly interrupted by violent rapping at the street door.

"Who can that be, knocking at this hour of the night?" said James Darc, rising, as much surprised as his wife at the interruption, to open the door.

The door was hardly ajar when an aged man of venerable and mild appearance, but at that moment pale with fear, hastily dismounted from his horse and cried, breathlessly, "Woe is us! Friend, the English! the English! the country is about to be invaded!"

"Great God! What is it you say, uncle!" exclaimed Isabelle, recognizing Denis Laxart, her mother's brother.

"The French troops have just been routed at the battle of Verneuil. The English, re-inforced in Champagne, are now overflowing into our valley. Look! Look!" said Denis Laxart, drawing Isabelle and James Darc to the threshold of their street door and pointing to the horizon towards the north, where wide streaks of reddish light went up and accentuated the darkness of the night, "the village of St. Pierre is in flames and the bulk of the troop of these brigands is now besieging Vaucouleurs, whence I managed to flee. One of their bands is raiding the valley, burning and sacking in their passage! Flee! Flee! Pick up whatever valuables you have. The village of St. Pierre is only two leagues from here. The English may be this very night in Domremy. I shall hasten to Neufchateau to join my wife and children who have been there for the last few days visiting a relative. Flee! there is still time. If you do not you may be slaughtered within two hours! Flee!"

Uttering the last word, the distracted Denis Laxart threw himself upon his horse and disappeared at full gallop, leaving James Darc and his wife stupefied and terror stricken. Until now the English never had approached the peaceful valley of the Meuse. James Darc's sons, whom the violent raps given at the door by Denis Laxart had frightened out of their slumbers, hastily slipped on their clothes and rushed into the main room.

"Father, has any misfortune happened? What makes you look so frightened?"

"The English!" answered Isabelle, pale with fear; "we are lost, my dear children! It is done for us!"

"The village of St. Pierre is on fire," cried James Darc. "Look yonder, at the border of the Meuse, towards the Castle of Ile. Look at those tongues of flame! May God help us! Our country is now to be ravaged like the rest of Gaul! Woe is us!"

"Children," said Isabelle, "help to gather whatever is most valuable and let us flee."

"Let us drive our cattle before us," added James. "If the English seize or kill them we shall be ruined. Woe is us!"

"But whither shall we flee?" asked Peter, the elder son. "In what direction shall we run without the risk of falling into the hands of the English?"

"It is better to stay right here," observed John. "We cannot fare worse than if we flee. We shall try to defend ourselves."

"Try to defend ourselves! Do you wish to see us all killed? Alack! The Lord has forsaken us!"

Weeping and moaning and scarcely knowing what she did, poor Isabelle tugged at her trunks, all too heavy to be carried far, and threw about pell-mell on the floor the best clothes of herself and her husband. Her wedding dress, carefully packed up; pieces of cloth and of wool woven by her during the long winter evenings; Jeannette's christening gown, a pious maternal relic;— all lay strewn about. She put around her neck an old chain, inherited from her mother, which was her main ornament on holidays. She stowed away in her pocket a little silver cup, won long ago by her husband in a shooting contest.

Awakened, like her brothers, Jeannette also had hurriedly put on her clothes, and now entered the room. Her father and brothers, taking no notice of her, were arguing with increasing anxiety the point of fleeing or of waiting at all hazards the approach of the English. From time to time they stepped to the door and, with despair plainly depicted on their faces, pointed at the conflagration which, only two leagues away, was devouring the village of St. Pierre. The flames now leaped up only by fits and starts; evidently the fire had little left to consume.

"A curse upon the English! What shall we do?"

So suddenly appraised of the enemy's invasion, seeing the distant conflagration, and near by her father and brothers distracted with fear and her mother nervously heaping up whatever she thought might be carried away, Jeannette, overcome by terror, trembled in every limb; and a mortal pallor overcast her face. Her eyes became suffused with tears and, her blood rushing to her head, she was, for a moment, seized with vertigo. A cloud passed before her eyes, she staggered and fell almost fainting on a stool. But her weakness was short. She soon became herself, and heard her mother calling: "Come quick, Jeannette, and help me to pack up these clothes! We shall have to flee for our lives! The English are coming and will pillage everything—and kill everything!"

"Where shall we flee for safety?" asked James. "We may run up against the English on the road and that would be running towards danger!"

"Let us stay here, father," John insisted, "and defend ourselves. I said so before. It is the best course to take."

"But we have no arms!" cried Peter, "and those brigands are armed to the teeth! They will slaughter us all!"

"What shall we do?" cried in chorus James and his sons, "what shall we do? Oh, Lord, have pity on us!"

Isabelle did not listen; she heard neither her husband nor her sons. She thought only of fleeing; and she ran from one room to the other and hither and thither, to make sure that she had left nothing of value behind; and quite unable to resign herself to the giving up of her copper and tin utensils that she had so industriously polished and spread upon the dresser.

After her temporary fright and feebleness, Jeannette rose, dried her eyes and helped her mother to pack up the articles that lay about on the floor; occasionally rushing to the door, contemplating the distant and dying reflections of the conflagration that still fitfully reddened the horizon in the direction of the Castle of Ile and the village of St. Pierre. She then turned to her father and, guided by her innate good sense, said in a calm voice: "Father, there is but one place where we can take refuge—the Castle of Ile. The castellan is kind. We would have nothing to fear behind fortified walls; and his yard will hold twenty times more cattle than either we or all of our neighbors possess."

"Jeannette is right," cried her two brothers, "let us to the Castle of Ile. We and our cattle will cross over on the ferry. Sister is right."

"Your sister is crazy!" replied James stamping on the ground. "The English are at St. Pierre. They are burning and killing everything! To go in that direction is to run into the very jaws of the wolf."

"Father, your fear is unfounded," explained Jeannette. "The English, after having burnt the village, will have abandoned it. It will take us more than two hours to reach the place. We shall take the old path through the forest. We are sure not to meet the enemy on that side. We shall cross the ferry and find refuge in the castle."

"That is right," said the two boys; "their mischief is done and the brigands will have decamped and left the ruins behind them."

James Darc seemed convinced by his daughter's reasoning. Suddenly one of the lads cried out, pointing to a new conflagration much nearer to Domremy:

"See, Jeannette is not mistaken; the English have left St. Pierre and are approaching by the open road. They burn down everything on their way. They must have just set fire to the hamlet of Maxey!"

"May God help us!" answered James. "Let us flee to the Castle of Ile by the old forest road. Jeannette, run to the stable and gather your sheep; you, boys, hitch up our two cows to the wagon. Isabelle and myself will carry the bundles to the yard and put them in the wagon while you are hitching up the cows. Quick, quick, children, the English will be here within two hours. Alack! If we ever again come back to Domremy we shall find only the ashes of our poor house!"

CHAPTER IX.

THE FLIGHT.

The family of Darc had not been the only ones to discover the nocturnal raid of the English. The whole parish was on foot, a prey to consternation and terror.

The more frightened gathered a few eatables, and abandoning all else, fled to the forest. Others, hoping that the English might not advance as far as Domremy, took the chances of remaining in the village. Finally, others there were who also decided to flee for safety to the Castle of Ile. The Darc family soon left their house, Jeannette calling her sheep, which obediently followed, James leading the cows that hauled the wagon on which his wife was seated in the midst of her bundles of goods, a few bags of wheat and the household utensils that she had managed to get together. The two lads carried on their shoulders the implements of husbandry that were portable.

The flight of the inhabitants of Domremy, in the darkness of the night, that was reddened only on the horizon by the reflection of the conflagrations, was heartrending. The imprecations uttered by the men, the moanings of the women, the cries of the children who clung weeping to their mothers' skirts, not a few of which latter held babies to their breasts; the mass of peasants, cattle and wagons promiscuously jumbled, striking against each other and getting in each others' way; all presented a distressing picture of that desperate flight for life. These poor people left behind them their only wealth—their granaries filled with the grain of the last harvest—expecting soon to see them devoured by the flames along with their humble homes. Their distress escaped in sobs, in plaintive cries, and often in curses and expressions of hatred and rage against the English. The spectacle left a profound and indelible impression upon Jeannette, now for the first time made acquainted with the horrors of war. Soon was she to contemplate them at still closer range and in their most appalling forms.

The fugitives arrived near the hamlet of St. Pierre, situated on the Meuse. There was nothing left but a heap of blackened debris, with here and there a wooden beam still burning—nothing else was left of the village. Walking a little ahead of her herd, Jeannette stood still, stupefied at the spectacle.

A few steps from where she stood a column of smoke rose from the ruins of a cottage that had been sheltered under a large walnut tree, the leaves of which were now singed and its branches charred by the fire. From one of the branches of the tree hung, head down, a man suspended by his feet over a now nearly extinct brazier. His face, roasted by the fire, retained no human form. His arms, twisted and rigid, betokened the intensity of his dying agony. Not far from him, two almost naked corpses, one of an old man and the other of a lad, lay in a pool of blood. They must have attempted to defend themselves against their assailants; a butcher's knife lay near the old man's corpse, while the lad still held in his clenched hands the handle of a pitchfork. Finally, a young woman, whose face was wholly concealed under her thick blonde hair and who must have been dragged from her bed in her night clothes, lay disemboweled near a still smoking heap of faggots; while a baby, apparently forgotten in the midst of the carnage, crept toward its dead mother crying loudly.

Such had been the savage war waged in Gaul for the last fifty years since the defeat of the French nobility at Poitiers.

The shocking spectacle unnerved Jeannette and, seized again with vertigo, she tottered and fell to the ground; Peter, her elder brother, coming close behind, raised her, and, with the help of his father, placed her on the wagon with her mother.

The wife of the castellan of Ile and her husband, a brave soldier, allowed the fugitives from Domremy to camp with their cattle in the yard of the castle, a vast space within the fortifications that were situated between the arms of the Meuse. Unfortunately the inhabitants of St. Pierre, who were taken by surprise at night, had not been able to reach this hospitable place of refuge. After ravaging the valley the English gathered near Vaucouleurs and concentrated their forces before that place, the siege of which they pressed vigorously for a short time. A few nights later a few of the peasants who had taken refuge in the Castle of Ile, among them Peter, Jeannette's elder brother, went out on a reconnoitering expedition and on their return reported that the enemy had departed from that part of the country. Tired of arson and carnage, the English had withdrawn from the neighborhood of Domremy after pillaging only a few of the houses and killing some of its inhabitants.

Back again at their home in Domremy the family of Darc busied themselves in repairing the damage that their house had sustained.

CHAPTER X.

"BURGUNDY!"—"FRANCE!"

During her sojourn in the Castle of Ile Jeannette had been the prey of severe attacks of fever. At times during her delirium she invoked St. Catherine and St. Marguerite, her good saints, believing that she saw them near her, and beseeching them with her hands clasped to put an end to the atrocities of the English. At other times the shocking scene of the hamlet of St. Pierre would rise in her troubled brain and she would cry out aloud or would sob at the sight of the victims that rose before her, livid and blood-bespattered. At still other times, her eyes shooting fire and her cheeks aflame she spoke of a martial virgin clad in white armor and mounted on a milk white steed whom, she said, she saw falling upon and exterminating the English. At such times Jeannette repeated with a quivering voice the refrain of Merlin's prophecy—

> "Gaul, lost by a woman, will be saved by a virgin
> From the borders of Lorraine and a forest of old oaks."

Isabelle sat up night and day nursing her daughter, imputing the ravings of the poor child to the violence of the fever and to the recollections of the horrible spectacle at St. Pierre. Great dejection of spirit and extreme feebleness succeeded Jeannette's malady. Back in Domremy, she was compelled to remain in bed several weeks; but her dreams reflected the identical pictures of her delirium. Moreover a deep sorrow had fallen upon her, for, strangely, her god-mother was one of the few victims of the English raid into Domremy. Her corpse was found riddled with wounds; and Jeannette wept for Sybille as much on account of her tender affection for her god-mother as on account of her regret at being separated forever from her who told such marvelous legends.

Two months passed and Jeannette was now nearly fourteen. She seemed to have regained her normal health, but the symptoms of puberty had disappeared and she frequently suffered from intolerable headaches followed by severe attacks of vertigo.

Feeling all the more uneasy as she remembered the words of the physician, Isabelle once more consulted him and he answered that the violent emotion caused by the invasion of the English and the spectacle of their cruelty must have deeply disturbed the girl's organization and checked her sexual development; but that her ailments would cease and the laws of nature resume their course in her physical being as the mental effects of her deeply stirred emotion wore off.

The physician's answer allayed Isabelle's fears. Moreover Jeannette again busied herself with her wonted household and field labors and she redoubled her activity in the effort to conceal from public gaze the spells of sadness and absent mindedness that now no longer were wholly without cause since she had witnessed some of the disasters to which her country was subject. Jeannette reflected to herself that the horrors she had seen at St. Pierre stained with blood all other sections of the land and fell heaviest upon those of her own class, the peasants. In pitying them she pitied her own. Since that fatal day Jeannette felt perhaps sadder at and wept more over the ghastly ills, an example of which she had seen with her own eyes, than at or over the misfortunes of the young Dauphin whom she did not know. The girl looked with increasing impatience for the advent of the warrior maid who was to bring deliverance to Gaul by driving the stranger out of the country, and by restoring his crown to the King and peace and rest to France.

These thoughts ever absorbed Jeannette's mind when alone in the woods or the field grazing her herd. Then would she yield unrestrained to revery and to the recollections of the legends that had had so much to do in forming her mind.

The undefinable emotion produced in her by the chiming of the bells began to raise visions before her eyes. The distant tintinnabulations, expiring on her ears, seemed to her transformed into a murmur of celestial voices of inexpressible sweetness.[11] At such moments Jeannette felt the blood rush to her head; her eyes were covered as with a mist; the visible world disappeared from her sight and she fell into a kind of ecstasy from which she recovered worn out as if awakened from some painful dream.

One day when Jeannette was grazing her herd while plying the distaff under the old beech tree near the Fountain of the Fairies a singular incident occurred that had a decisive influence over the fate of the young shepherdess. Reinforced by several bands of Burgundians, furnished by Marshall John of Luxemburg, the English had persisted in the siege of Vaucouleurs; which latter was defending itself heroically. The invasion by the English of that valley, otherwise so peaceful, incited a schism among its inhabitants. Many of them, especially the people of St. Pierre and of Maxey, who had been so cruelly dealt with by the invaders, were inclined to pass over to the English in order to save their property and lives. These formed, in the valley, the "English" or "Burgundian" party. Others, on the contrary, more irritated than frightened, preferred to resist the English. These poor people counted upon the support of their sovereign, the King of France, who, they said, would not longer leave them exposed to such miseries. The latter comprised the

"Armagnac" or "Royalist" party. The children, ever the imitators of their parents, likewise became "Armagnacs" and "Burgundians" when they played war. In these games the two parties ever finished by taking their roles seriously; when imprecations and actual blows with sticks and stones exchanged by the two "armies" gave these affairs the actual semblance of war.

The people of Domremy belonged mostly to the royalist, and those of St. Pierre and Maxey to the English party; and, of course, the children of these several localities shared, or rather aped, the political opinions of their respective families. It thus often happened that the lads of Maxey, while guarding their cattle, came to the borders of the commune of Domremy and flung insults at the little shepherds of the latter village. The dispute often became heated and hard words would be exchanged, when it would be decided to settle the difference of opinion by force of arms, that is with their fists and sticks accompanied by volleys of stones that figured as cross-bow bolts or cannon balls.[12]

Guarding her sheep, Jeannette spun her hemp under the trees of the forest of old oaks. In her revery she repeated in a low murmur the passage from Merlin's prophecy:

> "For whom that royal crown? That steed? That armor?
> Oh, how much blood! It spouts up, it flows in torrents!
> Oh, how much blood I see! How much blood I see!
> It is a lake, a sea of blood.
> It steams—its vapor ascends—
> It ascends like an autumn mist to the sky,
> To the sky where the thunder peals and the lightning flashes.
> Athwart these peals of thunder, these flashes of lightning,
> That blood-red mist, I see a martial virgin.
> White is her armor, white her steed.
> She battles—
> She battles and battles still in the midst of a forest of lances
> And seems to ride on the backs of the archers—"

Suddenly Jeannette heard in the distance a noise, at first indistinct, but drawing nearer and nearer accompanied by clamorous cries of "Burgundy! England!" uttered by infantile voices and answered by the counter cries of "France and Armagnac!" Almost immediately a crowd of Domremy boys appeared at the turn of the forest's skirt, fleeing in disorder under a shower of stones fired at them by the boys of Maxey. The engagement had been lively and the victory hotly contested, to judge by the torn clothes, the bruised eyes and the bleeding noses of the more heroic ones of the urchins. But yielding to a panic, they were now in full flight and rout. Their adversaries, satisfied with their victory, out of breath with running, and no doubt afraid of drawing too close to Domremy, the stronghold of the retreating army, prudently stopped near the forest which now hid them and repeated three times the cry: "Burgundy and England!"

The cry of victory caused Jeannette to bound to her feet transported with anger and shame at the sight of the boys of her village who battled for Gaul and the King fleeing before the partisans of Burgundy and England. A lad of about fifteen years, named Urbain, who captained the fleeing troop, and who was personally a brave soldier, seeing that his scalp was cut by a stone and his cap remained in the hands of the enemy, ran past Jeannette.

"Are you running for safety, Urbain?"

"Sure! That's what I'm doing," answered the mimic captain, raising his head and wiping the blood from his forehead with a handful of grass. "We fought as long as we could—but those of Maxey are about twenty and we are only eleven!"

Jeannette stamped on the ground with her foot and replied: "You have strength to run—and yet you have no strength to fight!"

"But they have sticks, and that is not fair—we are the weaker side."

"Fall upon them and capture their sticks!"

"That is easy to say, Jeannette!"

"As easy to do as to say!" cried the shepherdess.

"You will see—Come! Come back with me!"

Without noticing whether she was followed or not, but yielding to an involuntary prompting, Jeannette walked toward the enemy, then masked by a clump of trees, and cried out in ringing tones, while brandishing her distaff in lieu of a banner: "France! France! Off with you Burgundians and English!"

With her feet and arms bare, in her short white sleeves and scarlet skirt, her little straw hat on her long black hair, her cheeks aflame, her eyes sparkling, her poise heroic, Jeannette was at that moment so inspiring that Urbain and his followers felt themselves all at once strengthened and exalted. They picked up stones and rushed after the young shepherdess, who in her rapid course now barely seemed to touch the sward with her feet, crying, with her, "France! Off with you Burgundians and English!"

In the security of their triumph, the soldiers of the hostile army, who never expected to see their adversaries rally, had stopped about a hundred yards away and were resting on their laurels; and stretching themselves on the flower-studded grass, picked wild strawberries and played with stones.

Presently some of them climbed up in the trees looking for birds' nests, and the others scattered among the bushes picking and eating berries. The unexpected resumption of hostilities, the sudden cries hurled at them by the royalist army and by Jeannette, who now led it, greatly surprised the Burgundians, who, nevertheless, did not show the white feather. Their chief recalled his soldiers to arms. Immediately the plunderers of birds' nests slid down the trees, the berry pickers rushed up with crimson lips and those who had begun to fall asleep on the grass jumped up and rubbed their eyes. But before the line of battle could be formed the soldiers of Jeannette, anxious to avenge their former defeat, and carried away by the inspiring conduct of their present chief, fell valiantly upon the foe with redoubled cries of: "France! France!" Our heroes seized the Burgundians and English by the hair, boxed their ears and thumped them with such fury that the tables were completely turned; the erstwhile victors now became the vanquished, broke ranks and took to their heels.

The triumph redoubled the ardor of the assailants, who were now animated with the desire to carry off a few bonnets as spoils and trophies. The French army rushed breathlessly upon the English, with Jeannette ever in the lead. She fought intrepidly and made havoc with her distaff, which was garnished with a thick bunch of hemp—a terrible weapon, as many discovered that day. In the meantime, the English, stupefied by the sudden apparition of the young shepherdess in scarlet, who emerged so strangely from the neighborhood of the Fountain of the Fairies, the mystic reputation of which place extended far over the valley, took Jeannette for a hobgoblin. Fear lent them wings and the French were again vanquished—but only in running. The swiftest ones of the army pushed forward in pursuit of the enemy, but were obliged to desist for want of breath. Urbain and two or three of the most resolute kept up the pursuit with Jeannette, who, now seized with heroic exaltation, no longer thought of her own soldiers or took cognizance at all of her surroundings, but kept her flashing eyes fixed upon a number of fleeing English whom she wished to capture. Could she accomplish this it seemed to her that her victory would be complete.

But the runaways had so much the lead and ran so fast that she was almost despairing of being able to come to close quarters with them, when, still running, she perceived a donkey peacefully grazing on the meadow, totally unconcerned as to the battle or its outcome. Agile and robust, as became a child of the field, she leaped with one bound upon the back of the ass, urged it with heels, distaff and voice, and forced it into a gallop. The animal yielded all the more readily to the desires of Jeannette, seeing that the direction whither it was going was that of its own stable. It pricked up its ears and kicked up its heels with great joy, without, however, throwing Jeannette, and ran toward the English, who, unfortunately for themselves, were also on the route to the ass's stable and who, still more unfortunately for themselves, in the heat of their flight had never thought to look behind. Suddenly, however, hearing the hoof beats of the animal galloping at their heels and the victorious cries of the young shepherdess, they thought themselves pursued by devils; and fearing to see some horrible apparition, they threw themselves upon their knees with their eyes shut, their hands joined as if in prayer and begging for mercy. The enemy was decidedly vanquished.

Jumping off the ass, Jeannette allowed it to continue its route; and threatening with her innocent distaff the soldiers, who surrendered at discretion, she shouted to them in a resonant voice:

"Wretches! Why do you call yourselves Burgundians and English, seeing that we are all of France? It is against the English that we must all take the field! Oh, they do us so much harm!"

Saying this, the young shepherdess, a prey to an undefinable emotion, broke into tears, her knees trembled and she fell to the ground beside the vanquished foe, who, rising in inexpressible terror, incontinently resumed their headlong flight, leaving Jeannette alone so confused in mind that she knew not whether she was awake or dreaming.

Nevertheless, her heart still palpitating from the effects of the recent struggle, vague but exhilarating aspirations began to ferment in her being. She had just experienced for the first time the martial ardor caused by a glorious victory, won to the orchestration of the cries of "France!" and "Armagnac!" Forgetting that this childish battle was but play, indignant at and aroused by the check suffered by her party, she had seen her boys cheered and re-encouraged by her voice and, carried away by her example, return to the fray and vanquish the hitherto victorious enemy.

These aspirations were vaguely mixed with the recollections of the horrible butchery in the village of St. Pierre and the prophecy of Merlin, and caused the young shepherdess to raise her thoughts to St. Catherine and St. Marguerite, her two good saints, to whom she now prayed fervently to chase the English from France and to take pity on the gentle Dauphin. The chaotic jangle of these apparently disconnected and aimless thoughts that clashed together in the burning brain of Jeannette immediately brought on one of those painful spells of dizziness to which she had been ever more subject since the profound perturbation of her health. She relapsed into a sort of ecstasy; again a misty curtain was drawn before her eyes; and when she regained consciousness the sun had gone down and it was dusk.

On arising Jeannette hastened back to the Fountain of the Fairies, near which she had left her lambs browsing. The walk was long, she lost much time in getting her scattered flock together, and it was dark night ere she reached Domremy, trembling at having incurred the anger of her father by her delay; and above all fearing the scolding that she expected for the part she had taken in the combat between the boys. Urbain, full of pride at his victory, might, upon his return to the village, have boasted of the battle. Thus the poor child felt her heart beat with dismay when, arriving near her house, she saw the uneasy and angry face of James Darc. The moment he caught sight of his daughter he went toward her with a threatening look, saying: "By the Savior, is it in the dark of night that you must gather the sheep?" And approaching her with increasing irritation and with his hand raised over her head, he continued: "Bad and shameless child! Have you not been battling with the boys of the village against the boys of Maxey?"

In his rage James was on the point of beating the guilty girl, when Isabelle ran to him and caught his arm, crying, "James, I beg of you to pardon her this time!"

"Very well—I will be indulgent this time; but let her never again take a notion to romp with the boys. If she does it again, as sure as I am her father, I shall punish her severely; but for this time she can go to bed without supper."

CHAPTER XI.

THE VISION.

The fast to which Jeannette's father had sentenced her was destined to lead to grave consequences. Grieved at the reprovals he had heaped upon her, the young shepherdess led her sheep to the fold and retired to bed without sharing the family's evening meal.

At Jeannette's age hunger is peculiarly imperious. If the stomach is empty the brain is doubly active, as appears from the hallucinations of the anchorites who had long abstained from food. The poor child, overcome by her father's severity, sought solace in the recollections of the day's happenings and wept a great deal before she fell asleep from sheer exhaustion. Never had her sleep been so troubled by bizarre dreams, in which the marvelous legends that her god-mother Sybille had told her reappeared in various grotesque shapes. In her dreams, Hena, the virgin of the Isle of Sen, offered her blood as a sacrifice for the deliverance of Gaul and, erect with her harp in her hand, expired amidst the flames on the pyre. But, Oh, horror and surprise! Jeannette recognized her own features in those of Hena.

Another moment, Merlin, followed by a black dog with flaming eyes, rose before her, holding his knotted staff in his hand and with his long white beard streaming in the wind, looking for the red egg of the sea-serpent upon a desert beach and chanting his prophecy:

> "Gaul, lost by a woman, will be saved by a virgin
> From the borders of Lorraine and a forest of old oaks."

Then, again, it was the infantile combat of the day that surged uppermost in her disordered mind and now assumed the gigantic proportions of an immense battle. Thousands of cuirassed and casqued soldiers, armed with lances and swords, pressing hard, undulating, combing and breaking like the waves of the sea, were hurled against each other and were cut to pieces— opposing floods of iron in mutual clash. The clash of armors, the cries of the combatants, the neighing of horses, the fanfare of trumpets, the discharges of artillery resounded from afar. The red flag of England quartered with the gold fleur-de-lis floated over the blood-stained embattled ranks. A martial maid, cased in white armor and mounted on a white steed held the French flag—and once more Jeannette recognized her own features in those of the martial maid. St. Catherine and St. Marguerite hovered over her in the azure sky and smiled down upon her while St. Michael, the archangel, with his wide wings outspread and his face half turned toward her, pointed with his flaming sword to a brilliant star-like golden crown held by two angels in dazzling white.

The long dream, now and then interrupted by periods of semi-wakefulness and feverish starts, during which it would melt into the realities of her surroundings in the disordered mind of Jeannette, lasted until morning. When it was again day Jeannette awoke exhausted, her face wet with the tears that had flowed during her sleep. She made her customary morning prayer and besought her two good saints to appease her father's anger. She found him in the stable, whither she went to take her flock to the field; but James Darc informed her with austere severity that she was no longer to take the sheep to pasture, seeing that she paid so little attention to them. Her younger brother was to lead them out and she was to remain at the house to sew or spin.

This sentence was a severe punishment to Jeannette. It was to her a grievous sorrow to renounce going every day to the clear fountain and the shady spot where she derived so much pleasure from listening to the chimes of the bells, the last vibrations of which had latterly reached her ears as a celestial whisper of silvery voices. She submitted to the paternal will, however, and occupied herself during the morning with household duties.

More indulgent than her husband, Isabelle said to her daughter shortly before noon, "Go and play in the garden until the meal hour."

The summer's sun darted its burning rays upon Jeannette's head. Enfeebled by the fast of the previous night[13] and fatigued by her distressing dreams, she sat down upon a bench with her forehead resting on her hands and dropped into a revery, thinking of the prophecy of Merlin. Presently, as the bells of Greux began to sound from afar, she listened to their chimes with rapture, wholly forgetful of the fact that the sun's rays beat down perpendicularly upon her head. As the sound of the bells was gradually dying away the child suddenly saw a light, so intense, so dazzling in its splendor, that the sunshine reflected from the white wall of the church opposite seemed darkness in comparison.[14] At the same moment it seemed to her that the dying vibrations of the bells, instead of vanishing altogether, as usual, in an unintelligible murmur, were now changed into a voice of infinite sweetness that whispered to her:

"JOAN, BE WISE AND PIOUS—GOD HAS A MISSION FOR YOU—YOU SHALL CHASE THE STRANGERS FROM GAUL."[15]

The voice stopped and the dazzling splendor disappeared. Distracted and seized with an uncontrollable fear, Jeannette took a few steps in the garden and, falling upon her knees, joined her hands in prayer, invoking the aid of her good saints, St. Marguerite and St. Catherine, as she believed herself possessed of the devil.[16]

That July day of the year 1425 decided the future of Joan Darc. The brilliant light that had dazzled her eyes, the mysterious voice that had sounded in her ear, were the first communications of the spirits that protected Joan, or of *her saints*, as she expressed herself in later years. Differently from most other visionaries, whose hallucinations, disconnected and aimless, floated at the caprice of their disordered minds, the communications to Joan from the invisible world were ever connected with their original cause—her horror of the English and her wish to drive them out of Gaul. Finally, her spirit, nursed by the mysterious legends of her godmother; her imagination struck by the prophecy of Merlin; her heart filled with ineffable compassion for the young King, whom she believed worthy of interest; above all deeply affected by the shocking ills to which the rustics of her condition were exposed by the acts of rapine and sanguinary violence of the English; and, finally, feeling against the invaders the dauntless hatred with which William of the Swallows and Grand-Ferre—obscure heroes, sons of the Jacquerie and precursors of the shepherdess of Domremy—pursued them, Joan was driven to look upon herself as called upon to thrust the strangers out of France and restore to the King his throne.

CHAPTER XII.

RETURNING VISIONS.

During the next three years, from July, 1425, to February, 1429, that is from Joan's fourteenth to her seventeenth year, the communications from the spirit world became ever more and more frequent. Joan saw St. Marguerite and St. Catherine approach her with smiles on their faces and tenderly embrace her.[17] At other times it was the archangel St. Michael who appeared before her, holding his flaming sword in one hand and in the other the crown of France. Again, a multitude of angels played before her wondering eyes in the midst of an immense and dazzling ray of light that shot out from heaven, wherein they gamboled like the atoms that swarm before our eyes in a ray of sunlight across a dark space.[18] Hardly a day went by but that, especially after the ringing of the bells, Joan heard the voice of her dear saints saying to her:

"Joan, run to the assistance of the King of France! You will drive away the English! You will restore the crown to the gentle Sire!"

"Alack! I am but a poor girl, I would not know how to ride a horse nor to lead armed men,"[19] the naïve shepherdess would answer. But the recollections of the prophetic legend of Merlin at times dispelled these doubts, and she would then ask herself why she should not be called to fulfil the prediction. Was not the Lord urging her by the voices of her saints: Go to the assistance of the King? Was she not born and brought up on the borders of Lorraine and near a forest of oaks? Was she not a virgin? Had she not voluntarily consecrated herself to eternal celibacy, yielding perhaps in that matter no less to the repugnance of an invincible chastity than to the desire of giving an additional pledge to the fulfilment of the prophecy of the Gallic bard? Did she not, when only sixteen years of age, in the presence of a large assemblage, confute and prove a liar, by the irresistible sincerity of her words, a lad of her village who pretended to have received from her a promise of marriage?[20] The shy bashfulness of Joan recoiled at the bare thought of marriage. Finally, did she not remember how, on the occasion of the infantine battle between the urchins of Maxey and those of Domremy, her courage, her prompt decisiveness, her enthusiasm changed defeat into victory? With the aid of God and His saints, could she not be victorious in an actual battle, also?

Joan was a pious girl. She was instinct with that genuine piety that raises and connects all things to and with God, the creator of the universe. She thanked Him effusively for manifesting Himself to her through the intermediation of her saints, whom she ever continued to see and hear. At the same time, however, she did not feel for the priests the confidence that St. Catherine and St. Marguerite inspired her with. She piously fulfilled her Catholic duties: She confessed, and often attended communion service, according to the common usage, without, nevertheless, ever speaking either with Master Minet, the curate, or with any other clergymen on the subject of her communications with the beings of the invisible world.[21] She locked in the most secret recesses of her heart her vague aspirations after the deliverance of Gaul, hiding them even from her little girl friend, Mangeste, and from her grown female friend, Hauguette, thus guarding her secret also from her father, her mother and her brothers. During three years she imposed upon herself an absolute silence regarding these mysteries. Thanks to the powerful control that she exercised over herself, Joan showed herself, the same as before, industrious, taking her part in the field and household labors, despite her being increasingly beset by her "voices," that, ever more imperiously, repeated to her almost daily:

"Go, daughter of God! The time has come! March to the rescue of the invaded fatherland! You will drive away the English, you will deliver your King, you will return to him his crown!"

The communications of the spirits became more and more pressing in the measure that Joan approached her seventeenth year. The great designs, that she felt driven to be the instrument of, took an ever stronger hold upon her. Unremitting and painful the obsession pursued her everywhere.

"I felt," said she later, "I felt in my spirit that which a woman must feel when about to be brought to bed of a child."[22]

St. Marguerite and St. Catherine appeared before the young girl, encouraged her, reassured her, promised her the help of God in the deeds that she was to achieve; when the vision vanished the poor child would break out in tears, regretting, as she later expressed it, that her good saints did not take her with them to the angels in the paradise of the good God.[23]

Despite these alternations between faith and doubt concerning her mission, Joan gradually familiarized herself with the thought at which her modesty and simplicity had at first recoiled, the thought of commanding armed men and of vanquishing the English at their head.

In that wonderful organism a rare sagacity, an excellent judgment, an astonishing military aptitude were, without losing any of these qualities, without losing aught of virtue, blended with the exaltations of an inspired woman. Often, recalling as she constantly did, the infantine battle in which victory remained with her, Joan would say:

"Men and children, when known how to be handled, can not choose but obey the identical impulses, the identical generous sentiments; with the aid of heaven it will be with the men of the royal army as it was with the urchins of Domremy; they will follow my example."

Or again:

"To raise the courage of a discouraged and disheartened army, to exalt it, to lead it straight upon the enemy, whatever the number of these may be, to attack it daringly in the open field or behind its entrenchment, and to vanquish it, that is no impossible undertaking. If it succeeds, the consequences of a first victory, by rekindling the fire of an army demoralized by the habit of defeat, are incalculable."

Thoughts like these revealed in Joan a profound intuition in matters of war. Joan, moreover, was not of those puling visionaries, who expect from God alone the triumph of a good cause. One of her favorite sayings was: "Help yourself, and heaven will help you."[24] She ever put in practice that adage of rustic common sense. When on a later occasion a captain said to her disdainfully: "If God wished to drive the English out of Gaul, He could do so by the sole power of His will; He would need neither you, Joan, nor any men-at-arms," Joan answered:

"The men-at-arms will battle—God will give the victory."

CHAPTER XIII.

WRESTLING WITH THE ANGELS.

The three years of mysterious obsessions—between 1425 and 1429—which preluded her glory were for Joan a period of secret and distressing struggles. In order to obey her "voices," in order to carry out her divine mission and fulfil the prophecy of Merlin she would have to battle—and her horror of blood was such that, as she one day said, her "hair stood on end at the sight of French blood flowing."[25] She would have to live in the field with the soldiers—and one of her leading virtues was a delicate sense of modesty. She would have to leave the house in which she was born, renounce her humble, domestic occupations in which she excelled, "being afraid of none at her needle or her distaff," as she was wont to say in her naïve pride. She would, in short, be forced to bid adieu to her young friends, her brothers, her father and her mother, all of whom she tenderly loved, and move—she, a poor and unknown peasant from a corner of Lorraine—to the court of Charles VII, and say to him: "Sire, I am sent to you by our Lord God; confide to me the command of your troops; I shall drive the English out of France and shall restore your crown to you!"

When these thoughts assailed Joan during her intervals of doubt when, her ecstasy over, she fell back upon actual reality, the poor child recoiled before an abyss of difficulties and of impossibilities without number. She derided and pitied herself. The past would then seem a dream; she would ask herself whether she was not out of her mind; she would beseech "her voices" to speak, and her saints to appear before her, in order that her faith in her divine mission might be revived, and prove to her that she had not been the sport of some mental aberration. But Joan's crisis had passed. Even if on such occasions the mysterious voices remained silent and she began to look upon herself as a demented wretch, the next day, perhaps that very night, she again saw her beautiful saints approaching, adorned with their golden crowns draped in brocade, exhaling a celestial odor,[26] and, smiling, say to her: "Courage, Joan, daughter of God! You will deliver Gaul. Your King will owe his crown to you! The time approaches! Stand ready to fulfil your mission!"

The young virgin would then again recover confidence in her predestination, until the day when fresh doubts would assail her, and again melt away. Nevertheless, the doubts were on the decrease, and the moment came when, no longer faint-hearted, but invincibly penetrated with the divine source of her mission, Joan decided to fulfil it at any price, and only awaited an opportue circumstance. From that moment on, above all, and realizing then more than ever the necessity of practicing her favorite adage, *Help yourself, and heaven will help you,* Joan turned the full bent of her mind upon quickly gathering information on the condition of Gaul, and of acquiring the elementary knowledge of arms.

Public events, together with the geographic location of the valley, joined in meeting Joan's wishes. The borders of Lorraine were frequently crossed by the messengers to and from Germany. Anxious for news, as are all people living at a distance from the country's center, James Darc often extended the hospitality of his house to these riders. They gossiped on the English war, the only concern of those sad days. Always reserved before her parents, who were foreign to the vast designs fermenting within her brain, Joan silently worked away at her distaff, losing not a single word of the reports that she heard. At times, however, she would venture one question or another to the travelers, suggested by her secret thoughts, and gradually enlightened herself. Nor was that all. The heroic resistance of the inhabitants of Vaucouleurs several times forced the English to raise the siege; towards the approach of the bad season these took up their winter quarters in Champagne, always to return with the spring. During these marches and counter-marches the hostile army ravaged anew the valley of the Meuse. James Darc and other peasants were more than once obliged to resort to the Castle of Ile for refuge, which, on such occasions, was frequently attacked and valiantly defended. When the danger was over the peasants returned to the village.

The frequent sojourns of the family of Darc at the Castle of Ile, which was well fortified and garrisoned with experienced soldiers; the military alarms, the watches, the assaults that the garrison had to sustain—all this familiarized Joan with the profession of arms. Concentrated within herself, yielding to her martial vocation, attentively observing all that passed around her, explaining to herself the means and manoeuvres of defense, listening, meditating over the orders issued to the soldiers by their superiors, Joan learned or guessed at the elementary principles of the military art. The ideas thus conceived germinated, budded, matured in the quick and penetrating mind of the young girl. She mistrusted herself less when her voices said to her:

"The time approaches—You will drive the English out of Gaul—You are the virgin prophesied by Merlin."

Joan's grand uncle, Denis Laxart, lived in Vaucouleurs; he had long known Robert of Baudricourt, a renowned captain of the country, who abhorred the English and was ardently devoted to the royalist party. Joan often interrogated her uncle about Captain Robert of Baudricourt, upon his nature, upon his affability, upon the manner in which he treated the poor. In his simplicity, the good Denis had no suspicion of the purpose of his niece's interrogatories; he attributed them to girlish curiosity, and answered that Robert of Baudricourt, as brave a soldier as he was brutal and violent, usually sent everybody to the devil, was a terrible man, much feared by himself, and finally, that he never approached the captain but in trembling.

"It is a pity that so good a captain should be of so intractable and so rough a nature," Joan would say with a sigh, to her uncle, and sad and discouraged she would drop the subject only to return to it again.

Grown to a handsome maid, Joan was approaching the end of her sixteenth year—the time predicted by her voices had arrived.

CHAPTER XIV.

"THE TIME HAS ARRIVED."

Towards the end of February of 1429, a small troop of soldiers, on their way back to their duke in Lorraine, and belonging to the party of the Armagnacs, halted at Domremy. The hospitable villagers cordially quartered the strangers at their houses. A sergeant fell to James Darc. The family gave him a friendly reception; they helped him to ease himself of his casque, his buckler, his lance and his sword, and the brilliant weapons were deposited in a corner of the apartment where Joan and her mother were busy preparing the family meal. The sight of the arms that the soldier had laid aside caused the young girl to tremble. She could not resist the desire of secretly touching them, and profiting by a moment when she was left alone, she even put the iron casque upon her young head and took in her virile hand the heavy sword which she drew from its scabbard and brandished, thrusting and cutting.

At seventeen Joan was tall and strong. The superb contours of her virginal bosom[27] filled and rounded her corsage, scarlet as her skirt. Her large black eyes, pensive and mild, her ebony hair, her clear complexion, slightly tanned by the sun, her cherry lips, her white teeth, her chaste physiognomy, serious and candid, imparted an attractive aspect to her appearance; as she now donned the soldier's casque the young girl was resplendent with martial beauty. The sergeant and James Darc entered the room. The latter frowned with severity; the soldier, however, charmed at seeing his casque on the head of the beautiful peasant girl, addressed to her some complimentary words. The anger of James redoubled, but he controlled himself. Blushing at being thus surprised, Joan quickly took off the casque and returned the sword to its scabbard. The family sat down to table. Although the sergeant was still young, he claimed to have often been among the royal troops that had taken the field against the English. He dilated upon his own prowesses, caressed his moustache, and threw side glances at Joan.

To the great astonishment of her family, and despite the obviously increasing though still controlled anger of her father, Joan came out of her ordinary reserve. She drew her stool near that of the soldier, seemed greatly to admire the hero, and overwhelmed him with questions concerning the royal army—its strength, its tactics, its present location, the number of its pieces of artillery, the names of the captains who inspired their soldiers with confidence.

Greatly flattered by the curiosity of the beautiful young girl concerning his military feats, even imagining that she was perhaps more interested in the warrior than in the war, the sergeant answered gallantly all the questions put by Joan. On her part, she listened to him with such rapt attention, and seemed by the fire in her eyes and the animation on her face to take so profound an interest in the conversation, that James Darc felt indignant thinking that the military carriage of the soldier was turning Joan's head. The eyes of the indignant father shot daggers at the soldier. Joan, too much preoccupied with her own thoughts, did not notice the rising anger of her parent, but plied her questions. With secret sorrow she learned then that, driven back beyond the Loire after a recent battle called the "Battle of the Herrings," the royal army had fled in disorder; that the English were besieging Orleans; and that, once the city was taken and Touraine invaded, the fate of the King and of France would be sealed, all his domains would then be in the hands of the English.

"Is there then no help for Gaul?" cried Joan, a prey to inexpressible exaltation. "Is all lost?"

"If the siege of Orleans is not raised within a month," answered the sergeant; "if the English are not driven back far from the Loire, then France will cease to exist! And this is as true as you are the most beautiful maid of Lorraine. Blood of Christ! When a little while ago you had my casque on your head, I thought I had before me the goddess of war. With a captain such as you, I would attack a whole army single-handed!"

At these words James Darc rose abruptly from the table; he told his guest that night was approaching, and country people, who rose with the sun, also retired with the sun. Cross at being thus bade to go, the sergeant slowly picked up his arms and sought to catch Joan's eyes. But the maid, wholly forgetful of the soldier, now sat on her stool steeped in painful meditations, thinking only of the fresh disasters of Gaul, at which her tears flowed freely.

"There can now be no doubt left," the peasant said to himself, "my daughter, so chaste and so pious until this day, has suddenly gone crazy over this braggart; she is weeping over his departure. Shame upon her and us! A curse upon the hospitality that I have extended to this stranger! May the devil take him!"

After the guest had gone, James Darc's face assumed an expression of intense severity. Barely repressing his indignation, he stepped up to his daughter, took her rudely by the arm, motioned her imperiously to the stairs, and cried:

"Go upstairs! There has been enough palavering to-day. I shall talk to you to-morrow!"

Still absorbed in her own racking thoughts, Joan obeyed her father mechanically. When she regained her own room, the latter proceeded, addressing his sons, both of whom were surprised at their father's rudeness towards their sister:

"May God help us! Did you notice the manner in which Joan looked at the sergeant? Oh, if she ever fell in love with a soldier, it would be your duty to drown her with your own hands; or, I swear it, I would sooner strangle her myself."[28]

The peasant uttered the words with such an explosion of rage that Joan heard him. She understood the mistake her father had fallen into, and wept. But soon "her voices" whispered to her:

"The time has arrived. Without you France and her King are lost—Go, daughter of God!—Save your King—Save France!—The Lord is with you—You are about to enter upon your mission."

CHAPTER XV.

CAPTAIN ROBERT OF BAUDRICOURT.

Robert of Baudricourt, the commander-in-chief of Vaucouleurs, a man in the prime of life, of military bearing and of a face whose harshness was relieved by intelligent and penetrating eyes, was walking in nervous excitement up and down a hall in the castle of the town. Instructed by a recent despatch of the desperate position of Charles VII and the danger Orleans ran from the close siege of the English, the captain walked at a rapid pace, grumbling, blaspheming and shaking the floor under the impatient beat of his spurred heels. Suddenly a leather curtain, that concealed the principal entrance to the hall, was pushed aside and revealed a part of the timid and frightened face of Denis Laxart, Joan's grand uncle. Robert of Baudricourt did not notice the good man; he stamped with his feet on the floor, struck the table a violent blow with his fist near where lay the fatal despatch he had just received, and cried:

"Death and fury! It is done for France and the King! All is lost, even honor!"

At this exclamation of exasperation, the courage of Denis Laxart failed him; he dared not approach the captain at such a moment, and he reclosed the curtain, behind which, however, he remained standing awaiting a more opportune moment. But the rage of Robert of Baudricourt redoubled. He again stamped on the floor and cried:

"Malediction! All is lost—all!"

"No, sir! No, all is not lost!" said the good Denis Laxart, resolutely overcoming his fear, but still remaining behind the shelter of the curtain. A second later he pushed his head through the portiere and repeated: "No, sir; all is not lost!"

Hearing the timid voice, the captain turned around; he recognized the old man, whom he rather esteemed, and asked in a rough voice:

"What are you doing at that door? Walk in—why do you not walk in?" But seeing that Denis hesitated, he added still more gruffly: "The devil take it! Will you come in!"

"Here I am, sir—Here I am," said Denis stepping in; "but for the love of God, do not fly off in such a temper; I bring you good news—news—that is unexpected—miraculous news. All is not lost, sir—on the contrary—all is saved. Both King and Gaul!"

"Denis!" replied the captain, casting a threatening look at Joan's uncle, "If your hair were not grey, I would have you whipped out of the castle with a sword's scabbard! Dare you joke! To speak of the safety of King and France under such circumstances as we find ourselves in!"

"Sir, I beseech you, listen without anger to what I have to tell you, however incredible it may seem! I do not look like a clown, and you know me long. Be good enough to listen to me patiently."

"I know you, and know you for a good and wise man; hence your incongruous words shock me all the more. Come on, speak!"

"Sir, as you see, my forehead is bathed in perspiration, my voice chokes me, I am trembling at every limb; and yet I have not even begun to inform you why I came here. If you interrupt me with outbursts of rage, I shall lose the thread of my thoughts—"

"By the bowels of God! Come on! What is it!"

Denis Laxart made a great effort over himself, and after having collected his thoughts he said to the captain in a hurried voice:

"I went yesterday to Domremy to see my niece, who is married to James Darc, an honest peasant from whom she has two sons and a daughter. The daughter is called Jeannette and is seventeen years—"

Noticing that the captain's ill restrained impatience was on the point of exploding at the exordium, Denis hastened to add:

"I am coming to the point, sir, which will seem surprising, prodigious to you. Last evening, my little niece Jeannette said to me: 'Good uncle, you know Captain Robert of Baudricourt; you must take me to him.'"

"What does your niece want of me?"

"She wants, sir, to reveal to you what she told me yesterday evening without the knowledge of her parents, without the knowledge even of Master Minet, the curate—that mysterious voices have long been announcing to her that she would drive the English from Gaul by placing herself at the head of the King's troops, and that she would restore to him his crown."

Struck dumb by the extravagance of these words, Robert of Baudricourt could now hardly contain himself; he was on the point of brutally driving poor Denis out of the hall. Nevertheless, controlling his rage out of consideration for the venerable old man, he retorted caustically:

"Is that the secret your niece wishes to confide to me? It is a singular revelation!"

"Yes, sir—and she then proposes to ask you for the means to reach the gentle Dauphin, our Sire, whom she is absolutely determined to inform of the mission that the Lord has destined to her—the deliverance of Gaul and the King. I must admit it to you, I was struck by the sincerity of Jeannette's tone when she narrated to me her visions of saints and archangels, when she told me how she heard the mysterious voices that have pursued her for the last three years, telling her that she was the virgin whose advent Merlin foretold for the deliverance of Gaul."

"So you have confidence in your niece's sincerity?" asked the captain with a mixture of contempt and compassion, interrupting the old man whom he considered either stupid or crazy. "So you attach credence to the words of the girl?"

"Never did anyone reproach my niece with falsehood. Therefore, yielding to her entreaties, I yesterday evening obtained from her father, who seemed greatly irritated at his daughter, permission for her to accompany me, under the pretext of spending a few days in town with my wife. This morning I left Domremy at dawn with my niece on the crupper of my horse. We arrived in town an hour ago. My niece is waiting for me at home, where I am to take her your answer."

"Well! This is my answer: That brazen and insane girl should have both her ears soundly cuffed, and she should be taken back to her parents for them to continue the punishment.[29] Master Denis Laxart, I took you for a level-headed man. You are either an old scamp or an old fool. Are not you ashamed, at your age, to attach any faith to such imbecilities, and to have the impudence of coming here with such yarns to me? Death and fury! Off with you! By the five hundred devils of hell—get out, on the spot!"

CHAPTER XVI.

AT THE CASTLE OF VAUCOULEURS.

Poor Denis Laxart tumbled out of the room and the Castle of Vaucouleurs at his wits' end; but he soon returned. He did not now come alone. He was accompanied by Joan; his mind was troubled and he trembled at the bare thought of again bearding the bad humor of the Sire of Baudricourt. But so persistently had Joan begged and beseeched her uncle to take her to the terrible captain that he had yielded. The plight of the good man's mind may be imagined when, now accompanied by the young girl, he again approached the leather curtain or portiere of the hall. The captain was just conversing with John of Novelpont,[30] a knight who lived at Vaucouleurs, and was saying to him, evidently towards the end of a talk: "She is a crazy girl fit for a good cuffing. Don't you think so too?"

"What of it, if advantage could be drawn from her craziness!" answered John of Novelpont. "Imagine a man afflicted with some incurable disease and given up by his physicians; being by them condemned to die, someone proposes that he try *in extremis* a philter of pretended virtue, concocted by some crazy person. Should not our patient try that last chance of recovery? Soldiers and the masses are credulous folks; the announcement of celestial, supernatural help might revive the hopes of the people and the army, raise their courage, and perchance bring victory to them after so many defeats. Would not the consequence of a first success, of a victory over the English, be incalculable?"

"If but one victory were won," answered Robert of Baudricourt somewhat less determined in his first views, "our soldiers would regain courage, and they might finally overpower the English."

"Why not consent to see the girl? You could question her yourself, and then form an opinion."

"A visionary—a cowherd!"

"In the desperate condition that France is in, what risk is run by resorting to empiricism? It would be sensible to hear the peasant girl. Whether absurd or not, the prophecy of Merlin that she invokes is popular in Gaul. I remember to have heard it told in my infancy. Moreover, everywhere, prophecies are just now afloat in our unhappy country. Tired of looking for deliverance from human, our people are now expecting help from supernatural agencies. Have not the learned clerks of the University of Paris, and even the clergy, resorted to the clairvoyance of men versed in Holy Writ and habituated to a contemplative life? There are conditions when one must risk something—aye, risk everything."

"By the death of Christ! Are you there again!" cried Robert of Baudricourt, interrupting his friend at seeing the timid face of Denis Laxart appearing at the slit of the leather curtain. "Are you not afraid of exhausting my patience?"

Denis made no answer, but vanished behind Joan, who pushed the curtain aside and resolutely stepped towards the two cavaliers. Her uncle followed her with his eyes raised to heaven, his hat in his hands, and trembling at every limb.

Had Joan been old or homely she would undoubtedly have been instantly driven out by Robert of Baudricourt with contumely. But he, as well as the Sire of Novelpont, was struck with the beauty of the young girl, with her firm yet sweet expression, with her modest and yet confident demeanor. Seized with admiration, the two cavaliers looked at each other in silence. The Sire of Novelpont, shrugging his shoulders, seemed to say to his friend: "Was I wrong when I advised you to see the poor visionary?"

Robert of Baudricourt was still uncertain as to what reception he should bestow upon Joan, when his friend, meaning to test her, interpellated her, saying: "Well, my child, so the King is to be driven out of France and we are all to become English? Is it to prevent all that that you have come here?[31] Speak up! We shall listen."

"Sir," said Joan in a sweet yet firm voice that bore the stamp of unquestionable sincerity, "I have come to this royal city in order to request the sire Robert of Baudricourt to have me taken to the Dauphin of France. My words have been disregarded. Nevertheless, it is imperative that I be with the King within eight days. If I could not walk, I would creep thither on my knees. There is in the world no captain, duke or prince able to save the kingdom of France without the help that I bring with the assistance of God and His saints;"[32] Joan emitted a sigh, and, her eyes moist with tears, added naïvely: "I would much prefer to remain at our house and sew and spin near my poor mother—but God has assigned a task to me—and I must perform it!"[33]

"And in what manner will you perform your task?" put in Robert of Baudricourt, no less astonished than his friend at the mixture of assurance, of ingenuous sweetness and of conviction that pervaded the young girl's answer. "How will you, a plain shepherdess, go about it, in order to vanquish and drive away the English, when Lahire, Xaintrailles, Dunois, Gaucourt, and so many other captains have been beaten and failed?"

"I shall boldly place myself at the head of the armed men, and, with the help of God, we will win."

"My daughter," replied Robert of Baudricourt with a smile of incredulity, "if God wished to drive the English out of Gaul, He could do so by the sole power of His will; He would need neither you, Joan, nor men-at-arms."[34]

"The men-at-arms will battle—God will give the victory,"[35] answered Joan laconically. "Help yourself—heaven will help you."

Again the two knights looked at each other, more and more astonished at the language and attitude of this daughter of the fields. Denis Laxart rubbed his hands triumphantly.

"So, then, Joan," put in John of Novelpont, "you desire to go to the King?"

"Yes, sir; to-morrow rather than the day after; rather to-day than to-morrow. The siege of Orleans must be raised within a month.[36] God will give us victory."

"And it is you, my pretty child, who will raise the siege of Orleans?"

"Yes, with the pleasure of God."

"Have you any idea what the siege of a town means, and in what it consists?"

"Oh, sir! It consists of besieged and besiegers. That is very plain."

"But the besieged must attempt sallies against the enemy who are entrenched at their gates."

"Sir, we are here four in this hall. If we were locked up in here, and we were determined to go out or die, would we not sally forth even if there were ten men at the door?"

"How?"

"Fighting bravely—God will do the rest![37] The besieged will sally forth."

"At a siege, my daughter, sallies are not all there is of it. The besiegers surround the town with numerous redoubts or bastilles, furnished with machines for darting bolts and artillery pieces for bombarding, and all are defended with deep moats. How will you take possession of such formidable entrenchments?"

"I shall be the first to descend into the moats and the first to climb the ladders, while crying to the armed men: 'Follow me! Let us bravely enter the place! The Lord is with us!'"[38]

The two knights looked at each other amazed at Joan's answers. John of Novelpont especially experienced a rising sensation that verged on admiration for the beautiful girl of so naïve a valor. Denis Laxart was thinking apart:

"My good God! Whence does Jeannette get all these things that she is saying! She talks like a captain! Whence did she draw so much knowledge?"

"Joan," resumed Robert of Baudricourt, "if I grant your desire of having you taken to the King, you will have to cross stretches of territory that are in the power of the English. It is a long journey from here to Touraine; you would run great risks."

"The Lord God and His good saints will not forsake us. We shall avoid the towns, and shall travel by night rather than by day. Help yourself—and heaven will help you!"

"That is not all," persisted Robert of Baudricourt, fixing upon Joan a penetrating look; "you are a woman; you will have to travel the only woman in the company of the men that are to escort you; you will have to lodge pell-mell with them wherever you may stop for rest."

Denis scratched his ears and looked at his niece with embarrassment. Joan blushed, dropped her eyes, and answered modestly:

"Sir, I shall put on man's clothes, if you can furnish me with any; I shall not take them off day or night;[39] moreover, would the men of my escort be ready to cause annoyance to an honest girl who confides herself to them?"

"Well, would you know how to ride on horseback?"

"I shall have to learn to ride. Only see to it that the horse be gentle."

"Joan," said Robert of Baudricourt after a moment's silence, "you claim that you are inspired by God; that you are sent by Him to raise the siege of Orleans, vanquish the English and restore the King on his throne? Who is to prove that you are telling the truth?"

"My acts, sir."[40]

This answer, given in a sweet and confident voice, made a lively impression upon the officers. Robert of Baudricourt said:

"My daughter, go back with your uncle to his house—I shall shortly notify you of my decision. I must think over your request."

"I shall wait, sire. But in the name of God, I must depart to the Dauphin, and let it be rather to-day than to-morrow; the siege of Orleans must be raised before a month is over."

"Why do you place so much importance upon the raising of that siege?"

"Oh, sir!" answered Joan, smiling, "I would place less importance upon delivering the good town if the English did not place so much importance upon taking it! The success of the war depends upon that with them; it also depends upon that with us!"

"Well, now, Sir Captain," said the radiant Denis Laxart in a low voice to Robert of Baudricourt, "should I cuff both the ears of the brazen and crazy girl? You advised me to do so."

"No; although a visionary, she is a stout-hearted girl!" answered the knight, also in a low voice. "For the rest, I shall send the curate of Vaucouleurs to examine her, and, if need be, to exorcise her in case there be some sorcery at the bottom of this. Go back home."

Denis and Joan left the hall; the two cavaliers remained in a brown study.

CHAPTER XVII.

JOHN OF NOVELPONT.

Shortly after Joan left, Robert of Baudricourt hastened to the table and prepared to write, while saying to John of Novelpont: "I now think like you; I shall forward the odd adventure to the King and submit to him the opinion that at the desperate pass of things it may not be amiss to try to profit by the influence which this young girl, who claims to be inspired and sent by God, might exercise upon the army, which is completely discouraged. I can see her, docile to the role that she will be put to play, passing before the troops, herself clad in armor and her handsome face under a casque of war! Man is captivated through his eyes as well as through his mind." Robert of Baudricourt stopped upon noticing that the Sire of Novelpont was not listening, but was pacing the length of the hall. He cried: "John, what in the name of the devil are you thinking about?"

"Robert," gravely answered the cavalier, "that girl is not a poor visionary, to be used *in extremis* like an instrument that one may break if it does not meet expectations."

"What else is she?"

"Her looks, her voice, her attitude, her language—everything reveals an extraordinary woman—an inspired woman."

"Are you going to take her visions seriously?"

"I am unable to penetrate such mysteries; I believe what I see, what I hear and what I feel. Joan is or will be an illustrious warrior-maid, and not a passive instrument in the hands of the captains. She may save the country—"

"If she is a sorceress the curate will play the holy-water sprinkler upon her, and report to us."

"I am so much impressed by her answers, her candor, her daring, her good sense, her irresistible sincerity, that if the King sends word back with your messenger that he consents to see Joan—I am resolved to accompany her on her journey."

"Ah, Sir John," said Robert of Baudricourt, laughing; "that is a sudden resolve! Are you smitten by the pretty eyes of the maid?"

"May I die if I am yielding to any improper thought! Such is the proud innocence of that young girl that however lustful I might be, her looks would instantly silence my lust.[41] I am ready to stake my salvation upon it that Joan is chaste. Did you not see how she blushed to the roots of her hair at the idea of riding alone in the company of the horsemen of her escort? Did you not hear her express her wish to assume man's clothes, which she would not take off day or night during her journey? Robert, chastity ever proclaims a beautiful soul."

"If, indeed, she is chaste, she could not be a sorceress; demons, it is said, can not possess the body of a virgin! But be on your guard, dear sire; without your knowing it, the maid's beauty is seducing you. You wish to be her cavalier during the long journey; lucky chances may offer themselves to your amorous courtesy. But," added Robert of Baudricourt in answer to an impatient gesture from his friend, "we shall drop joking. This is what I think concerning the young girl: If she is not a sorceress, her brain is disordered by visions, and she believes herself, in good faith, inspired of God. Such as she is, or seems to be, the girl can become a valuable instrument in the hands of the King. Soldiers and the people are ignorant and credulous. If they see in Joan an emissary of God, if they believe she brings them supernatural aid, they will regain courage, and will make strenuous efforts to wipe out their defeats. Her exaltation, if skilfully exploited by the chiefs of the army, may have happy results. And that is the important point with us."

"The future will prove to you your error. Joan is too sincere, and right or wrong, too deeply imbued with the divinity of her mission, to accept the role that you imagine for her, to resign herself to being a machine in the hands of the chiefs of the army. She will act upon her own impulse. I take her to be naturally endowed with military genius, as have been so many other captains who were at first unknown. Whatever may happen, you must write to the King and inform him of what has happened."

"I think so, too."

"Which King are you writing to?"

"Have we two masters?"

"My dear Robert, I accompanied to court the Count of Metz, under whom I commanded a company of a hundred lances. I have had a near look of things at Chinon and at Loches. I have formed my opinion of our Sire."

"From which it follows that there are two Kings?"

"There is a King of the name of Charles VII, whose mind runs only upon ruling the hearts of easy-going women. Unnerved by indulgence, ungrateful, selfish, regardless of his honor, that prince, hemmed in at Chinon or Loches by his favorites and his mistresses, allows his soldiers to fight and die in the defence of the fragments of his kingdom, but has never been seen at the head of his troops."

"It is a disgrace to the royalty!"

"There is another King. His name is George of La Tremouille, a jealous despot, consumed with malice and vainglory, resentful. He rules supreme over the two or three provinces that the kingdom of France now consists of, and he dominates the royal council. He is the real master."

"I knew that the steward of the palace of our do-nothing King was the Sire of La Tremouille; it is to him I meant to write."

"Do no such thing, Robert; take my advice!"

"You say yourself he is the master—the King in fact!"

"Yes; but anxious to remain master and King in fact, he will not tolerate that any other than himself find the means to save Gaul. The Sire of La Tremouille will, you may rest assured, reject Joan's intervention. Write, on the contrary, direct to Charles VII. He will be struck by the strangeness of the occurrence. If only out of curiosity he will want to see Joan. He finds the day long in his retreat of Loches or Chinon. The blandishments even of his mistresses are often unavailing to draw him from his ennui. The arrival of Joan will be a novelty to him; a pastime."

"You are a good adviser. I shall write direct to the King and expedite a messenger to him on the spot. Should the answer be favorable to Joan, would you still think of accompanying her?"

"Then more than ever!"

"The journey is long. You will have to traverse part of Burgundy and of Champagne, both of them occupied by the enemy."

"I shall take with me my equerry Bertrand of Poulagny, a prudent and resolute man. I shall join to him four well armed valets. A small troop passes more easily unperceived. Moreover, as Joan wisely proposed, we shall avoid the towns all we can by traveling by night, and shall rest by day in isolated farm-houses."

"Do not forget that you will have to cross many rivers; since the war, the bridges are everywhere destroyed."

"We will find ferries at all the rivers. From here we shall go to St. Urbain, where we can stay without danger; we shall avoid Troyes, St. Florentin, and Auxerre; arrived at Gien, we shall be on friendly soil. We shall then proceed to Loches or Chinon, the royal residences."

"Admit it, Sire of Novelpont, are you not slightly smitten by the beauty of Joan?"

"Sire Robert of Baudricourt, I feel proud of being the knight of the warrior-maid and heroine, who, perhaps, may yet save Gaul."

CHAPTER XVIII.

"GOOD LUCK, JOAN!"

Towards sun-down of February 28 of the year 1429, a large crowd consisting of men, women and children pressed around the Castle of Vaucouleurs. The crowd was impatient; it was enthusiastic.

"Are you sure the pretty Joan will leave the castle by this gate?" asked one of the crowd, addressing at random his nearest neighbor.

"I think so—she can not go out on horseback by the postern gate. She is to ride along the ramparts with the Sire of Novelpont, who is to escort her on her long journey. We shall be able to get a good view of her here on her fine white horse."

"Our hearts all go out to her," remarked a third.

"The prophecy of Merlin is fulfilled. Well did he say—*Gaul, lost by a woman, will be saved by a virgin from the borders of Lorraine and a forest of old oaks!*" said a fourth.

"She will deliver us from the English! The poor will again be able to breathe! Peace and work for all!"

"No more war alarms; no more conflagrations; no more pillaging; no more massacres! May her name be blessed!"

"It is God who sent us Joan the Maid—Glory to God!"

"And yet a daughter of the field—a simple shepherdess!"

"The Lord God inspires her—she alone is worth a whole army. The archangels will fight on her side."

"Do you know that Master Tiphaine, the curate of the parish of St. Euterpe, undertook to exorcise the Maid in case she was a sorceress and was possessed of a demon? The clerk carried the cross, the choir-boy the holy-water, and Master Tiphaine carried the sprinkler. But he did not dare to approach the Maid too near, fearing some trick of the spirit of Evil. But Joan smiled and said: 'Come near, good Father, I shall not fly away.'"[42]

"She felt quite sure that she was a daughter of God!"

"Evidently she is a virgin. After the exorcism no clawy demon leaped out of her mouth!"

"Everybody knows that the devil can not inhabit the body of a virgin. Consequently Joan can not be a sorceress, whatever people may have said of her god-mother Sybille."

"So far from suspecting that Joan was an invoker of demons, Master Tiphaine was so edified with her mildness and modesty that the day after the exorcism he admitted her to holy communion—she ate the bread of the angels."

"That was lucky! Who, if not Joan, could eat angels' bread?"

"Do you know, friends, that while the Sire of Baudricourt was waiting for the answer of the King, and, by God, it seems the answer was long in coming, the Duke of Lorraine, hearing the report that Joan was the maid foretold by Merlin, wished to see her?"

"And did he?"

"The Sire of Novelpont took Joan to the duke. 'Well, my young girl,' said the duke to her, 'you who are sent by God should be able to give me advice; I am sick, and, it looks to me, near my end—'"

"So much the worse for him! Who does not know that the duke is suffering from the consequences of his debaucheries, and that, in order to indulge them at his ease, he has bravely cast off his own wife?"

"No doubt Joan must have known all that, because she answered the duke: 'Monseigneur, call the duchess back to your side, lead an honest life, God will not forsake you.[43] Help yourself and heaven will help you.'"

"Well answered, holy girl!"

"It is said that those are her favorite words—'Help yourself and heaven will help you!'"

"Well, may heaven and all its saints protect her during the long journey that she is to undertake!"

"Is it credible?—a poor child of seventeen years to command an army?"

"Myself and five other archers of the company of the Sire of Baudricourt," said a sturdy looking soldier, "requested him as a favor to allow us to escort Joan the Maid. He refused! By the bowels of the Pope, I would have liked to have that beautiful girl for a captain! Led by her, I would defy all the English put together! Yes, by the navel of Satan, I would!"

"Armed men commanded by a woman! That surely is odd!" observed an impressed cynic.

"Two beautiful eyes looking upon you and seeming to say: 'March upon the enemy!' are enough to set one's heart on fire! And if, besides, a sweet voice says to you: 'Courage—forward!' that would be enough to turn the biggest coward into a hero!"

"Above all if the voice is inspired by God, my brave archer."

"Whether she be inspired by God, by the devil or by her own bravery, I care as little as for a broken arrow. If one were but alone against a thousand, he must have the cowardice of a hare not to follow a beautiful girl, who, sword in hand, rushes upon the enemy."

"I can not help thinking of the pain it must give Joan's family to have her depart, however glorious the Maid's destiny may be. Her mother must feel very sad."

"I have it from Dame Laxart that James Darc, a very strict and rough man, after having twice had his daughter written to, ordering her return home, and objecting to her riding away with men-at-arms, has invoked a curse upon her. Furthermore, he forbade his wife and his two sons ever again to see Joan. She wept all the tears in her poor body upon learning of her father's curse. 'My heart bleeds to leave my family,' said the poor child to Dame Laxart, 'but I must go whither God bids me.[44] I have a glorious mission to fill.'"

"The Maid's father is a brute! He must have a bad heart! The idea of cursing his daughter—who is going to deliver Gaul."

"She will do so—Merlin foretold it."

"It will be a beautiful day for us all when the English are thrust out of our poor country which they have been ravaging for so many years!"

"The fault lies with the knighthood," put in a civilian; "why did it prove so cowardly at Poitiers? This nobility is a costly luxury."

"And on top of all, oppressed and persecuted, Jacques Bonhomme has had to pay the ransom for the cowardly seigneurs with gilded spurs!"

"But Jacques Bonhomme got tired and kicked in his desperation. Oh, once at least did the scythe and fork get the better of the lance and sword! The Jacquerie revenged the serfs! Death to the nobles!"

"But what a carnage was not thereupon made of the Jacques! The day of reprisals will come!"

"Well, the Jacques had their turn; that is some consolation!"[45]

"Now it will be the turn of the English, thanks to Joan the Maid—the envoy of God! She will throw them out!"

"Aye, aye! Let her alone—she promised that within a month there will not be one of these foreigners left in France."[46]

"Glory to her! The shepherdess of Domremy will have done what neither King, dukes, knights nor captains were capable of accomplishing!"

"Good luck to you, Joan, born like ourselves of the common people! A blessing on her from all the poor serfs who have been suffering death and all the agonies of death at the hands of the English!"

"They are letting down the drawbridge of the castle!"

"There she is! That's she!"

"How well shaped and beautiful she is in her man's clothes! Prosperity to Joan the Maid!"

"Look at her! You would take her for a handsome young page with her black hair cut round, her scarlet cape, her green jacket, her leather hose and her spurred boots! Long live our Joan!"

"By my soul, she has a sword on her side!"

"Although not a generous man, the Sire of Baudricourt presented her with it."

"That's the least he could do! Did not the rest of us in Vaucouleurs go down in our pockets to purchase a horse for the warrior maid?"

"Master Simon, the cloth merchant, answered for the palfrey as a patient animal and of a good disposition; a child could lead it; it served as the mount to a noble dame in the hunt with falcons."

"Upon the word of an archer," again put in the archer of the Sire of Baudricourt's company, "Joan holds herself in the saddle like a captain! By the bowels of the Pope! She is beautiful and well shaped! How sorry I am not to be among the armed men of her escort! I would go with her to the end of the world, if only for the pleasure of looking at her!"

"Indeed, if I were a soldier, I would prefer to obey orders given by a sweet voice and from pretty little lips, than given by a rough voice and from hairy and coarse lips."

"Look at the Sire of Novelpont with his iron armor! He rides at Joan's right. Do you see him? He is a worthy seigneur."

"He looks as if he would guard her as his own daughter. May God guard them both!"

"He is adjusting a strap on the bridle of the Maid's palfrey."

"At her left is the Sire of Baudricourt; he will probably accompany her part of the way."

"There is the equerry Bertrand of Poulagny, carrying his master's lance and shield."

"Jesus! They have only four armed men with them! All told six persons to escort Joan from here to Touraine! And through such dangerous territories! What an imprudence!"

"God will watch over the holy Maid."

"Look—she is turning in her saddle and seems to wave good-bye to someone in the castle."

"She is taking her handkerchief to her eyes; she is drying her tears."

"She must have been waving good-bye to her uncle and aunt, the old Laxarts."

"Yes; there they are, both of them, at the lower window of the tower; they are holding each other's hands and weep to see their niece depart, perhaps forever! War is so changeable a thing!"

"Poor, dear girl! Her heart must bleed, as she said, to go all alone, far from her folks, and to battle at the mercy of God!"

"She will now turn around the corner of the rampart—"

"Let her at least hear our hearty adieus—Good luck, Joan the Maid! Good luck to Joan! Good luck! Good luck! Death to the English!"

"She hears us—she makes a sign—she is waving good-bye to us. Victory to Joan!"

"Mother! Mother! Take me up in your arms! Put me on your shoulders. Let me see her again."

"Come child! Take a good look! Always remember Joan! Thanks to her, no longer will desolate mothers weep for sons and husbands massacred by the English."

"Good luck to Joan—Good luck!"

"She has turned the corner of the rampart—she is gone!"

"Good luck to Joan the Maid! May the good God go with her!"

"May she deliver us from the English! Good luck, Joan!"

PART II.

CHINON.

CHAPTER I.

THE COUNCIL OF CHARLES VII.

Three of the principal members of the Council of King Charles VII—George of La Tremouille, chamberlain and a despotic, avaricious and suspicious minister; the Sire of Gaucourt, an envious and cruel soldier; and Regnault, Bishop of Chartres, a double-dealing and ambitious prelate—were assembled on the 7th of March of 1429 in a hall of the Castle of Chinon.

"May the fever carry off that Robert of Baudricourt! The man's audacity of writing direct to the King inducing him to receive that female cowherd!" cried George of La Tremouille. "And Charles considers the affair a pleasant thing and wants to have a look at the crazy girl! The fools claim she is sent by God—I hold she has been sent by the devil to thwart my plans!"

"There is but one way of eluding the formal orders of the King," observed the Bishop of Chartres. "That accursed John of Novelpont has made so much noise that our Sire is determined to see the vassal whom, since her arrival, we have kept confined in the tower of Coudray to await the royal audience. The brazen and vagabond minx feels greatly elated at the imbecile enthusiasm that she has been made the object of by the clouts of Lorraine, and is surprised at not having been presented to Charles VII! Blood of Christ! Our do-nothing King is quite capable, as a means both of ridding himself of us and of dropping all care on the score of the kingdom's safety, of tempting God by accepting the aid of this Joan—In that event, my seigneurs, it will be all over with the influence of the royal council! All that will be left for us to do will be to quit our posts."

"And I, Raoul of Gaucourt, who served under Sancerre and under the Constable of Clisson, I who vanquished the Turks at Nicopolis, I am to take orders from a woman who tended cattle! Death and massacre! I sooner would break my sword!"

"These are hollow words, Raoul of Gaucourt," said the Sire of La Tremouille thoughtfully; "words are powerless against facts. Our Sire, indolent, fickle and cowardly, may, at the desperate pass his affairs are in, wish to try the supernatural influence of this female cowherd. Let us not deceive ourselves. Since the day that Joan was at my orders relegated to the tower of Coudray, half a league from here, the outcry raised by John of Novelpont has had its effect upon a part of the court. His enthusiasm for the said Joan, his reports of her beauty, her modesty, her military genius, have awakened a lively curiosity among a number of courtiers."

"Mercy!" cried Raoul of Gaucourt. "The idea of pretending that peasant possesses military genius! The man must be crazy enough for a strait-jacket."

"Raoul, collect yourself," replied the Bishop of Chartres; "my son in God George of La Tremouille, has stated the facts. He is right. A part of the court, greedy after novelties, jealous of our power, and tired of seeing a portion of their domains in the hands of the English has given an ear to the excited reports of John of Novelpont upon the visionary girl. A goodly number of these courtiers have beset the King. He wishes to see her. It would be absurd and impolitic to try to struggle against the current that has set in."

"So, then, we are to yield, are we?" cried Raoul of Gaucourt, wrathfully striking the table at which they were seated. "Yield before this sorceress who should be roasted on fagots!"

"We may avail ourselves of the fagots later on, my brave Raoul; but at present we must yield.—You know it better than I in your capacity of an experienced captain, Sire of La Tremouille; the position that can not be carried by a front attack, may yet be flanked."

"Your words are golden, dear tonsured companion. Among friends agreed upon the same end and having identical interests, the full truth is due to each by all. I shall, accordingly, open my mind to you upon the present situation. I have for some time succeeded in removing the princes of the blood from the councils of the King. We reign. Moreover, as regards myself, I am, just at present, far from desiring to see the war with the English and Burgundians come to an end. I have need of its continuance. My brother, who is on familiar terms with the Regent of England and the Duke of Burgundy, has obtained from both protection for my domains. Only this year, when the enemy pushed forward as far as the walls of Orleans, my lands and my seigniory of Sully were spared.[47] That is not all. Thanks to the civil troubles and to the numerous partisans whom I keep in pay in Poitou, that province is at my mercy. I do not lose the hope of annexing it to my possessions,[48] provided the war is prolonged a little. You see, I have a powerful interest in thwarting the projects of this female envoy of God, should they ever be realized. I do not wish for the expulsion of the English, I do not wish for the end of the war, for the reason that the war serves my purposes. Such, in all sincerity, are my personal motives. Now, let us see whether your interests, Regnault, Bishop of Chartres, and yours, Raoul of Gaucourt are not of the same nature as mine. As to you, Bishop of Chartres, should the war end suddenly by force of arms, what becomes of all the negotiations that for a long time you have been secretly conducting with the Regent of England on one side, and the Duke of Burgundy on the other—negotiations that have cost so much toil and that, justly so, give the King so high an opinion of your importance? What becomes of the guarantees and the pecuniary advantages that, like a shrewd negotiator, you demand and know how to obtain from the princes that you negotiate with?"

"All my hopes will be shattered if our troops, fanaticized by this girl, should gain but one victory in a single encounter with the English," cried the Bishop of Chartres. "The Regent of England wrote to me only recently that *he was not disinclined to entertain my propositions for a treaty*, in which case, added the Duke of Bedford, *I could be sure of obtaining all that I have demanded of him*. But if the fires of war should flare up again under the inspiration of this bedeviled peasant girl, all negotiations will be broken off, and then good-bye to the profits that I sought to derive. So that you were right, George of La Tremouille, when you said that our interests command us to join hands against Joan."

"And as to you, Raoul of Gaucourt," replied the Sire of La Tremouille, "I hope you are not ignorant of the fact that Dunois, Lahire, Xaintrailles, the Constable of Richemont, the Duke of Alençon, and other leading commanders, are all jealous of your ability and of your seat in the royal council, and that they will rank themselves on the side of the girl, whom they will turn into a docile instrument to overthrow you. If the royal army wins but one victory, your influence and military prestige will be eclipsed by the success of your rivals. Our King, fickle, ungrateful and irresolute as we know him to be, will sacrifice you at the first suspicion of treason or incompetence."

"Thunder and blood!" cried Raoul of Gaucourt, "I have a good mind to go straight to the tower of Coudray and order the execution of the sorceress without the formality of a trial! We shall find priests enough to affirm that Satan carried her off."

"The method is violent and clumsy, dear captain!" replied George of La Tremouille. "The same end can be reached by other methods. It is understood that I, you, and the Bishop of Chartres have common interests which bind us against the girl. What we must now do is to consider how to ruin her. Let's begin with you, holy Bishop of Chartres, the spiritual director of our Sire. However debauched he is, occasionally he is afraid of the devil. Could you not insinuate to the good King that he would endanger the salvation of his soul if he were, precipitately and without a previous inquest, to attach faith to the creature that calls herself a deputy of the Lord, but who is more likely a deputy of Satan?"

"An excellent idea!" exclaimed the Bishop of Chartres. "I shall convince Charles VII that it is imperative to have Joan examined by the clerks of theology, they being alone qualified to ascertain and solemnly declare whether she is obeying a divine inspiration, or whether, on the contrary, she is not a brazen impostor possessed of the evil spirit, in which case, by placing confidence in the girl, our Sire would then render himself the accomplice in a sorcery. I shall then empanel a canonical college that shall be charged with pronouncing finally and infallibly upon the degree of faith that may be accorded to the alleged divine mission of Joan. Obedient to my secret instructions she shall be pronounced a heretic, a sorceress and possessed of the evil spirit. The fagots will soon be in full flare to receive her to the heart's content of our brave Gaucourt. We shall have her burned alive."

"Blood of God!" cried the soldier. "I shall myself set fire to the pyre. There is the infamous female serf, who meant to command noble captains, burnt to a crisp!"

"She is not yet roasted, dear Gaucourt!" observed the Sire of La Tremouille. "Let us suppose that the plan of our friend the Bishop of Chartres fails; let us suppose that by some fatal accident and contrary to the instructions issued to it by our worthy bishop, the canonical council declares the said Joan truly and duly inspired by God—"

"I answer for the clerks whom I shall choose for the examination! They will all be men entirely devoted to me."

"Dear Bishop, it sometimes happens that the soldiers we think we can answer for man for man, slip us at the moment of action. It may happen that way with your clerks. Let us proceed from the theory that King Charles, finding himself *in extremis*, is inclined to take the risk of placing the said Joan at the head of his armies. It will then rest with you, Raoul of Gaucourt, more than with anyone else, to ruin the insolent girl, who has but one fixed thought—to raise the siege of Orleans. You must then demand of the King the command of the town of Orleans, and you must consent to serve under her orders."

"May hell confound me if ever, even for a single hour, I should consent to receive orders from that she-cowherd!"

"Be not all tempest and flame, brave Gaucourt. Remember that the bulk of the troops would then be under your immediate orders. Joan will issue orders to you, but you can disregard them, you can cross and thwart all her plans of battle; you can cause well calculated delays in the movements of the troops; above all you could—well—manoeuvre in such a way as to have the crazy girl fall into the hands of the English. In short, it would lie with you, more than with us, to prevent her from winning her first battle."

"At the first check that she meets," added the Bishop of Chartres insinuatingly to Raoul of Gaucourt, "the enthusiasm that she now excites will change into contempt. The people will feel ashamed of having allowed themselves to be duped by so clumsy an imposition. The revulsion against her will be immediate. If, contrary to all expectations—I should say certainty—the canonical council appointed by myself should declare Joan truly inspired by God;—if the King then places her at the head of his troops—then, brave Gaucourt, the loss of her first battle, brought on by your skilful manoeuvres, will deal a fatal blow to the adventuress! Victorious, she would be the envoy of God; vanquished, she becomes the envoy of Satan!—Then we may proceed against her in regular form under the pretext of heresy and sorcery—then will the fagots that you are in such a hurry to set fire to soon be kindled to receive her. It depends upon you whether she shall be burned alive by us, or allowed to be taken by the English, who will execute her."

"Well," answered Raoul of Gaucourt meditatively, "let us suppose the she-cowherd orders a sally against the besiegers; the bridge is lowered; the bedeviled girl rushes out over it; a few of our men follow her;—I give the signal to retreat; my people hasten to re-enter the town; the bridge is raised—and the wench remains in the power of the enemy! Is that it?"

"Yes; can we rely upon you?"

"Yes; I perceive the way, either by a false sally or some other manoeuvre, to settle the she-devil!"

"And now," resumed the Sire of La Tremouille, "let us feel hopeful; our plot is well laid; our nets are skilfully spread. It will be impossible for the visionary to escape; either you, Gaucourt, or you, worthy Bishop, will prevent it. As to me, I shall not be idle. But first of all, holy Bishop, is it not an established fact that a demon can not possess the body of a virgin?"

"It is an unquestionable fact, according to the formula of exorcism—We shall attend to that."

"Now, then, Joan claims to be a virgin. Her fanatical and imbecile followers call her Joan the Maid. Either the street-walker, indecently clad in man's clothes, is the concubine of John of Novelpont, to judge by the interest he takes in her, or she is really chaste and a virgin. It shall be my part to prick the libertine curiosity of the King on the subject by proposing to him to assemble a council of matrons. Such a council, presided over, let us suppose, by the King's mother-in-law, Yolande of Sicily, will be commissioned to ascertain whether Joan is really a virgin. If she is none, the most violent suspicions of imposture and sorcery immediately rise against her. Then she no longer is the alleged saint whom God has inspired, but an audacious cheat, a worthy companion of the easy wenches who follow the encampments. She will then be shamefully whipped, and then driven away, if not burned for a sorceress."

"I am ready to accept your theory that she is a ribald," replied the Bishop of Chartres, "and, with you, I feel sure that John of Novelpont, who is so fascinated with her, is her lover. Nevertheless, if by accident she does not lie and is justified in allowing herself to be called the Maid, and if it is solemnly established that she is still pure, would not that greatly redound to her advantage? Would not then the presumption of her divine mission be strengthened? On the other hand, by not submitting Joan to any such trial, the field remains free for suspicions, which it would then be an easy thing for us to fan; we could easily set calumny afloat."

"Your objection is serious," answered the Sire of La Tremouille. "Nevertheless, just supposing the girl to be chaste, what must not be her shame at the thought of so humiliating an investigation! The more conscious she be of the chastity of her life, that they say has been irreproachable until now, all the more will the creature feel grieved and indignant at a suspicion that so outrages her honor! The chaster she is, all the more will she revolt at the shamefulness of the verification! She will scorn the proposition as an unbearable insult, and will refuse to appear before the council of matrons!— Skilfully exploited, her refusal will turn against her."

"Upon the word of a soldier, the idea is ingenious and droll! I foresee that our wanton Sire will himself want to preside over the council that is to do the examining!"

"And yet, should Joan submit to the trial, and come out triumphant, she will then have a great advantage over us."

"No greater than if she is believed to be a maid upon her own word. The convocation of a council of matrons offers us two chances: if Joan submits to the disgraceful examination she may be declared a strumpet; if she refuses, her refusal makes against her!"

"There is nothing to answer to that," said Raoul of Gaucourt; "I adhere to the plan of a council of matrons to pass upon her virginity."

"Now, let us sum up and lay down our plan of conduct. First, to obtain from the King that a council of matrons be summoned to pass and publicly pronounce itself upon the maidenhood of our adventuress; secondly, in case she issues triumphant from that trial, to convoke a canonical council, instructed to put to the girl the most subtle, the hardest, the most perplexing theological questions, and to announce from her answers whether or not she is inspired by God; thirdly, and lastly, in the next to impossible event that this second examination also result in her favor, to manoeuvre in such manner that she lose her first battle and remain a prisoner in the hands of the English—one way or another she is bound to go down."

At this moment the equerry of Charles VII knocked at the door of the council hall, and entered to announce to the Sire of La Tremouille that the King demanded his minister's immediate presence.

CHAPTER II.

ALOYSE OF CASTELNAU.

Charles VII—the "gentle Dauphin" of France and object of the fervent adoration of Joan, who now for several days lay sequestered in the tower of Coudray—soon tired of the interview to which he had summoned his minister, and sought recreation elsewhere. He found it in the company of his mistress, Aloyse of Castelnau. Indolently stretched upon a cushion at her feet he chatted with her. Frail and slight of stature, the prince, although barely twenty-three years of age, was pale, worn-out and unnerved by excesses. Aloyse, on the other hand, in the full splendor of her beauty, soon found occasion to answer a joke of her royal lover on the subject of Joan the Maid. She said smiling:

"Fie, Charles! Fie, you libertine! To hold such language about an inspired virgin who wishes to restore to you the crown of France!"

"If it is to be that way, the ways of the Lord are strange and inscrutable, as our tonsured friends say. To have the crown and kingdom of France turn upon the maidenhood, upon the virginity of a cowherd!"

"Are you still at it?" responded Aloyse, interrupting Charles. "I guess your villainous thoughts regarding the poor girl."

"I ask myself, how could the idea have germinated in the mind of that poor girl of restoring my crown to me!"

"You display very little concern about your kingdom!"

"On the contrary—I think a good deal of my crown. It is the cares of royalty that cause me to speak in that way, my beautiful mistress."

"If the English take Orleans, the key of Touraine and Poitou, and they then invade those provinces, what will then be left to you?"

"You, my charmer! And if I must make the confession, it has often occurred to me that my great-grandfather, King John II, of pious memory, must have recorded among the happy days of his life the one on which he lost the battle of Poitiers—"

"The day when your great-grandfather, taken prisoner by the English, was transported to their own country? You must be crazy, my dear Charles!"

"Without any doubt, I am crazy; but crazy with love for you, my Aloyse! But let us come back to King John, made prisoner at the battle of Poitiers. He is taken to England. He is received with chivalrous courtesy and unheard-of magnificence. A sumptuous palace is assigned to him for prison, and he is invited out to exquisite banquets. The handsomest girls of England are charged to watch him. The forests that are at his disposal teem with game; the fields are vast; the rivers limpid. Thus his time is divided between love, play, the table, fishing, hunting—until he dies of indigestion. While King John was thus peaceably enjoying life in England, what was his son doing, the unhappy Charles V? Driven out of Paris by a vile populace that rose in rebellion at the voice of Marcel, the unhappy Charles the Wise, as he was called, frightened out of his senses by the ferocities of the Jacquerie, beset by the bustle of royalty, broken with the fatigues of war, ever on horseback, ever sleeping on the hard ground, and never sleeping with both eyes shut, living on poor fare and on poorer love, rushing hither and thither over hill and dale, was ever out of breath running after his crown! By the glories of Easter! Do you call that 'wisdom'?"

"He at least had the glory of re-conquering his crown, and indulged the pleasure of executing his enemies."

"Oh, I well understand the happiness of revenge. I abominate those insolent Parisians, those chasers of kings. If I had that accursed town in my power, I would order the most inveterate Burgundians to be hanged. But I would be careful not to establish my residence there, out of fear of fresh seditions. Charles V revenged himself; he reigned, but at the price of what anxieties, torments and incessant civil wars! While his father, King John, was all the while living happily in England, surrounded by abundance and love! To want this, to oppose that in matters of public concern, are intellectual labors that I leave to the Sire of La Tremouille and his fellows of the royal council to rack their brains over. Without alarming myself over the future, my Aloyse, I allow the current to carry me, rocked in your arms. Whatever may happen, I laugh! Long live love!"

"Oh, you do not speak like a King."

"A plague upon royalty! A burning crown of thorns! I'd rather have your white hands weave me a chaplet of myrtle, and fill my cup. If they do, I would gladly see the debris of my throne crumble and vanish. When the English will have conquered the provinces that still are left to me, they will take care of me as they did of my predecessor, King John! So, then, long live wine, idleness and love! If, on the contrary, in His ill will towards me, the Lord has stirred up this raging Maid, who is obstinately set upon restoring to me the crown of my fathers with all its escort of uneasiness, bluster and troubles—let it be! Let my fate be fulfilled! But, I swear to God, I shall budge not one step to insure the success of the warrior maid!"

"Then you have no faith in the inspiration of Joan, the Maid?"

"I have faith in your pretty eyes, for the reason that they keep all their promises; and I have none in the shepherdess. Were it not that I am daily beset with the outcry of people who have the royalty more at heart than I myself, I long ago would have sent her back to her muttons. But the Sire of La Tremouille himself inclines to yielding to these clamors. Some insist on seeing in Joan a divine instrument; others hold that in the desperate state of things we should try to profit by the influence that the Maid may exert over the minds of the soldiers. I am, accordingly, compelled to receive her at court to-day. But the Sire of La Tremouille is of the opinion that a council of matrons should first decide whether the pretty girl really possesses the magic charm with the aid of which I am to reconquer my kingdom."

"Come, Charles! A truce to your villainous jokes!"

"If Diana were your patron you could not be more intractable, my Aloyse! I do not recognize you to-day."

"Ah, I have one more proof of how indolent you are, how cowardly and how neglectful of your own honor. How often have not I said to you: Place yourself at the head of your troops, who are indignant at seeing the King refusing to share their hardships! Take a bold resolve; don your cuirass and go to battle!"

"A pest! My Amazon, you speak at ease of the hardships and perils of war. I am no Caesar—that much is certain!"

"Shameless heart! Miserable coward!"

"I wish to live to love you."

"You make me blush with shame!"

"You blush at being the mistress of the poor 'King of Bourges' as I am called—at reigning over so sorry a kingdom! You would like to reign over the kingdom of all France!"

"Am I wrong in wishing that you should reign gloriously? I wish you were more ambitious."

"Oh, my beloved! Would I, if I again were to become King of France, find the satin of your skin whiter and smoother? wine to taste better? or idleness more agreeable?"

"But glory! Glory!"

"Vanity! Vanity! I never have envied any glory other than that of the great King Solomon, of that valorous hero of six hundred concubines and more than four hundred legitimate wives! But unable to reach the heights of that amorous potentate, I content myself with aspiring after the destiny of King John, my great-grandfather."

"Shame upon you, Charles! Such sentiments are disgraceful, and will prevent a single captain from taking the field for you."

"Oh, those valiant captains who combat my enemies have no thought to my interests. They fight at the head of companies of mercenaries in order to pillage the populace and to recover their own seigniories that have fallen into the hands of the English."

The belle Aloyse was about to answer Charles VII when George of La Tremouille entered the royal apartment after repeatedly knocking at the door. The minister said:

"Sire, everything is ready for the reception of Joan. We await your orders."

"Let us go and receive the Maid! I greatly approve your idea of putting the inspired girl to the test, and finding out if she can pick me out among the courtiers, while Trans will play the role of King. The comedy is to start."

CHAPTER III.

THE TEST.

Animated by conflicting sentiments, the men and women of the court of Charles VII, gathered in a gallery of the Castle of Chinon, awaited the arrival of Joan the Maid. Some, and they were few, believed the girl inspired; most of the others regarded her either as a poor visionary, a docile instrument that might be turned to account by the heads of the State, or an adventuress whom her own audacity, coupled to the credulity of fools, was pushing forward. All, however, whatever their opinion concerning the mission that the peasant girl of Domremy claimed for herself, saw in her a daughter of the rustic plebs, and asked themselves how the Lord could have chosen his elect from such a low condition.

Splendidly dressed, the Sire of Trans sat on what looked like a throne—an elevated seat placed under a canopy at one end of the gallery. He was to simulate the King, while Charles VII himself, mixing in the crowd of his favorite courtiers, was laughing in his sleeve, satisfied with the idea of the test that Joan's sagacity was to be put to. Joan presently entered, conducted by a chamberlain. She held her cap in her hand and was in man's attire—a short jacket, slashed hose and spurred boots. Intimidated at first by the sight of the courtiers, Joan quickly regained her self-possession; holding her head high and preserving a modest yet confident bearing, she stepped forward in the gallery. Vaguely suspecting the ill-will of many of the seigneurs of the King's household, the girl scented a snare, and said to the chamberlain who escorted her:

"Do not deceive me, sir; take me to the Dauphin of France."[49]

The chamberlain motioned toward the Sire of Trans, who lolled ostentatiously on the raised and canopied seat at the extremity of the gallery. The mimic King was a man of large size, corpulent and of middle age. On her journey, Joan had often interrogated the knight of Novelpont on Charles VII, his external appearance, his features. Being thus informed that the prince was of a frail physique, pale complexion and short stature, and finding no point of resemblance between that portrait and the robustious appearance of the Sire of Trans, Joan readily perceived that she was being trifled with. Wounded to the heart by the fraud, the sign of insulting mistrust or of a joke unworthy of royalty, if Charles was an accomplice in the game, Joan turned back toward the chamberlain, and said, with indignation mantling her cheek:

"You deceive me—him that you point out to me is not the King."[50]

Immediately noticing a few steps away from her a frail looking and pale young man of small stature, whose features accorded perfectly with the description that she preserved as a perpetual souvenir in her mind, Joan walked straight towards the King and bent her knee before him, saying in a sweet and firm voice: "Sir Dauphin, the Lord God sends me to you in His name to save you. Place armed men at my command, and I shall raise the siege of Orleans and drive the English from your kingdom. Before a month is over I shall take you to Rheims, where you will be crowned King of France."[51]

Some of the bystanders, convinced as they were that the peasant girl of Domremy obeyed an inspiration, considered supernatural the sagacity that she had just displayed in recognizing Charles VII from among the courtiers; they were all the more impressed by the language that she held to the King. A large number of others, attributing Joan's penetration to a freak of accident, saw in her words only a ridiculous and foolish boast, and they suppressed with difficulty their jeering disdain at this daughter of the fields daring so brazenly to promise the King that she would clear his kingdom of the English, until then the vanquishers of the most renowned captains.

Charles fixed upon Joan a defiant and libertine look that brought the blush to her cheeks, ordered her to rise, and said to her with an air of nonchalance and sarcasm that revealed mistrust in every word:

"My poor child, we are thankful for your good intentions towards us and our kingdom. You promise us miraculously to drive away the English and to restore to us our crown. That is all very well. Finally, you claim to be inspired by God—and on top of all, that you are a maid. Before placing any faith in your promises we must first make sure that you are not possessed of an evil spirit and that you are virgin. On the latter head, your pretty face at least justifies doubt. In order to remove it the venerable Yolande, Queen of Sicily and mother of my wife, will preside over a council of matrons that will be commissioned by us duly, authentically and notarially to verify your virginity.[52] After that, my pretty child, if you issue triumphant from the trial, we shall then have to establish whether you are really sent to us by God. To that end, an assembly of the most illustrious clerks in theology, convened in our town of Poitiers, where our parliament is in session, will examine and interrogate you, and it will then declare, according to the answers that you make, whether you are inspired by God or possessed of the devil. You will admit, my little girl, that it would be insane to confide to you the command of our armed men before we have become convinced that God really inspires you—and, above all, that you are really a virgin."

At these words, so full of indifference, of mistrust, and of insulting immodesty, which were received with lewd smiles by the surrounding courtiers, and that, moreover, were pronounced by the "gentle Dauphin of France," whose misfortunes had so long been rending her heart, Joan felt crushed, and her chastity and dignity revolted at the bare thought of the disgraceful and humiliating examination that her body was first to be submitted to by the orders of that very Charles VII.

A prey to bitter sorrow, for a moment, in accord with the expectations of the Sire of La Tremouille, who was the promotor of the unworthy plan, Joan thought of renouncing her mission and abandoning the King to his fate. But it immediately occurred to the warm-hearted girl that not that indolent, ungrateful and debauched prince alone was concerned in her mission, but also Gaul, for so many years the bleeding victim of the foreigners' rapacity. Gaul's deliverance was at stake, Gaul, that having drained the cup of suffering to the very dregs, had attracted the compassion of the Lord! Accordingly, strengthening her faith and her energy in the recollection of the mysterious voices that guided her, recalling the prophecies of Merlin, confident in the military genius that she felt developing within her, and drawing from the consciousness of her own chastity and from the ardor of her love of country the necessary courage to resign herself to the ignominy that she was threatened with, yet anxious to make an effort to escape it, she raised to Charles VII her eyes bathed in tears and said to him: "Oh, Sire! Why not believe me and try me! I swear to you, I have come to you by the will of heaven!"[53]

CHAPTER IV.

THE HALL OF RABATEAU.

Upon her arrival at Poitiers, where the parliament was then in session and where she was to undergo the two examinations—on her virginity and her orthodoxy—Joan was placed in the house of Master John Rabateau, in charge of the latter's wife, a good and worthy woman whom Joan charmed with her piety, her innocence and the sweetness of her disposition. Joan shared her hostess's bed, and spent the first night weeping at the thought of the indecorous examination that she was to be subjected to the next day. The examination took place in the presence of Queen Yolande of Sicily and several other dames, among whom was the wife of Raoul of Gaucourt. Being an agent of the perfidious projects of George of La Tremouille, the soldier had succeeded in securing a place for his own wife on the commission that was to inquire into the chastity of Joan. He thought thereby to promote the chances of Joan's conviction. He failed. The infamous investigation was held, and Joan emerged triumphant from the disgraceful ordeal that deeply wounded her chaste and maidenly heart.

More serious and more arduous was the second examination; it lasted longer; and was unnecessarily prolonged.

A large number of royal councilors and members of parliament, assisted by several clerks in theology, among the latter of whom was Brother Seguin of the Carmelite Order and Brother Aimery of the Preachers' Order, and among the former of whom were Masters Eraut and Francois Garivel, proceeded at noon to the house of John Rabateau, in order to conduct the interrogatories that were to be put to Joan, who, always in her man's attire, awaited them and stood ready to answer them.

The inquisition took place in a spacious apartment. In the center of the hall stood a table, around which the men appointed to determine whether or not Joan the Maid was possessed of an evil spirit took their seats. Some of the inquisitors wore brown or black robes with black capes, others had on red robes lined with ermine. Their aspect was threatening, derisive and severe. They were all carefully picked by the Bishop of Chartres, who joined them after they arrived at Rabateau's house, and who presided in his quality of Chancellor of France. The holy man, whose very soul was sold to George of La Tremouille, saw with secret annoyance the purity of Joan established by the council of matrons. Though defeated there, the Bishop relied upon being able so to disconcert the poor peasant girl by the imposing appearance of the learned and redoubtable tribunal, and so to confuse her with subtle and insidious questions on the most arduous possible of theological points, that she would compromise and convict herself with her own answers. Several of the courtiers who had faith in the mission of the inspired young woman, followed her to Poitiers in order to witness the interrogatory. They stood at one end of the hall.

Joan was brought in. She stepped forward, pale, sad and with eyes cast down. So delicate and proud was the girl's susceptibility that at the sight of the councilors and priests, all of them men informed upon the humiliating examination that she had undergone shortly before, Joan, although pronounced pure, now felt as confused as if she had been pronounced impure. To so chaste a soul, to a soul of such elevation as Joan's, the shadow of a suspicion, even if removed, becomes an irreparable insult. This notwithstanding, the Maid controlled her feelings, she invoked the support of her good saints, and it seemed to her that she heard their mysterious voices softly murmur at her ear:

"Go, daughter of God! Fear naught; the Lord is with you. Answer in all sincerity and bravely. You will issue triumphant from this new trial."

The Bishop of Chartres motioned to Joan to approach nearer to the table, and said to her in a grave, almost threatening voice: "Joan, we have been sent by the King to examine and interrogate you. Do not hope to impose upon us with your lies and falsifications."

The interrogatory, being thus opened, proceeded as follows:

JOAN—"I have never lied! I shall answer you. But you are learned clerks, while I know not A from B. I can say nothing to you but that I have a mission from God to raise the siege of Orleans."

BROTHER SEGUIN (harshly)—"Do you pretend that the Lord God sends you to the King? You can not be believed. Holy Writ forbids faith being attached to the words of people who claim to be inspired from above, unless they give a positive sign of the divinity of their mission. Now, then, what sign can you give of yours? We want to know."

JOAN—"The signs I shall give will be my acts.[54] You will then be able to judge whether they proceed from God."

MASTER ERAUT—"What acts do you mean?"

JOAN—"Those that I have to accomplish by the will of God."

FRANCOIS GARIVEL—"Well, tell us what acts those will be. You will have to give more definite answers."

JOAN—"They are three."

BROTHER SEGUIN—"Which is the first?"

JOAN—"The raising of the siege of Orleans, after which I shall drive the English out of Gaul."

MASTER ERAUT—"And the second?"

JOAN—"I shall have the Dauphin consecrated at Rheims."

BROTHER SEGUIN—"And the third?"

JOAN—"I shall deliver Paris to the King."

Despite their prejudice against Joan and the ill will they entertained for the girl, whom they now saw for the first time, the members of the tribunal were struck no less by the Maid's beauty and conduct than by the exactness of her answers, that bore an irresistible accent of conviction. The audience, composed mainly of France's partisans, among whom was John of Novelpont, indicated by a murmur of approbation the increasingly favorable impression made upon them by the girl's answers. Even some of the members of the tribunal seemed to begin to feel an interest in her. Alarmed at these symptoms, the Bishop of Chartres addressed Joan almost in a rage: "You promise to raise the siege of Orleans, to drive the English out of Gaul, to consecrate the King at Rheims and to place Paris in his hands? These are idle words! We refuse to believe you unless you give some sign to show that you are truly inspired by God, and chosen by Him to accomplish these truly marvelous things."

JOAN (impatiently)—"Once more, I say to you, I have not come to Poitiers to display signs! Give me men-at-arms and take me to Orleans. The siege will be speedily raised, and the English driven from the kingdom. That will be the sign of my mission. If you do not believe me, come and fight under me. You will then see whether, with the help of God, I fail to keep my promise. These will be my signs and my actions."

MASTER ERAUT—"Your assurance is great! Where do you get it from?"

JOAN—"From my confidence in the voice of my dear saints. They advise and inspire me in the name of God."

BROTHER SEGUIN (roughly)—"You speak of God. Do you believe in Him?"

JOAN—"I believe in Him more than you do, who can imagine such a thing possible as not to believe in Him!"

BROTHER AIMERY (with a grotesque Limousin accent)—"You say, Joan, that voices advise you in the name of God? In what tongue do those voices speak to you?"

JOAN (slightly smiling)—"In a better tongue than yours, sir."[55]

The humorous and keen retort caused Joan's partisans to laugh aloud, a hilarity in which several members of the tribunal shared. They now began to think that despite the lowliness of her condition, the cowherdess, as they called her, was no ordinary being. Some of the members of the tribunal began to look upon her as inspired; others, of a less credulous turn of mind, thought to themselves that, thanks to her beauty, her brightness and her valiant resolution, she might, at the desperate state of things, actually become a valuable instrument in the war. In short, it occurred to them that to declare Joan possessed of a demon, and thus reject the unexpected help that she brought the King would be to expose themselves to serious reproaches from the partisans of Joan who were witnesses to the interrogation, and that the reproaches would soon be taken up and repeated by public clamor. The Bishop of Chartres, the accomplice of the Sire of La Tremouille and of Gaucourt, was not slow to scent the disposition of the tribunal. In a towering passion he cried to his fellow judges: "Messires, the holy canons forbid us to attach faith to the words of this girl; and the holy canons are our guide!"

JOAN (proudly raising her head)—"And I tell you that the book of the Lord which inspires me is worth more than yours! In that book no priest, however learned he may be, is able to read!"

MASTER ERAUT—"Religion forbids women to wear male attire under pain of mortal sin. Why did you put it on? Who authorized you to?"

JOAN—"I am compelled to assume male attire, seeing I am to battle with men to the end of my mission. Evil thoughts will thus be removed from their minds. That is the reason for my disguise."

FRANCOIS GARIVEL—"And so you, a woman, are not afraid of shedding blood in battle?"

JOAN (with angelic sweetness)—"May God preserve me from shedding blood! I have a horror of blood! I wish to kill nobody; I shall carry in battle only a staff or a standard, to guide the armed men. I shall leave my sword in its scabbard."

MASTER ERAUT—"Suppose our assembly declares to the King our Sire that, with a safe conscience, he may entrust you with armed men to enable you to undertake the raising of the siege of Orleans, what means would you adopt to that end?"

JOAN—"To the end of avoiding, if it is possible, any further shedding of blood, I shall first summon the English, in the name of God who sends me, to raise the siege of Orleans and return to their country; if they refuse obedience to my letter, I shall march against them at the head of the royal army, and with the help of heaven, I shall drive them out of Gaul!"

BISHOP OF CHARTRES (disdainfully)—"You would write to the English, and you have just told us you do, not know A from B?"

JOAN—"I do not know how to write, but I could dictate, Seigneur Bishop."

BISHOP OF CHARTRES—"I take you at your word. Here are pens and a parchment. I shall be your secretary. Let us see! Dictate to me the letter to the English. Upon my faith, its style will be singular!"

A deep silence ensued. Triumphantly the Bishop took up a pen, feeling sure he had laid a dangerous trap for the poor peasant girl, incapable, as he thought, of dictating a letter equal to the occasion. Even the partisans of Joan, although greatly incensed at the manifest ill will of the Bishop towards her, feared to see her succumb at this new trial. The minds of all were on tenterhooks.

BISHOP OF CHARTRES (ironically)—"Come, now, Joan, here I am ready to write under your dictation."

JOAN—"Write, sir."

And the maid dictated the following letter with a mild but firm voice:

"IN THE NAME OF JESUS AND MARY.

"King of England, submit to the kingdom of heaven, and place in the hands of Joan the keys of all the towns that you have forced. She comes sent by God to reclaim those towns in the name of Charles. She is ready to grant you peace if you are willing to leave France.

"King of England, if you do not do as I request you, then I, Joan, chief of war, will everywhere smite your men; I shall drive them out, whether they will or no. If they surrender at mercy, I shall grant them mercy; if not, I shall do them so much damage that nothing like it will have been seen in France for a thousand years back. What is here said will be done.

"You, archers and other companions in arms who are before Orleans, be gone, by the Lord's command, back to England, your own country. If not, fear Joan. You will remember your defeat! You shall not keep France! France will belong to the King to whom God gave the kingdom!"

Joan broke off her dictation, and addressing herself to the Bishop of Chartres, who was stupefied at the virile simplicity of the letter, that, despite himself, he had been compelled to write, she said:

"Sir, what are the names of the English captains?"

BISHOP OF CHARTRES—"The Count of Suffolk, Lord Talbot and the knight Thomas of Escall, lieutenants of the Duke of Bedford, Regent for the King of England."

JOAN—"Write, sir!

"Count of Suffolk, Lord Talbot, Knight Thomas of Escall, all of you lieutenants of the Duke of Bedford, who styles himself Regent of the Kingdom of France for the King of England, make answer! Will you raise the siege of Orleans? Will you cease the great cruelty that you heap upon the poor people of the country of France? If you refuse the peace that Joan demands of you, you will preserve a sad remembrance of your rout. The most brilliant feats of arms ever accomplished by the French in Christendom will be seen. We shall then see who will prevail, you—or heaven!

"Written on Tuesday of the great week of Easter, of the year 1429."[56]

JOAN (addressing the Bishop of Chartres after having dictated)—"Sir, sign for me, if you please, my name at the bottom of this letter. I shall make my cross in God beside the signature, seeing I cannot write, and write the following address on the parchment: 'To the Duke of Bedford who styles himself Regent of the Kingdom of France for the King of England."

The partisans of Joan, the members of the tribunal, even the Bishop of Chartres could hardly believe the evidence of their own senses: a poor rustic girl, only recently arrived from the heart of Lorraine, to hold in that letter a language that was at once so courteous, so dignified and so sensible—it bordered on a miracle.

Aye, a miracle of courage! A miracle of sense! A miracle of patriotism!—readily accomplished by Joan, thanks to her superior native intelligence and her confidence in her own military genius, of which she now began to be conscious; thanks to her faith in the heavenly support promised to her by her mysterious voices; finally, thanks to her firm resolve to act bravely obedient to the proverb that she delighted in repeating—*Help yourself, and heaven will help you!*

Much to the secret anger of the Bishop of Chartres, the declaration that the tribunal would make was no longer doubtful. Joan's triumph in the hall of Rabateau was complete. The tribunal declared that, Joan's virginity having been established, a demon could possess neither her body nor her soul; that she seemed inspired of God; and that the enormity of the public misfortunes justified the King to avail himself with a clean conscience of the unexpected and seemingly providential help. Despite his own shameful indolence, despite the opposition of the Sire George of La Tremouille, and fearing to exasperate public opinion, that was waxing ever more pronouncedly in favor of Joan, Charles VII found himself compelled to accept the aid of the peasant girl of

Domremy; whom, however, he cursed and swore at in secret. Inclined now to believe Joan inspired, the slothful King fretted at the thought of the trials and cares that the threatened vigorous renewal of hostilities against the English was to inflict upon him. He feared to see himself compelled by the force of circumstances to show himself at the head of his troops, to ride up hills and down dales, to endure fatigue, to face danger. But he was compelled to yield to the current of enthusiasm produced by the promises of deliverance made by Joan the Maid. It was decided that Joan was to proceed to Blois, and thence to Orleans, where she was to confer with Dunois, Lahire, Xaintrailles and other renowned captains upon the raising of the siege of Orleans. An equerry named Daulon was attached to the service of the Maid, together with a young page of fifteen named Imerguet. She was given battle horses, and servants to attend to her needs. A special suit of armor was ordered for her. In remembrance of the prediction of Merlin, she demanded that the armor be white, as also one of her chargers, her pennon and her standard, on the latter of which she ordered two blue-winged angels to be painted, holding in their hands the stalk of a lily in blossom. Furious at not being able to catch Joan in the snares that they had spread for her, George of La Tremouille and his two accomplices, the Bishop of Chartres and the Sire of Gaucourt, pursued their darksome plots with increased intensity. It was agreed among them, and in line with their previously laid plans, that Gaucourt was to demand of Charles VII the command of the town of Orleans. The three intriguers expected by that means to block the Maid's movements, ruin her military operations, and expose her to a first check that would forever confound her, or to allow her to be captured by the English in some sally when she was to be left in the lurch.

On Thursday the 28th of April, 1429, Joan Darc left Chinon for Blois, where she was to join Dunois and Marshal Retz, before proceeding to Orleans. The peasant girl, now fast maturing into a warrior, started on the journey, her mind occupied with recollections of the child's combat between the urchins of Maxey and of Domremy, a battle where she had for the first time vaguely felt her vocation for war, and also recalling the passage in the prophecy where the Gallic bard declared:

> "I see an angel with wings of azure and dazzling with light.
> He holds in his hands a royal crown.
> I see a steed of battle as white as snow—
> I see an armor of battle as brilliant as silver.—
> For whom is that crown, that steed, that armor?
> Gaul, lost by a woman, will be saved by a virgin
> From the borders of Lorraine and a forest of oaks.—
> For whom that crown, that steed, that armor?
> Oh, how much blood!

It spouts up, it flows in torrents!
Oh, how much blood do I see! It is a lake,
It is a sea of blood!
It steams; its vapor rises—rises like an autumn mist to heaven,
Where the thunder peals and where the lightning flashes.
Athwart those peals of thunder, those flashes of lightning,
That crimson mist, I see a martial virgin.
White is her armor and white is her steed.
She battles—she battles—she battles still
In the midst of a forest of lances.
And seems to be riding on the backs of the archers.
The steed, as white as snow, was for the martial virgin.
For her was the armor of battle as brilliant as silver.
But for whom the royal crown?
Gaul, lost by a woman, will be saved by a virgin
From the borders of Lorraine and a forest of oaks."

PART III.

ORLEANS.

CHAPTER I.

FRIDAY, APRIL 29, 1429.

In one week the martial Maid, inspired by the love for her people and country, vanquished the English, triumphant since the battle of Poitiers, more than seventy years before, when John II and the coward nobility of France took to their heels. In one week the brave daughter of the people accomplished what for over seventy years had proved beyond the strength of the most illustrious captains. The week has been called THE WEEK OF JOAN DARC.

Night had set in, but it was a balmy night of spring, and anyone on the evening of April 29, 1429, who stood on the street leading to the Banier Gate, one of the gates of the town of Orleans, would have thought it was bright day. All the windows, at which the inhabitants crowded, were illuminated with lamps. To the light of these was joined that of torches with which a large number of armed bourgeois and artisans had furnished themselves and were ranged in a double row along the full length of the thoroughfare for the purpose of keeping back the crowd. The courage of these town soldiers had been severely tested by the perils of the siege which they had long sustained single handed, having at first refused to admit into the city the companies of soldiers that consisted of insolent, thievish and ferocious mercenaries. However, after many a brave attempt, and seeing their numbers reduced from day to day under the shot and fire of the besiegers, the townsmen of Orleans had found themselves compelled to accept and support the mercenary bands of Lahire, of Dunois, of Xaintrailles and of other professional captains, who hired themselves and their men for cash to whomsoever paid for their services. They were dangerous auxiliaries, ever drawing in their train a mob of dissolute women who were themselves no less thievish than the English.

Accordingly, often had the councilmen of Orleans—resolute citizens, who bravely led their militia to the ramparts when these were assailed, or outside of the city when they made a sally—had lively disputes with the captains on the score of the misconduct of their men, or of their timidity in battle. These men, to whom arms was a trade, not having as the inhabitants themselves, families, property, their own hearths, to defend, were not particularly anxious about the speedy raising of the siege, well quartered and paid as they were by the town. It was, accordingly, with inexpressible impatience that the people of Orleans awaited the arrival of Joan Darc. They relied upon her help to drive the English from their redoubts, and to free themselves from the heavy burden of the French captains.

A compact crowd of men, women and children, held back by a military cordon, filled the two sides of the thoroughfare, at the end of which the residence of Master James Boucher, the treasurer, was situated, and was even more brilliantly illuminated than any other. Presently the hum of the multitude was silenced by the loud and rapid peals from the belfry of the town hall, together with the roar of artillery, announcing the arrival of the Maid. The faces of the citizens, until recently sad and somber, now breathed joy and hope. All shared and expressed the opinion that the virgin girl of Lorraine, prophesied by Merlin, was coming to deliver Orleans. She was announced to be of divinely dazzling beauty, brave and instinct with a military genius that struck even Dunois, Lahire and Xaintrailles, all of them renowned captains at the time defending the city for pay, when on the previous day they met her at Blois. Two of their equerries, who had ridden ahead into Orleans during the day, reported the marvel, which spread from mouth to mouth, and they announced the entry of Joan Darc for that evening.

Everywhere on her passage from Chinon to Blois, the equerries added, her march had been a continuous ovation, in which she was greeted by the joyful cries of the peasants, who for so long a time had been exposed to the ravages of the enemy, and was acclaimed by them as their redeeming angel sent by God. These, and similar accounts that were rife, revived the confidence of the townsmen. The crowd was especially dense in the neighborhood of the residence of Master James Boucher, where the heroine was to lodge.

Nine o'clock struck from the tower of the Church of St. Croix. Almost at the same instant the sound of trumpets was heard at a distance. The music approached slowly, and presently the brilliant light of the torches revealed a cavalcade riding in. The little page Imerguet and the equerry Daulon marched ahead, the one carrying the pennon, the other the white standard of the warrior maid, on which two azure-winged angels were painted holding in their hand a stalk of lilies in blossom. Behind them followed Joan Darc, mounted on her white charger, caparisoned in blue, while she herself was cased in a light plate armor of iron that resembled pale silver—a complete suit, leg-pieces, thigh-pieces, and coat of mail, arm-pieces and a rounded breast-plate that protected her virginal bosom. The visor of her casque, wholly raised, exposed her sweet and handsome face, set off by her black hair cut round at the neck. Profoundly moved by the acclamations that the good people of Orleans greeted her with, and which she received as a homage to her saints, a tear was seen to roll down from her large black eyes, adding to their brilliancy. Already familiarized with the handling of a horse, she elegantly guided her mount with one hand, while with the other she held a little white baton, the only weapon that, in her horror of blood, she wished to use in leading the soldiers to battle. Behind her rode Dunois, accoutered in a brilliant suit of armor, ornamented in gold; behind these came, mixed among the councilmen of Orleans, Marshal Retz, Lahire, Xaintrailles and other captains. Among the latter was the Sire of Gaucourt, leading a reinforcement of royal troops to Orleans and invested with the command of the town. With a sinister look, and hatred in his heart, the sire meditated dark schemes. Equerries and bourgeois deputations from the town brought up the rear of the train, which soon was pressed upon from all sides by so compact a mass that for a moment Joan Darc's steed could not move a step. Enraptured at her beauty and at her carriage at once so modest and yet so martial, men, women and children contemplated her with delirious joy and covered her with blessings. Some were even carried to the point of wishing to kiss her spurred boots half covered with the scales of her leg-pieces. As much touched as confused, she said naïvely to Dunois, turning towards him:

"Indeed, I will not have the courage to protect myself against these demonstrations, if God does not himself protect me."[57]

At that moment one of the militiamen who held a torch approached the Maid so closely in order to obtain a better view of her that he involuntarily set fire to the fringe of the standard borne by Daulon. Fearing the flag was in danger, Joan uttered a cry of fright, clapped the spurs to her horse before which the crowd rolled back, and approaching the equerry at a bound seized the burning banner, smothered the flames between her gauntlets and then gracefully waved it over her casque,[58] as if to reassure the people of Orleans, who might construe the accident into an evil omen. Such was the presence of mind and the horsemanship displayed by Joan on the occasion that the enraptured crowd broke out into redoubled acclamations. Even the mercenaries, who, not being on guard that night upon the ramparts, had been able to join the crowd, saw in the Maid an angel of war and felt stronger; like the archer of Vaucouleurs, it seemed to them that, led to battle by such a charming captain, they were bound to vanquish the enemy and avenge their previous defeats. Dunois, Lahire, Xaintrailles, Marshal Retz, all of them experienced captains, noticed the exaltation of their mercenaries, who but the day before seemed wholly discouraged; while the Sire of Gaucourt, perceiving the to him unexpected influence that the Maid exercised, not upon the Orleans militiamen merely, but upon the rough soldiers themselves, grew ever somberer and more secretly enraged.

Joan was slowly advancing through a surging mass of admiring humanity towards the house of James Boucher, when the cavalcade was arrested for a moment by a detachment of armed men that issued from one of the side streets. They were leading two English prisoners, and were headed by a large-sized man of jovial and resolute mien. The leader of the squad was a Lorrainian by birth, who had long lived in Orleans and was called Master John. He had well earned the reputation of being the best culverin-cannonier of the town. His two enormous bomb-throwers, which he had christened "Riflard" and "Montargis," and which, planted on the near side of the bridge on the redoubt of Belle-Croix, ejected unerring shot, caused great damage to the English. He was feared and abhorred by them. Our merry cannonier was not ignorant of their hatred, his cannons seemed to be the objective point for the best aimed bolts of the enemy's archers. He, accordingly, at times amused himself by feigning to be shot dead, suddenly dropping down beside one of his culverins. On such occasions his fellow townsmen engaged at the cannons would raise him and carry him away with demonstrations of great sorrow, that were echoed by the English with counter-demonstrations of joy. But regularly on the morrow they saw again Master John, in happier trim than ever,[59] and ever more accurate and telling with the shot from Riflard and Montargis. A few days later he would again repeat the comedy of death and the miracle of resurrection. It was this jolly customer who headed the squad that was leading the two prisoners to jail. At the sight of the warrior maid, he drew near her, contemplated her for a moment in rapt admiration, and reaching to her his heavy gloved hand said with considerable pride:

"Brave Maid, here is a countryman of yours, born like yourself in Lorraine; and he is at your service, together with Riflard and Montargis, his two heavy cannons."

Dunois leaned over towards Joan and said to her in a low voice:

"This worthy fellow is Master John, the ablest and most daring cannonier in the place. He is, moreover, very expert in all things that concern the siege of a town."

"I am happy to find here a countryman," said the Maid, smiling and cordially stretching out her gauntleted hand to the cannonier. "I shall to-morrow morning see how you manoeuvre Riflard and Montargis. We shall together examine the entrenchments of the enemy, you shall be my chief of artillery, and we shall drive the English away with shot of cannon—and the help of God!"

"Countrywoman," cried Master John in a transport of delight, "my cannons shall need but to look at you, and they will go off of themselves, and their balls will fly straight at the English."

The cannonier was saying these words when Joan heard a cry of pain, and from the back of her horse she saw one of the two English prisoners drop on his back, bleeding, with his scalp cut open by the blow of a pike that a mercenary had dealt upon his head, saying:

"Look well at Joan the Maid. Look at her, you dog of an Englishman.[60] As sure as I have killed you, she will thrust your breed out of France!"

At the sight of the flowing blood, that she had a horror of, the warrior maid grew pale; with a movement more rapid than thought, and pained at the soldier's brutality, she leaped from her horse, pressed her way to the Englishman, knelt down beside him, and raising the unhappy man's head, called with tears in her eyes to the surrounding militiamen:

"Give him grace; the prisoner is unarmed—come to his help."[60a]

At this compassionate appeal, several women, moved with pity, came to the wounded man, tore up their handkerchiefs and bound up his gash, while the warrior maid, still on her knees, held up the Englishman's head. The wounded man recovered consciousness for a moment, and at the sight of the young girl's handsome face, instinct with pity, he joined his two hands in adoration and wept.

"Come, poor soldier; you need not fear. You shall not be hurt," said Joan to him, rising, and she put her foot into the stirrup that her little page Imerguet presented to her.

"Daughter of God, you are a saint!" cried a young woman with exaltation at the act of charity that she had just witnessed, and throwing herself upon her knees before the warrior maid at the moment that the latter was about to leap upon her horse she added: "I beseech you, deign to touch my ring!" saying which she raised her hand up to Joan. "Blessed by you, I shall preserve the jewel as a sacred relic."

"I am no saint," answered the warrior maid with an ingenuous smile. "As for your ring, touch it yourself. You are no doubt a good and worthy woman; your touch will be as good as mine."[61]

So saying, Joan remounted her horse, to be saluted anew by the acclamations of the throng; even the most hardened soldiers were touched by the sentiments of pity that she had displayed towards an unarmed enemy. So far from taxing her with weakness, they admired the goodness of her heart and her generosity.

Master John frantically cheered his countrywoman, and the cries of "Good luck, Joan!" "Good luck to the liberator of Orleans!" resounded like the roll of thunder. Almost carried off its feet by the crowding mass of people, Joan's horse finally arrived with its inspired rider before the house of Master James Boucher. Standing at the threshold of his door with his wife and his daughter Madeleine near him, Master James Boucher awaited his young guest, and led her, together with the councilmen and captains, into a large hall where a sumptuous supper was prepared for the brilliant train. Timid and reserved, the Maid said to Master Boucher:

"I thank you, sir, but I shall not take supper. If your daughter will be kind enough to show me to the room where I am to sleep, and to help me take off my armor, I would be grateful to her. All I wish, sir, is a little bread moistened in water and wine—that is all I shall need; I shall immediately go to sleep. I wish to be awakened at early morning, to inspect the entrenchments with Master John the cannonier."[62]

According to her wishes, the Maid retired, Master Boucher's daughter Madeleine showing her to her room. At first seized with fear of the inspired Maid, Madeleine was soon so completely captivated by her sweetness and the affability of her words, that she naïvely offered to share her room during her sojourn in Orleans. Joan accepted the offer with gladness, happy at finding a companion that pleased her so well Madeleine gently helped her to disarm and brought her her refection. Just before lying down to sleep Joan said to her:

"Now that I have met you and your parents, Madeleine, I feel all the happier that God has sent me to deliver the good town of Orleans."[63]

The Maid knelt down at the head of her bed, did her devotions for the night, invoked her two patron saints, implored them with a sigh to bestow their blessings upon her mother, her father and her brothers, and was soon plunged in peaceful sleep, while Madeleine long remained awake, contemplating the sweet heroine in silent admiration.

CHAPTER II.

SATURDAY, APRIL 30, 1429.

Just before daybreak, and punctual to his appointment made the previous evening, Master John the cannonier was at James Boucher's door. Immediately afterwards, Joan opened the window of her room, which was on the first floor, and looked out upon the street which still was dark. She called down:

"Oh, Master John, are you there?"

"Yes, my brave countrywoman," answered the Lorrainian, "I have been waiting for you."

Joan soon left the house and joined the cannonier. She had not resumed her full armor of battle, but had merely put on a light iron coat of mail which she wore under her coat. A hood took the place of her casque. Her baton was in her hand, and on her shoulder was flung a short mantle in which she meant to wrap herself on her return, in order to prevent being recognized and thus becoming the object of popular ovations. She asked Master John to make with her the rounds of the town outside the ramparts, in order to inform herself on the strength of the enemy's entrenchments. Joan departed with her guide, traversed the still deserted streets, and issuing by the Banier Gate, started on her excursion.

Twelve formidable redoubts, called "bastilles," surrounded the town from the side of the Beauce and the side of the Sologne districts, and only slightly beyond range of the town's cannon. The most considerable of these hostile fortifications were the bastille of St. Laurence to the west, of St. Pouaire to the north, of St. Loup to the east, and of St. Privé, of the Augustinians and of St. John-le-Blanc to the south and on the other side of the Loire. Furthermore, and opposite to the head of the bridge, which, on the side of the besieged, was protected by a fortified earthwork, the English had raised a formidable castle, flanked with frame towers, called by them "tournelles." All these redoubts, manned with large garrisons, were surrounded with wide and deep moats, besides a belt of palisades planted at the foot of thick earthworks that were crowned with platforms on which were placed culverins and ballistas intended to hurl bolts into the town or upon its sallying forces. The bastilles, raised at distances of from two to three hundred fathoms from each other, completely encircled the town, and cut it off from the roads and the upper river.

Joan Darc minutely questioned the cannonier upon the manner in which the English fought in the redoubts, which she frequently approached with tranquil audacity in order to be able to judge by herself of the besiegers' means of defence. During the examination, she came near being struck by a volley of bolts darted at her from the bastille of St. Laurence. She was in no wise frightened, but only smiled at the sight of the projectiles that fell a few paces short of her. Joan, astonished the cannonier no less by her calmness and bravery than by the relevancy of her observations. Her every word revealed surprising military aptitude, and a quick and accurate eye. Among other things, she said to the cannonier, after having inquired from him what were the tactics hitherto pursued by the besieged, that it seemed to her the better way was, not to attack all the redoubts at once in general sallies as had hitherto been done, but to concentrate all the troops upon one point, and in that manner attack the bastilles one after another with the certainty of carrying them, seeing that they could hold but a limited number of defenders, while in the open field nothing could limit the number of the assailants; their combined mass could be three and four times superior to the garrison of each redoubt taken separately. Finally, by a number of other observations Joan revealed the extraordinary intuition that has ever been the mark of great captains. More and more astonished at such a martial instinct, the cannonier cried:

"Well, countrywoman, in what book did you learn all that?"

"In the book that our Lord God inspires me to read. That book is ever open before me," naïvely answered Joan.[64]

While the Maid was thus examining the enemy's works and was meditating upon and maturing her plan of campaign, the Sire of Gaucourt, who had been appointed chief of the royal troops sent to Orleans, was meditating upon and maturing the dark plot of treason long before hatched by him together with his two accomplices of the royal council, the Sire of La Tremouille and the Bishop of Chartres. Early that morning Gaucourt visited the most influential captains. Envy and malice supplied the man's lack of acumen. Moreover, carefully instructed by La Tremouille, he appealed to the worst passions of these men of the sword. He reminded them of the frantic enthusiasm with which Joan was received by the populace, by the town militia, even by their own mercenaries. Did not they, celebrated warriors, feel humiliated by the triumph of the peasant girl, of that cowherdess? Were not the insensate expectations pinned upon the visionary girl an insult to their fame? Did they not feel wounded and angry at the thought that their companies until then dejected and discouraged, seemed inflamed with ardor at the bare sight of the seventeen-year-old girl, even before she had delivered her first battle? The insidious words found an echo in the perverse spirits of several of the captains. As has often been seen before and will be seen again in the future with people of the military trade, several of the captains gave a willing ear to the perfidious insinuations of Gaucourt, and agreed, if not openly to refuse their co-operation with the Maid, at least to thwart her designs, to prevent their successful execution, and ever to oppose her in the councils of war. Dunois and Lahire were the only ones who thought it would be "good policy" to profit by the exaltation that the Maid inspired in the people and even in the mercenaries; they were of the opinion that she should be seconded if she actually gave evidence of military genius. These views notwithstanding, the majority of the captains adhered to their ill will for the young girl of Domremy, of whom they were vilely jealous. Gaucourt augured well for his black designs without, however, as yet daring fully to reveal to his ready accomplices his infamous machination—to cause the Maid to fall into the hands of the English by leaving her in the lurch at a sally and raising the draw-bridge behind her—as, indeed, was one day to happen.

Back from her long excursion around the ramparts of Orleans in the company of Master John, Joan said to Gaucourt and other chiefs who called upon her, that she had consulted her voices and they advised a simultaneous attack on the next day, Sunday, by all the combined forces of the army upon the bastille of the Tournelles to the end of first of all freeing the head of the Orleans bridge, opening the roads from the side of Beauce for the entry of provisions, which the town began to run short of, and facilitating the entrance of the reinforcements that had been ordered from Tours and Blois. The captains crossed themselves at hearing the Maid, a daughter of God, propose such an enormity—to fight on Sunday! Would that not, they remonstrated with Joan, be to inaugurate her arms with a sacrilege? As to themselves, sooner should their hands shrivel than draw their swords on that day, a day devoted to rest and prayer! In vain did Joan cry: "Oh, sirs! He prays who fights for the welfare of Gaul!" The captains remained unshakable in their orthodoxy on the pious observance of the dominical rest. Much against her will Joan saw herself compelled to postpone the plan for Monday, but desirous of turning the postponement to account and avoiding all she could the effusion of blood that she had such a horror of, she requested her equerry Daulon to write at her dictation another and short letter to the English, the first one having been forwarded to them from Blois by a herald. The missive having been written and signed with her name, Joan attached to it her "cross in God" in the fashion of a counter-sign, placed the parchment in her leathern girdle-pouch and invited the captains to accompany her to the ramparts on the Loire that faced the bastille of the Tournelles, occupied by the English. The warrior maid wished once more to examine the important position, preparatorily to the Monday attack. The request was complied with, and several captains accompanied her, in the midst of a large concourse of people, of soldiers and of mercenaries, no less enthusiastic than the previous evening, to the gate of the little castle on the river. Joan advanced to the edge of the boulevard of the bridge, so near to the bastille of the Tournelles, that the voice of the besieged could be heard by the besiegers. A large number of the Orleans militiamen were on guard upon the embattled platform of their own entrenchment which was equipped with ballistas and other engines of war used in hurling bolts and large stones. Transported with joy at the sight of the Maid in their midst, the good people surrounded her and inquired with martial ardor and impatience: "When will the assault be?" She promised it for Monday, and ordered them to raise a white flag in order to propose a truce of an hour to the English at the Tournelles, to whom she desired to speak. The flag of peace rose in the air, the besiegers answered with a like signal that they accepted a momentary suspension of hostilities, and several of them appeared at the embrasures of their bastille, not yet aware of Joan's proximity. The Maid picked out a large arrow from one of the quivers that hung from each of the ballistas, pushed the iron through the parchment on which the missive that she had brought with her was written, and having thus securely fastened it, she gave the arrow to one of the cannoniers with the request to hurl it into the Tournelles. Stepping upon the parapet, Joan called out to the English:

"Stand aside that you may not be wounded by the arrow on which I have fastened the letter that I have written to you. Read it!"

The ballista was set in motion; the arrow whizzed through the air and carried into the enemy's encampment the missive of Joan, which ran as follows:

ALL OF YOU, MEN OF ENGLAND, WHO HAVE NO RIGHTS OVER THE KINGDOM OF FRANCE:—

I, Joan, call upon you by the order of God, to abandon your bastilles and to return to your own country. If not I shall do you such damage that you will eternally remember it. This is the second time that I write to you. I shall write no more.—JOAN.[65]

Informed by their spies of the incredible and menacing enthusiasm created in Orleans by the arrival of the Maid, the English soldiers began to believe her inspired of the devil, nor could the dangerous superstition any longer be easily combated by their chiefs. Learning from her missive that the Maid was now so near them, the more timid grew pale, while others uttered furious imprecations. One of the most rabid among the latter, an English captain of wide repute named Gladescal, a man of colossal size and armed cap-a-pie, still held the Maid's letter in his hand, and shook his fist at her, while he foamed at the mouth with rage.

"You and your men," cried out Joan to them in her kind and serious voice, "surrender yourselves, every man, at mercy. Your lives will be spared on condition that you agree to return to your own country."[66]

At these words of peace, Gladescal and his men answered with a new explosion of vituperation. The stentorian voice of Gladescal was heard above all the others: "I shall have you roasted, you bedeviled witch!"

"If you catch me!" Joan answered. "But I, if I overcome you, and I certainly shall, with the aid of God, I shall cast you far away from France, you and yours; I shall thump you out of the land, seeing that you refuse to surrender at mercy.[67] God battles on our side."

"Go back to your cows, vile serf!" yelled Gladescal. "Get you gone, you ribald and triple fraud!"

"Yes, yes!" repeated the English amidst hisses and jeers. "Go back and tend your cows! Go back, infernal fraud and strumpet!"[68]

The unworthy and obscene insults hurled at her in the presence of so many of her people fell short of the warrior maid, whose conscience was free from any blot. But they deeply wounded her delicate sense of modesty, the most salient feature of her character; she wept.[69]

Several of the captains who accompanied Joan smiled maliciously, and hoped that the invectives of the English would smirch the girl's character in the opinion of the Orleans militiamen and of the soldiers who had witnessed the insult. It was otherwise. Moved by her virginal beauty, her celestial appearance, her touching tears, and above all, affected by the religious respect that her person inspired in all who approached her, they could not repress their indignation. Inflamed with rage, they rushed to the battlements and in turn shook their fists at the English, returning insult for insult, and crying with fervor:

"Good luck! Good luck to Joan the Maid!"

"We shall cut you to pieces, you vagabonds and English swine!"

"Joan will throw you far from here!"

Some of the cannoniers even forgot the truce, and set the loaded ballistas in motion, to which the enemy replied with a volley of arrows. Joan, unsuspecting of danger, did not budge from the parapet, and seemed to defy death with serenity. Two men were wounded near her. Covering her with their bodies, the militiamen forced her to descend from the parapet, and implored her to spare herself for the great assault on Monday. On the other hand, most of the English attributed her escape from the murderous discharge of their arrows to a supernatural interposition, and their superstitious fears received fresh increment. They feared the devil and his sorceries.

CHAPTER III.

SUNDAY, MAY 1, 1429.

Unable to overcome the opposition of the captains to attacking the enemy on Sunday morning, Joan again proceeded at break of day and in the company of John the cannonier to examine the enemy's position. Master John conceived a singular attachment for the martial maid, and he later accompanied her in almost all her engagements, being charged by her with the command of the artillery. Due to his extensive experience at the siege of Orleans, the cannonier had acquired profound skill in matters connected with the attack and defence of fortifications. On her part, endowed with unusual perspicacity in martial matters, Joan derived in a short time great advantage from the practical knowledge of Master John. Back from her Sunday morning excursion, the Maid proceeded to the Church of St. Croix, where she attended high mass and took the communion in the presence of a vast concourse of people, upon all of whom the Maid's modesty and piety left a profound impression. Upon her return to the house of James Boucher, Joan entertained herself in the afternoon by joining in the family sewing, and she astonished not a little both Madeleine and her mother, who were charmed to see the warrior maid, from whom the deliverance of the town and even the kingdom was expected, display so much skill, ingenuity and familiarity in the labors of her own sex. More than once was she obliged to interrupt the sewing at which she was engaged and show herself at one of the casements in response to the clamors of the admiring crowds that pressed before the treasurer's house.

Towards evening, the captains who were hostile to Joan either from jealousy or any other cause, held a meeting and decided that the projected Monday attack should not take place. It was absolutely necessary, they claimed, to await a reinforcement that Marshal St. Sever was bringing from Blois and that was expected to attempt an entry during the night of Tuesday. This further postponement, of which Joan was notified by one of the captains, afflicted her profoundly. Guided by her good judgment, Joan considered the delays disastrous; they allowed the ardor of the troops to cool off after it had been rekindled by her presence, and gave the English time to recover from their dread, because, thrown into increasing consternation by the reports that they received concerning the Maid, the English had not, since her arrival, dared to quit their bastilles to skirmish against the town. But compelled to yield to the will of the captains, whom to oppose had not yet occurred to her, Joan could only weep at the further delay. But presently the scales began to drop from her eyes. Reflection showed her that the delays were intentional, and her voices, the echoes of her sentiments and her thoughts, said to her:

"They are deceiving you—the captains treasonably seek to oppose the will of heaven that you deliver Orleans and set Gaul free. Courage. God protects you. Rely only upon yourself for the fulfilment of the mission that He has entrusted to you."

CHAPTER IV.

MONDAY, MAY 2, 1429.

Strengthened by her "voices," Joan sent her equerry, Daulon, early in the morning to convoke the captains for noon at the house of her host. Most of them responded to the call. When they were assembled, the virgin warrior, nowise intimidated, declared to them with mildness but with firmness, that if on the next day, Tuesday, they did not in concert with her definitely arrange a plan of attack for Wednesday morning, she would then, without any further delay, mount her horse, raise her standard and, preceded by her equerry sounding the trumpet call and her page carrying her pennon, traverse the streets of the town and call to arms the good townsmen of Orleans, and the soldiers also; and that she alone would lead them to battle, certain of victory with the aid of God.

The Maid's resolute language and the fear of seeing her carry out her threat had their effect upon the captains. Several signs of popular dissatisfaction had manifested themselves on the inexplicable delay in using the unexpected help that Joan had brought from heaven. Pointing with becoming dignity to the numberless proofs that they had given of their bravery and of their devotion to the public cause, the councilmen complained bitterly of being ignored, in the councils where the fate of the town was decided upon; and no less than Joan they condemned the fatal, perhaps irreparable, delays of the captains. Yielding despite themselves to the pressure of public opinion, the captains promised the Maid to meet the next day and decide jointly with her upon a plan of battle.

Without the consciousness of her military genius, that every day rose mightier within her; without her invincible patriotism; without her settled faith in divine help, Joan would before now have renounced the painful and glorious task that she had set to herself. The indolence and craven egotism of Charles VII, his insulting doubts concerning her character, the infamous physical examination that she was forced to undergo, the ill will of the captains towards her since her arrival in Orleans, had profoundly grieved her simple and loyal spirit. But determined to deliver Gaul from its age-long foes and to save the King despite himself, seeing that she considered the safety of the country bound up in his throne, the heroine thrust her personal sufferings aside and only thought of pursuing her task of deliverance to its consummation.

CHAPTER V.

TUESDAY, MAY 3, 1429.

On Tuesday the council of war assembled at the house of James Boucher and in the presence of Joan. The Maid submitted briefly and spiritedly the plan of attack that she had matured and modified after the several reconnoitering tours which she had made during the last three days. Instead of first attacking the Tournelles, as she had at first contemplated, she proposed collecting all the disposable forces in an attack against the redoubt of St. Loup, situated on the left bank of the Loire and constituting one of the most important posts of the enemy, seeing that, as it commanded the road to Berry and the Sologne, it rendered difficult the revictualing of the town and the entry of reinforcements. That redoubt was to be carried, first; she was then to march successively against the others. The only forces that Joan proposed to keep from the expedition was a body of reserve, that was to be held ready to sally from the town for the protection of the assailants of the bastille of St. Loup, in case the English should issue from their other redoubts to the help of the attacked garrison and thus attempt a diversion. A few men placed in the belfry of the town hall were to watch the movements of the English, and if these were seen to sally in order to attempt either the junction of their forces or the diversion foreseen by Joan, the signal was to be given to the reserve corps to fall upon the enemy, intercept their march to St. Loup, drive them back, and keep them from taking the French in the rear. The plan, explained with a military precision that stupefied even the captains who envied Joan, was unanimously adopted. It was agreed that the troops were to set off at daybreak.

CHAPTER VI.

WEDNESDAY, MAY 4, 1429.

Feeling certain of battling on the morrow, Joan slept on Tuesday night the peaceful sleep of a child, while Madeleine, on the contrary, remained almost constantly awake, tossed about by painful uneasiness, and thinking with no little alarm that her companion was to deliver a murderous battle in the early morning. Joan awoke at dawn, made her morning prayer, invoked her good saints, and was assisted by Madeleine in putting on her armor. A touching and charming picture! One of the two girls, delicate and blonde, raising with difficulty the pieces of the iron armor that she helped her virile and dark complexioned friend to case herself in, and rendering the service with a degree of inexperience that caused herself to smile through the tears that she did her best to repress and that welled up at the thought of the near dangers that threatened the martial maid.

"You must excuse me, Joan, I am more in the habit of lacing my linen gorget than a gorget of iron," said Madeleine, "but with time I shall be able, I hope, to arm you as quickly as could your equerry. To arm you! Good God! I can not pronounce the dreadful word without weeping! Is it quite certain that you are to lead an assault this morning?"

"Yes; and if it please God, Madeleine, we shall drive hence these English who have caused so much damage to your good town of Orleans and to the poor people of France!"

The Maid said this as she strapped the jambards over her buckskin hose whose waistband outlined her supple and robust shape. Her shoulders and bosom were then almost exposed. She hastened to button up her chemise, while blushing with chaste embarrassment although she was in the presence of a girl of her own age; but such was Joan's modesty, that on a similar occasion she would have blushed before her own mother! Putting on a slightly padded skin jacket that the friction with her armor had already begun to blacken, she cased her breast in her iron corselet, that Madeleine strapped on as well as she could.

"May this cuirass protect you, Joan, against the enemy's swords! Alack! To have a young girl fight! To have her face such dangers!"

"Oh, dear Madeleine, before leaving Vaucouleurs, I said to the Sire of Baudricourt, the seigneur who helped me to reach the Dauphin of France: 'I would prefer to remain and sew and spin near my mother; but I must fulfil the orders of the Lord.'"

"What dangers you have run, my dear Joan, and still are to run in the fulfilment of your mission!"

"Danger troubles me little; I place myself in the hands of God. What troubles me is the slowness I encounter in having my services availed of. These delays are fatal to Gaul—because it seems to me that my days are numbered."[70]

The martial maid pronounced these last words with so sweet a melancholy that Madeleine's tears started to flow afresh. Placing back upon a table the casque that she was about to place upon her friend's head, she threw herself into her arms without uttering a word, and embraced her, sobbing, as she would have embraced her sister at the supreme hour of an eternal farewell. Dame Boucher entered at that moment precipitately and said:

"Joan, Joan, the Sire of Villars and Jamet of Tilloy, two councilmen, are downstairs in the hall. They wish to speak with you immediately. Your page has just led up your horse. It seems that something unexpected has happened."

"Adieu, till we meet again, my dear Madeleine," said Joan to the weeping girl. "Be comforted. My saints and the Lord will protect me, if not against wounds, at least against death until I shall have carried out the mission that they have laid upon me;" and hastily taking up her casque, her sword and the small baton that she habitually carried in her hand, the Maid descended quickly into the large hall.

"Joan," said the Councilman Jamet of Tilloy, an honest and brave townsman, "everything was ready, agreeable to yesterday's decision, to attack the bastille of St. Loup this morning. But before dawn a messenger ran in to announce to us the approach of a large convoy of provisions and munitions of war that the people of Blois, Tours and Angers send us, under the command of Marshal St. Sever, by way of the Sologne. The escort of the convoy is not strong enough to pass without danger under the bastille of St. Loup, which commands the only available wagon road. The English may sally from their redoubt and attack the train which the town has been impatiently expecting. The captains, who are assembled in council at this hour, are debating the point whether it is better to attack the bastille of St. Loup or to go forward to meet Marshal St. Sever, who is waiting for reinforcements before resuming his march."

"How far is the convoy from here, sir?" asked Joan.

"About two leagues. It can not choose but pass under the bastille of St. Loup. There is where the danger lies."

After a moment's reflection, Joan answered with composure:

"Let us first of all see to the provisions and munitions of war. We can not fight without victuals. Let us help the convoy to enter the town this morning; we shall immediately after attack and take the bastille with the help of God."

The Maid's advice seemed wise. She mounted her horse, and accompanied by the Sire of Villars rode to the town hall, whither the Councilman Jamet of Tilloy preceded her in haste while ordering the militia to be called to arms under its captains of tens and of forties and giving the Bourgogne Gate as the rendezvous. On this occasion the captains yielded without a contest to the will of Joan, who was strongly seconded by the councilmen. She marched out of the Bourgogne Gate at the head of two thousand men, who, loudly clamoring for battle, and impatient to wipe out their previous defeats, were fired by the sight of the martial maid, who gracefully rode her white charger with her banner in her hand. At a little distance from the bastille of St. Loup, a veritable fortress that held a garrison of over three thousand men, Joan took the command of the vanguard which was to clear the path for the column. Whether it was a superstitious terror caused by the presence of the Maid, whom they recognized from a distance by her white armor and standard, or whether they were merely reserving their strength to sally forth and attack the convoy itself, the English remained behind their entrenchments and limited themselves to shooting a few almost inoffensive volleys of arrows and artillery balls at the Orleans column. The obvious timidity of an enemy who was usually so daring increased the confidence of the French. They soon left the bastille behind them and met near St. Laurent, an advance post that covered the convoy. At the sight of the reinforcement from Orleans, that reached them without hindrance from the English in their bastille, the escort of the convoy attributed the successful operation to the influence of the Maid, and felt in turn elated. Himself struck by the successful move, that was due to the promptness of Joan's manoeuvre, Marshal St. Sever still feared, and not without good reason, that the enemy's purpose was to allow the French to pass out freely in order all the more effectively to fall upon them on their return, hampered as they would then be by the large train of carts and cattle that the convoy had to escort. The Marshal was undecided what to do.

"Forward and resolutely!" replied Joan. "Our bold front will impress the English; if they come out of their redoubt we shall fight them; if they do not come out, we shall soon be in Orleans with the convoy. After that we shall immediately return and attack the bastille, and we shall conquer with the aid of God. Have confidence, Marshal!"

These words, pronounced in a firm voice, overheard by some of the soldiers, repeated by them and carried from rank to rank raised the troop's enthusiasm. The march to Orleans was struck with the carts and cattle in the center, and Joan leading the van with a strong vanguard determined to sustain the first shock of the enemy. But the latter did not show himself. It was later learned from several English prisoners that their captains, aware of the decisive effect for good or evil that the first battle with the Maid would have upon the temper of their troops, and realizing that their courage had begun to waver at the marvelous accounts that reached them about her, had determined not to be drawn into a battle until conditions should render triumph certain. Hence their inaction at the passage of the convoy, which, without striking a blow, entered Orleans to the unutterable delight of the people and the militiamen. The people were carried away with a fanatic zeal at the successful stroke of the Maid. Wishing to turn their enthusiasm to immediate account, Joan proposed to turn about on the spot and attack the bastille of St. Loup. The captains argued that their men should first have time to eat, and promised to notify her when they should be ready for the assault. Joan yielded to these protestations, returned to the house of James Boucher, fed, as was her custom, on a little bread dipped in wine and water, had her cuirass unbuckled, and threw herself upon her bed, where, thus, half armed, she fell asleep. Her mind being full of the events of the morning, the Maid dreamed that the troops were marching without her against the enemy. The painful impression of the dream woke her up, and no sooner awake than she bounded out of bed at the distant noise that reached her of detonating artillery. Her dream had not deceived her.[71] They had begun to attack the redoubt. The Sire of Gaucourt, who had been commissioned to notify the Maid, had left her in ignorance. She ran to the window, saw her little page Imerguet holding his own horse by the bridle and talking at the door with Dame Boucher and her daughter. Neither the equerry nor the page of Joan had been informed of the sally.[72] But not aware of that, the martial maid leaned out of the window and addressed Imerguet in a reproachful tone:

"Oh, bad boy! They are attacking the entrenchments without me, and you did not come to tell me that French blood was flowing![73] Madeleine, come quick, I beg you, to help me put on my cuirass! Alack! We are losing time."

Madeleine and her mother quickly ascended to Joan's room. She was helped on with her armor, descended to the street and leaped upon the horse of her page. At that moment it occurred to her that she had forgotten her banner near her bed where she always placed it. She said to Imerguet:

"Run up quick for my standard! It is in the room. Hand it to me through the window in order to lose less time."[74]

The page hastened to obey, while Dame Boucher and her daughter paid their adieus to the Maid. The latter raised herself upon her stirrups, took the standard that Imerguet lowered to her from the window above, and plunging her spurs into the flanks of her horse, the warrior maid waved with her hand a last good-bye to Madeleine, and departed with such swiftness that the sparks flew from the pavement under the iron shoes of her steed.[75]

By concealing the hour of the assault from Joan, the Sire of Gaucourt had planned to keep her away and thus to injure her in the opinion of the soldiers, who would impute to cowardice her absence at the hour of danger. Planted at the Bourgogne Gate at the head of the reserves, Gaucourt saw with surprise and anger Joan approaching at a gallop, cased in her white armor and her white standard in her hand. She passed the traitor like an apparition, and soon disappeared from his sight in a cloud of dust raised by the rapid gait of her horse, that she drove with free reins down the Sologne road, while with pangs of despair she heard the detonations of the artillery increase in frequency. In the measure that she drew near the field of battle, the cries of the soldiers, the clash of arms, the formidable noise of battle reached her ear more distinctly. Finally the bastille of St. Loup hove in sight. It intercepted the Sologne road, dominating the Loire river, and was built at the foot of an old church that in itself was a powerful fortification. The church formed a second redoubt within the first, whose parapets were at that moment half concealed by the smoke of the cannons. Their fire redoubled, the last ranks of the French were descending almost perpendicularly into a deep moat, the first defense of the entrenchment, when, leaving her steaming horse, Joan rushed forward, her banner in her hands, to join the combatants who at that moment, instead of proceeding forward down into the moat were turning about and climbing out again crying:

"The bastille is impregnable!"

"The English are full of the devil!"

"The Maid is not with us!"

"God has forsaken us!"

The captains had calculated upon the enthusiasm produced by the heroine to lead the troops to the assault with the promise that she was soon to join them. Relying upon the promise the first rush of the assailants, who consisted mainly of Orleans militiamen, bourgeois and artisans, was intrepid. But the English, not seeing the Maid among the French, considered them deprived of a support that many of themselves looked upon as supernatural; the enemy's courage revived and they repelled the otherwise overpowering attack. The revulsion was instantaneous. A panic seized the front ranks of the assailants and the swiftest in the night were seeking to regain the home side of the moat when Joan appeared running towards them, with eyes full of inspiration and her face glowing with martial ardor. The fleers stopped; they imagined themselves strengthened by a superhuman power; the shame of defeat mounted to their cheeks; they blushed at the thought of fleeing under the eyes of the beautiful young girl, who, waving her banner, rushed to the moat crying in a ringing voice:

"Stand firm! Follow me! Ours is the battle by order of God! Victory to Gaul!"[76]

Carried away by the magic of the bravery and beauty of the heroine, the fleers fell in line behind her to the cry of:

"Good luck to Joan!"

"Joan is with us!"

These clamors, which announced the presence of the Maid, redoubled the energy of the intrepid ones who still held the middle of the moat, although they were being decimated by the stones, the bullets and the arrows hurled at them from the top of the boulevard of the redoubt. Joan, nimble, supple and strong, and supporting herself from time to time upon the shoulders of those who surrounded her, descended into the moat with them, crying:

"To the assault! Let's march bravely! God is with us! Victory to Gaul!"

The ranks opened before the heroine and closed behind her. Her bravery carried away the most timidly disposed. Arrived at the foot of the slope that had to be climbed under a shower of projectiles in order to reach a palisaded trench that protected the boulevard, Joan perceived Master John. Neither he nor the other sturdy cannoniers of Orleans had retreated an inch since the assault began. They were just making ready to climb out of the ditch on the enemy's side.

"Helloa, my good countryman," Joan called out cheerfully to the cannonier; "let us climb up there quick; the redoubt is ours!"

And supporting herself upon the staff of her standard in order to scale the steep slope, the Maid soon was several steps in the lead of the front ranks of the assailants. Inspired by her example, these soon reached the summit of the slope. Many fell dead or wounded by the shower of balls and bolts near the heroine. She was the first to set foot upon the narrow strip surrounding the moat and beyond which rose the palisaded entrenchment. Turning to those who followed her, Joan cried:

"To the palisade! To the palisade! Courage! The English are beaten! I tell you so by order of God!"[77]

Master John and his men hewed down the posts with their axes; a breach was effected; the flood of the assailants rushed through the gap like a torrent through a sluice; and a furious hand-to-hand encounter was joined between the French and the English.

"Forward!" cried Joan keeping her sword in its scabbard and merely waving her banner; "heaven protects us! Forward!"

"We shall see whether heaven protects you, accursed witch!" cried an English captain, whereat he dealt a furious blow with his sabre upon the head of the Maid. Her casque protected her. Immediately another blow from a heavy iron mace fell upon her right shoulder. Dazed by these repeated strokes, she staggered for a moment; Master John supported her while two of his cannoniers threw themselves before her to protect her with their bodies. The shock was quickly overcome. Joan recovered herself, stood daring and erect, and rushed into action with redoubled spirit. The enthusiasm of the warrior maiden was irresistible; the boulevard was soon heaped with the dead of both sides. Driven back, the English again succumbed to the superstitious terror that the Maid inspired them with and they sought safety behind the numerous frame buildings that served as barracks to the garrison of the bastille and as lodgings for the officers. The struggle continued with unabated fury, without mercy or pity, through the causeways that separated the vast frame structures. Each lodging of the captains, each barrack, became a redoubt that had to be carried. Fired by the presence of the Maid, the French attacked and carried them one after the other. The English who survived the fury of the first assault defended the ground inch by inch and succeeded in retreating in good order into the church that crowned the boulevard—a church with thick walls, surmounted by a belfry. Entrenched in this last fort, whose doors they barricaded from within, the English archers riddled their assailants with arrows, shot through the narrow windows, while other English soldiers, posted on the platform of the belfry, rolled down heavy stones, placed there in advance, upon the heads of the French. Gathered in a mass near the portico of the church, and entirely exposed, the French were being crushed and decimated by the invisible enemy, not an arrow or stone of whom was lost. The Maid noticed that her men began to waver. Banner in hand she rushed forward:

"Victory to Gaul! Break in the door! Let us boldly enter the church. It is ours by the order of God!"

Master John, together with several determined men, attacked with hatchets the iron studded door, while a shower of arrows, shot through a narrow slit in an adjoining building, rained upon the cannonier and his companions. Their efforts were vain. Many of Master John's aides fell beside him, his own arm was pierced by a shaft. The English who entrenched themselves in the tower of the church, sawed off the framework of the roofing, and with the aid of levers, threw it down upon their assailants. The avalanche of stones, lead, slates and beams despatched all those upon whom it fell. A panic now threatened.

"Forward!" cried Joan. "We needed beams to beat in the doors. The English now furnish us with them. Take up the heaviest of them. Ram the door. It will give. We shall have those Englishmen even if they are hidden in the clouds."[78]

Again reanimated by her words, the soldiers obeyed the orders of the Maid. Despite his wound, Master John directed the operation. An enormous beam was taken from the debris, raised by twenty men, and plied like a ram against the door of the church. Suddenly, the French soldiers, who, standing on the brow of the parapet, overlooked the plain, cried out:

"We are lost! The enemy is coming in large numbers out of the bastille of St. Pouaire!"

"They are going to take us in the rear!"

"We shall be between these fresh troops and the English entrenched in the church!"

This move, skilfully foreseen and prepared for by Joan, who had issued the necessary orders to meet it, was in fact made by the enemy.

"Fear not!" said the martial maid to those near her, who were petrified by the news, "a reserve troop will sally from the town and cut off the English. Look not behind, but before you! Fall to bravely! Take the church!"

Hardly had Joan uttered these words when the precipitate ringing of the town hall bell was heard, and it was immediately followed by a sally headed by a cavalry corps. The infantry marched out of the town at the double quick and in good order, and planted itself in battle array across the road that led from the bastille of St. Pouaire to that of St. Loup. Intimidated by the resolute attitude of the reserve corps, which was commanded by Marshal St. Sever, the English halted, and, giving up their plan of marching to the assistance of their fellows at St. Loup, returned to their own entrenchments. Seeing Joan's words thus verified, her soldiers placed implicit faith in her divine prescience. Feeling perfectly safe in their rear and fired by their own success, they turned upon the church with redoubled determination to carry it. Two enormous beams were now plied by twenty men apiece shattering the iron-studded door, despite all the arrows of the enemy. The dying and the wounded were quickly replaced by fresh forces. Joan, intrepid, ever near the combatants and her banner on high, encouraged them with voice and gesture while escaping a thousand deaths, thanks to the excellent temper of her armor. The door finally broke down under the unceasing blows of the beams, and fell inside the church, but at the same moment, a cannon, placed within and opposite the door, ready for action, vomited with a terrible detonation a discharge of stones and scraps of iron upon the assailants at the gap. Many fell mortally wounded, the rest rushed into the vast and dark basilica where a new hand-to-hand encounter, stubborn and murderous, took place. The struggle continued from step to step up the staircase of the tower to the platform, now stripped of its roof, and from the summit of which the English were finally hurled into space. Just as the sun was tinting with its westering rays the placid waters of the Loire, the standard of Joan was seen floating from the summit of the church, and the cry of the vanquishers echoed and re-echoed a thousand times:

"Good luck! Good luck to the Maid!"

The victory won and the intoxication of battle dissipated, the heroine became again a girl, full of tenderness for the vanquished. Descending from the belfry of the church whither her bravery had carried her, the Maid wept[79] at the sight of the steps red with blood and almost concealed under the corpses. She implored her men to desist from carnage and to spare the prisoners. Among these were three captains. Hoping thereby to escape death they had put on some friars' robes that had been left in a corner of the sacristy and had there lain unnoticed since the English had taken possession of the Church of St. Loup. The three false prelates were found hidden in a dark chapel. The vanquishers wished to massacre them. Joan saved them[80] and, together with others, they were taken prisoners. The frame barracks and lodgings were put to the flame, and the vast conflagration, struggling against the first shadows of the thickening night, threw consternation into the other redoubts of the English, while it lighted the departure of the French.

When, to the light of torches, Joan re-entered Orleans at the head of the troops, the belfry of the town hall and all the bells of the churches were ringing their loudest and merriest; cannon boomed; the whole town was in transports of joy, hope and enthusiasm. The Maid had by her first triumph given the "sign" so oft demanded of her that she was truly the envoy of God. She was received as a liberator by the people, idolatrous with thankfulness.

Upon her return to the house of Master James Boucher, where she was whelmed with caresses by his wife and Madeleine, Joan convoked the captains and said to them: "God has so far supported us, sirs; but we are only at the beginning of our task; let us finish it quickly. Help yourselves, and heaven will help you! We must to-morrow at daybreak profit by the discouragement into which our victory of to-day must have cast the English. We must bravely return to the attack of the other redoubts."[81]

The close of this day, so glorious to the martial maid, had a bitter sorrow in store for her. Even Lahire, Dunois and Xaintrailles, all of whom were animated with less ill will than the other captains towards Joan, recoiled before her brave resolution, and taxed her with foolhardiness. Promptly availing himself of the opportunity, Gaucourt and the captains who were openly hostile to the Maid caused the council of war to declare that "In view of the religious solemnity of the following day, Thursday, the feast of the Ascension, it would be outrageously impious to go to battle; the council would meet at noon only to consider what measures should be next taken."[82]

This deplorable decision afforded the English time to recover from the stupor of their defeat; it also ran the risk of losing the fruits of Joan's first victory. The blindness, the perfidy or the cowardice of the captains filled her with indignation. Steeped in sorrow she withdrew to her own room where, all in tears, she knelt down and implored the advice of her good saints; and with her eyes still wet with tears that her friend Madeleine wiped in sadness and surprise, unable to understand the cause of her friend's grief after so glorious a day, Joan fell asleep, evoking in thought as a means of solace the passage of the prophecy so miraculously fulfilled, in which Merlin announced:

> "Oh, how much blood do I see! How much blood do I see!
> It steams! Its vapor rises, rises like an autumn mist to heaven,
> Where the thunder peals and the lightning flashes!—
> Across that crimson mist, I see a martial virgin;
> White is her steed, white is her armor—
> She battles, she battles, she battles still,
> In the midst of a forest of lances,
> And seems to be riding on the backs of the enemy's archers!"

CHAPTER VII.

THURSDAY, MAY 5, 1429.

Despite the ingenuousness of her loyal nature, Joan could no longer doubt the ill will or jealousy of the captains. They hypocritically invoked the sanctity of the feast of the Ascension merely for the purpose of paralyzing her movements by calculated inertia. In this extremity she asked the advice of her mysterious "voices," and these were now more than ever the echo of her excellent judgment, of her patriotism and of her military genius. The mysterious "voices" answered:

"These captains, like almost all the nobles who make of war a trade, are devoured with envy. Their jealous hatred is irritated at you, poor child of the field, because your genius crushes them. They would prefer to see the English take possession of Orleans rather than have the siege raised by your valor. They may perhaps not dare openly to refuse to second you, fearing to arouse the indignation of their own soldiers, above all of the bourgeois militiamen and of the people of Orleans. But these captains will traitorously resist your plans until the day when the general exasperation will compel them to follow you with their bands of mercenaries. Accordingly, you can rely for the accomplishment of your mission of liberation only upon yourself, and upon the councilmen and the town militia of Orleans. These do not fight out of vainglory or as a trade; they fight in the defence of their hearths, their families, their town. These love and respect you. You are their redeeming angel. Their confidence in you, increased by the victory of yesterday, is to-day boundless. Lean boldly upon these loyal people; you will triumph over the envious and the enemy combined; and you will triumph with the aid of God."

The advice, given to Joan through the intermediary of her good saints, comforted her. Furthermore she learned in the morning that the capture of the bastille of St. Loup had an immense result. As that bastille commanded at once the roads to the Sologne district and to Berry, and the Loire above Orleans, it had rendered difficult the provisioning and reinforcing of the town. Learning, however, of the destruction of the formidable redoubt, the surrounding peasants promptly began to pour into town with their products as on a market day. Thanks to these fresh supplies, besides the convoy of the previous day, abundance succeeded scarcity, and the inhabitants glorified Joan for the happy change of things. There was another precious result. Numerous well armed bands, fanaticized by the accounts that they received of the Maid, entered the town from the side of the Sologne, and offered their help to march against the English with the urban militia. The heroine immediately realized that she had a powerful counterpoise to the ill will of the captains, and was not slow in putting it to use. Accordingly, she ordered her equerry Daulon to convoke the captains and councilmen for the hour of noon after high mass, at the house of Master Boucher, and she pressed upon her host to see that none of the magistrates be absent; the Maid then requested Madeleine to procure her a dress of one of the servants of the house and a hooded cloak, took off her male clothes, donned the attire of her sex, carefully wrapped herself so as to be discovered of none in the town, went to the banks of the Loire, took a boat and ordered the boatman to cross the river and land at a good distance from the bastille of St. John-le-Blanc situated on the opposite bank and face to face with the still smoldering debris of the bastille of St. Loup.

Joan disembarked and proceeded, according to her custom, to examine the entrenchments that she contemplated assailing. Not far from the bastille of St. John-le-Blanc rose the Augustinian Convent, composed of massive buildings that were strongly fortified. Beyond that, the bastille of the Tournelles, a veritable citadel flanked with high wooden towers, spread its wings towards the Beauce and Touraine and faced the bridge of Orleans that had long been cut off by the enemy. Still another formidable redoubt, that of St. Privé, situated to the left and not far from the Tournelles completed the besieging works of the English to the south of the town. The martial maid proposed to carry the four formidable positions one after the other, after which the English would be compelled to abandon the other and less important bastilles which they had raised to the west, these being incapable of resistance after the destruction of the more important works. Joan long and leisurely observed the approaches of these works and revolved her plan of attack. Her woman's clothes aroused no suspicion with the English sentinels. After she had gathered full information with a quick and intelligent eye, she returned to her boat and re-entered the house of Master Boucher so well wrapped in her mantle that she actually escaped the observation of all eyes. She forthwith resumed her male attire to attend the high mass, where she again took the communion. The enthusiastic acclamations that broke out along her route to and from the church proved to her that she could count with the support of the people of Orleans. She entered the house of Master James Boucher where the captains and councilmen were gathered. The council soon went into session, but Joan was not summoned at the start.

At this session there assisted the magistrates of the town as well as Xaintrailles, Dunois, Marshals Retz and St. Sever, the Sire of Graville, Ambroise of Loré, Lahire and other captains. The Sire of Gaucourt presided in his quality of royal captain.[83] The recent victory of the Maid, a victory in which several of the captains least hostile to her had played a secondary role, inspired them all with secret and bitter envy. They had expected to serve themselves with the young peasant girl as a passive instrument of their will, to utilize her influence to their own advantage and to issue their commands through her. It had turned out otherwise. Forced, especially after the battle of the day before, to admit that Joan excelled them all in the profession of war, irritated at the injury done to their military fame, and convinced that the military successes would be wholly placed to the credit of Joan, the one time less hostile captains now went wholly though secretly over to her pronounced enemies, and the following plan of battle was unanimously adopted for the morrow:

"A feint shall be made against the fortress of the Tournelles in order to deceive the enemy and cause it to sally out of the redoubts that lie on the other side of the Loire and hasten to bring help to the threatened position. The enemy will be readily duped. A few detachments shall continue skirmishing on the side of the Tournelles. But the royal troops and the companies of mercenaries will move upon and easily capture the other bastilles where the English, in their hurry to hasten to the defence of an important post, will have left but feeble garrisons behind."[84]

This plan of battle, whether good or bad from the viewpoint of strategy, concealed an act of cowardly perfidy, an infamous, horrible snare spread for Joan. Speaking in the name of the councilmen, and answering the Sire of Gaucourt, who explained the plan that the captains had adopted, Master James Boucher observed that the Maid should be summoned so as to submit to her the projects of the council.

The Sire of Gaucourt hastened to object in the name of all the captains, on the ground that they were not sure the young girl would know how to keep so delicate a matter secret, and that, seeing the doubt existed, she should be informed only upon the plan of attack against the Tournelles, but should not be apprised that the manoeuvre was only a feint, a ruse of war. Accordingly, during a skirmish commanded by the Maid in person, the bulk of the army was to carry out the real plan of battle, on which Joan was to be kept in the dark.[85]

The infernal snare was skilfully planned. The captains relied upon the Maid's intrepidity, certain that she would march without hesitation at the head of a small number of soldiers against the formidable Tournelles, and they did not doubt that in such an assault, as murderous as it was unequal, she would be either killed or taken, while the captains, sallying from Orleans at the opposite side and at the head of the bulk of the troops, would proceed against the other bastilles, that were expected to be found almost wholly deserted by the English, who would have hastened to the aid of the defenders of the Tournelles. Finally, Joan having on the previous day taken an emphatic stand against the captains' opinion, and maintained that the raising of the siege of Orleans depended almost wholly upon the capture of the Tournelles, and that that important work should be forthwith attacked, it was expected she would imagine her views had been adopted by the council of war after mature reflection, and that, carried away by her courage, she was certain to march to her death. Thus the plot concocted long before by the Sire of La Tremouille, Gaucourt and the Bishop of Chartres was now to be put into execution.

Despite their mistrust of the captains, the councilmen failed to scent the trap laid for the Maid. She was introduced, and Gaucourt informed her of the decision of the council omitting, however, to say that the attack upon the Tournelles was only to be a feint. Gifted with rare good sense and sagacity, the Maid had too many proofs of the constant opposition that until then all her plans had met from the captains not to be astonished at seeing them suddenly adopt a plan that they had so loudly condemned the day before. Suspecting a snare, she listened silently to Gaucourt while pensively pacing up and down the hall. When he ended she stopped walking, fixed her frank and beautiful eyes upon the traitor and said boldly:

"Seigneur Gaucourt, do not hide from me anything of what has been decided. I have known and shall know how to keep other secrets than yours."[86]

These words, through which the Maid's mistrust of the captains plainly peeped, confused them. They looked at each other dumbfounded and uneasy. Dunois, the least depraved of all, felt the pangs of remorse and could not decide to remain an accomplice in the execrable scheme of betrayal. Still, not wholly daring to uncover it, he answered:

"Joan, do not get angry. You can not be told everything at once. You have been made acquainted with the first part of our plan of battle. I must now add that the attack upon the Tournelles is to be a feint, and while the English come to the help of their fellows and cross the Loire, we shall attack in good earnest their bastilles over in the Sologne, which they will have left almost empty of defenders."

Despite the belated explanation, the heroine no longer doubted the perfidy of the captains. She nevertheless concealed her indignation, and with the full power of her military superiority she declared to them point blank and with her rustic frankness that the council's plan of battle was detestable— worse yet, shameful. Did not the plan resolve itself into a ruse of war that was not merely cowardly, but fatal in its consequences? Was it not necessary, by keeping the soldiers continually on their mettle by daring, if need be vast exploits, to restore the confidence of the defenders of the town who had been so long beaten? Was it not necessary to convince them that nothing could resist their daring? "Now, then," the martial maid proceeded to argue, "granted that this pitiful feint succeeds, what a wretched victory! To march upon an enemy whom one knows is not there, and thanks to the excess of numbers crush a handful of men! To thus expose the vanquishers to a cowardly triumph, at a time when the hour has struck for heroic resolutions! A hundred times preferable would be a heroic defeat! And, finally, always granting the success of the ruse, what would have been destroyed? A few defenceless redoubts of no farther importance since the capture of the strong and large redoubt of St. Loup, which alone cut off the town's communication with the Sologne and Berry. Assuredly the plan is worthless, it is at all points bad and inopportune."

After thus summarizing and disposing of the captains' plans, the Maid continued:

"On the contrary, we should not to-morrow *feign*, but really and boldly *attack* the Tournelles, by crossing the Loire a little above St. John-le-Blanc, the first redoubt to take, then marching against the fortified Convent of the Augustinians, and finally upon the Tournelles. These positions being taken, the English, no longer in condition to keep themselves a single day longer in the other bastilles, will find themselves forced to raise the siege."

This, Joan declared, was her plan of battle, and nothing in the world could turn her from her resolution, her "voices" having inspired her by order of God. She was accordingly determined, she declared, in case the captains opposed her project, to carry it to a successful finish despite them, demanding only the aid of the councilmen and the militia of the good town of Orleans, whom the Lord would take under his protection, because they would indeed be defending the town, France and the King against the English. Finally she would on that very day order the militia to stand ready for the next day at dawn, and, followed or not by the captains and their bands, she would march straight upon the enemy.

Laid down in a firm voice and fully approved by the councilmen, Joan's project aroused the most violent objections on the part of the captains; they declared it to be as hazardous as impracticable. The Sire of Gaucourt summed up the views of his accomplices, crying with scornful haughtiness: "The council of captains having taken a decision, it will be upheld, and they will oppose *with force*, if necessary, any attempt on the part of the soldiers of Orleans to make an attack on the morrow.[87] Such is the council's will."

"*Your* council has decided, say you?" replied Joan with serene assurance; "*my* council has also decided—it is God's. I shall obey Him despite you!"[88]

Saying this, the Maid left the room, wounded to the quick by the obvious perfidy of the captains. Firmly resolved to put an end to so many fatal delays, and in accord with the councilmen to demand the safety of their town only from the bravery of her own citizens if need be, Joan immediately turned her attention to the preparations for the morrow's attack, and commissioned the councilmen to gather a large number of barges for the transport of the soldiers, at whose head she was to attack the English at early dawn from the side of the Tournelles.

CHAPTER VIII.

FRIDAY, MAY 6, 1429.

Early in the morning the Sire of Gaucourt, with a squad of soldiers and mercenaries, took possession of the Bourgogne Gate, through which Joan had to pass to reach the river bank and effect the embarkation of the troops. Gaucourt ordered the soldiers, whom he planted under the arch, to allow none to leave the town, and to use their arms against anyone who tried to violate their orders. Stepping back a few paces, wrapping himself closely in his cloak, and listening from time to time for what was happening in town, the traitor waited.

Dawn soon appeared; its early glimmer lighted the horizon and set off the outlines of the crenelated Bourgogne Gate. A distant noise presently attracted the attention of Gaucourt; it increased and drew near; and soon he distinguished the muffled tread of many feet and the rattling of arms. He then repeated his orders to his soldiers and withdrew into the shadow of the vault that united the two towers at this entrance to the town. A few minutes later a compact column, marching in good order and composed of the urban militia and surrounding peasants, who had entered Orleans after the capture of the bastille of St. Loup, turned into the street that led to the Bourgogne Gate. Master John and about twelve other citizen cannoniers marched in the front ranks, dragging a cart on which were two portable culverins, christened by Master John "Jeannette" and "Jeanneton" in honor of his countrywoman; another cart, also hand-drawn, contained the munitions for the two pieces of artillery. The martial maid rode at the head of the column, escorted by several armed councilmen who had previously taken part in the defence of the town. One of these, intending to hasten the egress of the troops, quickened his horse's pace, and advanced toward the gate to have it opened. A sergeant in his cups seized the bridle of the councilman's horse and cried roughly:

"There is no passage here. It is forbidden to leave the town! Such are our orders!"

"The town gates are opened or closed by orders of the councilmen. I am a councilman. You must obey."

"I have my orders," replied the mercenary drawing his sword; "back, or I cut you to pieces!"

"You miserable drunken fellow! Do you dare to threaten a magistrate!"

"I only know my captain, and since you are trying to pass despite my orders, here is for you!" saying which he made a thrust at the councilman.

The sword glided over the magistrate's armor, and the soldier cried out: "This way, my men!"

About twenty soldiers rushed to the spot from under the gate. The squad of drunken men had surrounded and were hooting at and threatening the magistrate when Joan, her equerry Daulon, her page, and the other councilmen who, together with her, formed the head of the column, reached the scene of the wrangle. At the same moment the Sire of Gaucourt appeared. He was in a towering rage, made a sign to his soldiers to draw back, and himself stepped towards the heroine whom he insolently addressed:

"Joan, the council of war pronounced itself yesterday against your proposed plan for to-day. You shall not leave the town—"[89]

"You are a bad man!" cried the Maid indignantly. "I shall pass whether you will it or not. The men of Orleans will follow me—and we shall vanquish the English again as we have done before."[90]

The Maid's defiant answer to the impudent and imprudent words of the royal captain were heard by Master John and his cannoniers, and were repeated down the column from rank to rank of the militiamen, producing such exasperation against Gaucourt that from all parts the furious cries were heard:

"Death to the traitor! Cut the captain to pieces!"

"He dares to oppose the Maid's passage!"

"Death to the traitor! Death to his soldiers! They are worse than the English!"

In the midst of these cries, Master John and his cannoniers, together with a mass of armed citizens, fell upon Gaucourt and his mercenaries and drubbed them soundly with the handles of their pikes; not content with having almost killed the captain and his band, the more enraged of the militiamen insisted upon hanging them. With much difficulty, Joan and the councilmen obtained mercy for Gaucourt and his crew. On a later occasion he admitted that he had never before been as near death as on that day.

The Bourgogne Gate was opened, and the troops proceeded on their march towards the river whose waters began to glisten in the rays of the rising sun. Joan had several times the day before insisted with the councilmen to see that about twenty barges, capable of containing each from fifty to sixty men be safely moored and ready at daybreak for the embarkation of the troops. Never forgetful of any precautionary measure, fifty soldiers were to remain on guard during the night on board of the flotilla in order to defend it, if need be, against a "coup de main" of the English. The councilmen themselves superintended the execution of the Maid's orders. Nevertheless, seeing that her mistrust of the captains gained ground, especially after her last experience with Gaucourt, Joan wished to make sure that her transports were ready. She put the spurs to her horse and took the lead of the column toward the river bank which a high hill intercepted from her sight. What was the martial Maid's stupor at the sight before her! Only five or six barges and a few boats lay ready. She rode her horse almost to the saddle into the Loire to question an old skipper who sat aft on one of the lighters. From him she learned that towards midnight a captain had requisitioned most of the lighters for the royal army. The wind being favorable, the captain said he had orders to ascend the Loire with the flotilla as far as Blois in order to take reinforcements. Several master skippers, the one who spoke to Joan among them, had answered that they would not budge from their anchorage without counter-orders from the councilmen; but the captain threatened the skippers with bodily injury if they refused to obey. The majority yielded to the intimidation in the belief that the purpose was really to bring reinforcements from Blois, and spread their sails to the wind. There only remained six barges and a few boats.

This new machination of the captains wounded the Maid's heart without, however, abating her courage, or disturbing her presence of mind. With the number of barges that she had counted upon, her troops were to be landed in two or three trips; it would now require eight or ten. Precious time would thus be lost. Observing the movement from the tops of their redoubts, and taking cognizance of the small number of barges at her disposal, the English might attempt a sally and repel the descent upon them by hastening to the opposite river bank before all the troops had time to form in line of battle. Joan appreciated the extreme peril of the situation; but so far from being discouraged thereby, only felt that a stronger demand was made upon her audacity, calmness and foresight. Full of faith in her mission, she repeated her favorite saying—*Help yourself and heaven will help you!*

The sun was rising behind the wooded banks of the Loire and the curtain of poplars that shaded its shore when the first ranks of the militia arrived upon the scene. Their disappointment was profound at the sight of the small number of barges that awaited them. But leaving them no time to reflect, Joan said:

"Let the bravest follow me! The others will come after!"

A race ensued as to who was to be the first upon the barges so as to be considered the bravest by the heroine. She left her horse with a valet, and threw herself into one of the boats accompanied only by her equerry, her page and an oarsman; she had herself rowed several times around the barges to see that they were not overloaded. The militiamen vied with one another to be ranked among the most intrepid. The barges being finally full, their sails were spread, and the wind being favorable, blowing in the direction of the left bank, they moved swiftly, preceded by several boats in which were the councilmen, Master John and several of his cannoniers, the rest of whom were on board the barges with the two culverins Jeannette and Jeanneton. The first of the vanguard boats carried Joan cased in her white armor that now glistened in the sun. Standing erect and motionless in the prow of the light skiff, and leaning on the staff of her standard that fluttered in the morning breeze, the outlines of the martial maid stood off against the azure sky like the country's protecting angel.

Hardly had the boat reached the opposite bank when Joan leaped ashore and drew up her men in order of battle as fast as they disembarked. Master John and his cannoniers landed the two culverins from the barges, and these then returned and returned again bringing over the rest of the army from the right bank of the Loire. The work of transportation consumed over an hour, an hour of indescribable impatience and anxiety to the heroine. She feared at every moment to see the English issue from their entrenchments to rush at the small number that she at first landed with. But her fears were idle. The heroic capture of the bastille of St. Loup, that two days before had fallen into the hands of the French, spread consternation among the ranks of the English. Imputing her prowess to witchcraft, they dared not assail her in the open, and tremblingly awaited her under shelter of their own works. This evidence of timidity augured well for the happy issue of Joan's undertaking, nor was she slow to perceive and draw courage from it. When the last phalanx was successfully landed, Joan, now at the head of two thousand militiamen and peasants, marched straight upon the bastille of St. John-le-Blanc, that was similarly fortified to the bastille of St. Loup. To the end of protecting the descent of the assailants in the enclosing moat, Master John planted Jeannette and Jeanneton on the outer edge of the embankment and trained their muzzles at the parapet of the redoubt, whose own cannon and other engines began to pour their projectiles upon the French. Thanks, however, to the cannonier's marksmanship most of the English engines were speedily silenced. The assault was accordingly less murderous to the assailants. The Maid and her troop speedily crossed the moat, leaving a large number of their own dead and wounded behind; they rushed up and climbed the opposite escarpment, arrived at the palisade and forced it; and in an incredibly short time the white standard was seen floating from the boulevard of the entrenchment. The resistance of the English was at first desperate, but speedily yielding to a panic, they fled pell mell, crossed the Loire at a ford and retreated in utter disorder to the little neighboring island of St. Aignan.

This rough and bloody attack consumed only two hours. Without allowing her men a moment's rest, Joan ordered the barracks of the bastille to be set on fire, to the end of utterly ruining the works, and also signaling her new victory to the good people of Orleans. A short respite was taken, and the combatants, exalted and exhilarated with their triumph, followed the martial maid to the attack of the Augustinian Convent, still more strongly entrenched. This position had to be first carried, in order to undertake the siege of the Tournelles, itself a veritable fortress raised at the entrance of the town bridge. Thanks to the protection that her friends deemed divine, Joan had not until then been wounded, although ever at the head of her forces. But to offset this, her losses were serious. Despite the considerable reduction of her forces, she turned her back upon the burning redoubt of St. John-le-Blanc and marched to the attack of the Augustinians, which was defended by a garrison of over two thousand men, reinforced by about a thousand more from the Tournelles. Thanks to this reinforcement, instead of awaiting the enemy under shelter of the fortifications of the convent, the English decided to risk a decisive stroke and deliver battle in the open field, reliant upon the advantage of their own numbers and upon the aid afforded by the redoubt of St. Privé, whose garrison sallied forth to take the French in the rear. Joan had about fourteen hundred men under her command; before her stood over three thousand, and her right flank was threatened by another considerable force.

At the sight of the numerical superiority of the enemy, who advanced in a compact mass, cased in iron, with the red standard of St. George floating in the air, the martial maid collected herself, crossed her arms over her cuirassed bosom, and raised her inspired eyes to heaven. Suddenly she believed she heard the mysterious voice of her two good saints murmuring in her ear: "March, daughter of God! Attack the enemy boldly! Whatever their numbers, you shall vanquish!"

For the first time the Maid drew her sword, used it to point at the foe, turned towards her own troops and cried in tones that stirred their bosoms:

"Be brave! Forward! God is with us!"

The words, accompanied with a heroic gesture, the sublime expression of her beautiful countenance, all contributed to drag the soldiers at her heels. The hearts of all burned with the fires of intensest patriotism. Her men were no longer themselves; they were she! The wills of all seemed concentrated in one single will! The souls of all were merged into one! At that supreme moment the militiamen attained that superb contempt for death that transported our ancestors the Gauls when, half naked, they rushed upon the iron-cased and serried ranks of the Roman legions, throwing these into a panic and breaking through them by the very force of their foolhardiness. Thus it was with the intrepid attack of the Gallic virgin on this day. So far from yielding to numbers, as the English had hoped she would, she fell upon them at the head of her troop. Stupefied, terrified by such audacity, the

English ranks wavered and opened despite all the orders, threats, imprecations and desperate efforts to the contrary by their captains. A large breach was opened in the center of the enemy's line. Their success added fuel to the exaltation of the men of Orleans, and raised them to a delirium of heroism. They made havoc with their swords, pikes and maces among the English ranks. The breach widened amid floods of blood. The white standard of the Maid advanced—the red standard of St. George retreated. The arms of the English soldiers seemed paralyzed and struck but uncertain blows. Only a few of the French were wounded or killed; on the side of the English, however, the blood ran in torrents. Suffolk, who conducted himself gallantly, cried out, showing to his bewildered and panic stricken men his own sword dyed red:

"Look at this blood, you miserable cowards! Do you still deem these varlets to be invulnerable? Will you allow yourselves to be vanquished by a female cowherd? If she be a witch, let us capture her, by God, and burn her—the charm will end! But to capture her you must fight or die like soldiers of old England!"

This energetic language, the example of their chiefs, the impression, slowly asserting itself, of the vast numerical inferiority of the French, and the bray of the trumpets of the garrison of St. Privé that was hastening to the rescue, gradually revived the courage of the English. Shame and rage at their threatened defeat presently changed their panic into a furious exaltation. They closed ranks and took the offensive. Despite all the prodigies of valor on the part of their adversaries, they, in turn, now forced them to retreat in disorder. In the midst of the maddening struggle Joan would certainly have been killed but for the devotion of Master John and some twenty other determined men. With their bodies they made a rampart around her, determined to preserve her life that was so dear to them all. The ground was defended inch by inch. Every moment the handful of men grew thinner. Ten of them, fighting to her left, were scattered and crushed by the opposing numbers. During the movement of retreat Joan was driven despite herself towards the Loire, and already a few distracted men were heard crying:

"To the barges! Save himself who can! To the barges! The battle is lost!"

The triumphant English pursued the Maid with jeers and their accustomed insults. They pushed forward, crying:

"Strumpet!" "Cowherd!" "Thief!"

"We shall now capture and burn you, witch!"

The panic had now completely seized the ranks of the French. They no longer fought but fled wildly towards the Loire. In vain did the Maid seek to rally them. Suddenly and obedient to an inspiration of her genius, instead of resisting the current that was carrying her away, she outran it and overtook the swiftest fleers, waving her standard. These followed and rallied around her and thus naturally and perforce order was gradually restored. During this move, the jeers, imprecations and insults of the English, hurled at the Maid, redoubled in volume, especially when they saw the skippers, witnessing the French defeat, share the general panic, raise the sails of their barges, the only means of retreat for the French, and push off from the shore out of fear of being boarded by the vanquishers. The latter, now certain of the success of the day, even disdained to hasten the rout of the fleeing French, who, crowded against the Loire, were sure to be drowned or taken—Joan first of all. The bulk of the English troops halted to shout three cheers of triumph, a few companies advanced unsupported and with mocking slowness to make the assured capture.

"Come, now, Joan! Come!" cried the English captains from a distance. "Come now, strumpet, surrender! You shall be burned! That's your fate!"

The presumptuous confidence of the enemy afforded the heroine the necessary time to re-form her lines.

"Prisoners or drowned!" she said to them, pointing to the receding barges. "One more effort—and by the order of God we shall vanquish, as we have vanquished twice before! Let us first attack this English vanguard that boasts to have us in its clutches! Be brave! Forward!"

And turning about she rushed upon the enemy.

"Be brave! Forward! Forward!" repeated Master John and the most determined townsmen of Orleans, following the Maid.

"Be brave! Forward!" echoed all the others. "Let us exterminate the English!"

The scene that ensued was no longer one of courage, or of heroism; it was a superhuman frenzy that transported the handful of French and added tenfold strength to their arms. The enemy's companies, that had been detached from the main body and sent forward to make a capture deemed unquestionable, were stupefied at the offensive move, and unable to resist the superhuman shock of despair and patriotism. Driven in disorder, the sword in their flanks, towards the main body, they overthrew its front ranks and spread disorder and confusion in the English army.

The superstitious fears of the English, fears that they had once before succumbed to, now gained new empire over them that seemed justified by the unheard-of audacity of a body of men, once in full flight, suddenly returning to the attack with intrepidity. The front ranks of the English being broken through, the general panic spread all the quicker seeing that, in sharing it, those who stood away from the center of action were wholly in the dark as to the cause of the sudden rout. The English soldiers struck at and trampled one another; the orders of their captains were lost in the frightful tumult; their efforts were powerless to conjure away the defeat. The cry of the first soldiers to flee: "The witch has let loose her fiends upon us!" was carried from mouth to mouth. Finally, and as if to overfill the measure, the English of the bastille of St. Privé, upon arriving to the aid of their fellows, saw the barges, that had shortly left the near shore, now returning from the opposite side filled with fresh French soldiers. The French captains had been compelled by the exasperation of the inhabitants of Orleans to decide to co-operate with the Maid,[91] and they had marched out and reached the river bank just as the barges arrived on that side. At the sight of the re-inforcements, the corps from St. Privé hastened back to its own encampment, while the rest of the panic-stricken English ran to their respective bastilles for shelter behind the entrenchments of the redoubts of the Augustinians and the Tournelles. When the fresh French contingent brought by Marshal St. Sever and other captains disembarked, the martial maid was preparing to attack the Convent of the Augustinians, determined not to allow the enemy time to recover from their panic. Now supported by the reinforcements, Joan threw herself upon the convent, but at the moment when, in the lead of all she set foot upon a narrow passage leading to the palisade that she was to attack, she uttered a piercing cry. The teeth of a man trap had closed above her ankle; it penetrated her jambards and her skin and even reached the bone. It was an English "ruse of war," into which the Maid had put her foot.[92]

The pain was so keen that Joan, exhausted from the fatigues of the day, fainted away, and fell in the arms of her equerry Daulon. When she recovered consciousness, the day was nearing its end; the bastille of the Augustinians had been carried and its defenders were either dead or prisoners. The heroine had been transported to the lodgings of one of the English captains who had been killed in the combat. When Joan returned to consciousness, her equerry wished to remove the armor from her wounded limb and bathe the wound, but blushing at the exposure of even her foot to the surrounding soldiers, Joan obstinately refused all attention, and bestowed all her thought to the best use to be made of the capture of the Augustinian Convent. She forbade that it be set on fire, and ordered it to be held during the night by a strong garrison, that should lead the next day in a determined attack upon the Tournelles. After issuing these and other necessary orders with remarkable military sagacity, the warrior maid had herself conveyed to Orleans in a boat, feeling unable to walk by reason of the pain of her wound. The Augustinian Convent rose almost on the river's edge. Daulon, Master John and a few other cannoniers carried Joan to the river on a stretcher improvised out of the shafts of lances and placed her in a boat. Her page and equerry accompanied her, and she was rowed over to Orleans where she arrived at night. Modestly desiring to escape observation in her transit through the town to the house of her host, especially seeing that all the windows in the houses were illuminated, Joan asked Daulon to spread her cloak over her on the stretcher. Thus, although unseen of all, Joan was the witness of the delirious joy inspired by her last triumph. The town was in gala, hope radiated from all countenances. In two days, the Maid had destroyed or carried three of the most redoubtable fortifications of the English, and set free a large number of prisoners. More than eight hundred of these were found in the Augustinian Convent. By virtue of the confidence that she inspired, there was no doubt entertained on the success of the morrow's assault—the Tournelles would be taken, and, agreeable to the promise she had made in the name of God, the enemy would raise the siege.

Concealed under the cloak that covered her, the Maid was transported to the house of James Boucher. Informed of the victory by the wild cheers of the people, but full of anxiety for the heroine, his wife and daughter were at first thrown into terror seeing her carried on a stretcher. But the Maid soon calmed them, promising that with their help she would soon be restored. Assisted by the two she went up to her room, and there submitted to the tender nursing at which her modesty could take no offence. Madeleine and her mother, like most women of the time, were versed in the tending of wounds. They applied oil, balm and lint to the heroine's hurt after removing her armor, which, much to their alarm, they saw was indented in more than twenty places with sabre blows and lance thrusts. A large number of contusions, discolored and painful, the results of so many strokes, fortunately deadened by her cuirass and arm protectors, marked the body of Joan, who now only felt the reaction of her exertion during the warmly contested battle. She took a little nourishment, performed her evening devotions, thanked God and her saints for having sustained her during the bloody struggle, and implored their aid for the battle of the morrow. The warrior maid was about to compose herself for recuperative sleep, when Master Boucher requested admission to Joan upon an important and urgent matter. She quickly threw one of Madeleine's robes over herself in order to receive her host's visit and was struck by the signs of indignation and anger depicted on his face as he entered. His first words on entering were:

"What impudence! I can hardly believe it possible! Whom do you think I come from this minute, Joan? The Sire of Gaucourt," and answering an interrogating gesture of the heroine, her host proceeded: "Would you believe the man has forgotten the rude lesson of this morning? Would you believe that at his instigation the captains, assembled this evening after supper, decided that—*in view of the small number of the mercenary troops in town, the council opposes a battle for the morrow, and declares that the people should be satisfied with the successes they have so far won ... and until the arrival of reinforcements no further measures shall be taken against the English.*[93] I was commissioned to inform you of this decision on the spot and demand your submission—"

"It is nothing short of treason!" broke in Dame Boucher, who although ignorant of arms, nevertheless perceived the baseness of the act. "What, remain locked up within our walls, on the eve of the last triumph that is to free our town!"

"I spoke in that sense to the Sire of Gaucourt," replied James Boucher, "and I consented to communicate to Joan the decision of the captains, but declared at the same time that I was positive she would refuse to obey, and that in that case she should not lack the support of the councilmen and the good people of Orleans."

"You have answered, sir, as I myself would have answered," said the warrior maid with a smile of deep sorrow at this further evidence of the captains' perfidy. "Be at ease. Your brave militiamen occupy to-night the Augustinian Convent. I shall join them to-morrow at daybreak to lead them to the assault, and with God's help and their courage we shall carry the Tournelles. As to the captains' ill will, I have a sovereign means to thwart it. It is for that reason that I requested you to have me escorted to-morrow to the sound of the town's trumpets. Good night, sir; have faith and courage. The good town of Orleans will be set free. God so orders it."

James Boucher withdrew, followed by his wife. Madeleine alone remained with the warrior maid. The latter, before taking to her bed, and yielding to a vague presentiment, requested her companion, to whom she frankly avowed her utter ignorance of reading and writing, to write to her mother, Isabelle Darc, a letter that she proceeded to dictate—a simple, touching, respectful letter that revealed at every word her love for her family and the tender recollection of the happy days that she spent in Domremy. In that missive Joan did not forget even her village girl friend, nor the good old sexton who, to oblige her, when she was still little and loved so passionately to listen to the sound of the bells, purposely prolonged the morning chimes or the chimes of the Angelus. This missive, that bore the stamp of serious, religious and tender sentiment, breathed a vague presentiment concerning her chances of safety at the murderous battle contemplated for the morrow. Madeleine, who more than once, while writing the letter, had dried her tears, was struck by these apprehensions and asked her with a trembling voice:

"Oh, Joan, do you apprehend misfortune to yourself?"

"The will of God be done, dear Madeleine. I do not know why, but it seems to me I shall be wounded to-morrow again.[94] Oh, I was right! It was a mistake to delay employing me so long. I am not to live long!" Joan then relapsed into silence and presently added: "May God protect you, dear friend; I am going to sleep. I feel very tired and I must be on my feet to-morrow before dawn."

CHAPTER IX.

SATURDAY, MAY 7, 1429.

Before daybreak Joan re-armed herself with the help of Madeleine. The wound in her foot pained her severely. Although the distance was short from Orleans to the Convent of the Augustinians she asked for her horse. After tenderly embracing her companion, Madeleine helped her descend to the ground floor. There they found James Boucher, his wife and a female friend named Colette, the wife of the registrar Millet. All three had risen early to bid the warrior maid godspeed. Sadness overspread the faces of all at the thought of the fresh dangers that the heroine was about to brave, but the latter reassured her friends as well as she could, and pressed upon James Boucher the necessity of causing it to be proclaimed throughout the city that, in order to insure a successful issue to the assault on the Tournelles the fort should be attacked by the captains from the side of the bridge the instant that she began the attack from the side of the Augustinian Convent. Thus pressed upon by popular clamor, the captains would be forced to recede from their treasonable decision of the previous evening. Will they, nill they, they would co-operate with her. Joan had just given these last instructions to her host, when a fisherman stopped at the door to offer for sale to Dame Boucher an enormous river shad that he had just caught in the Loire. In order not to leave her hosts under a sad impression, Joan said mirthfully to James Boucher:

"Do buy this shad and keep it for this evening. I shall return by the Orleans bridge after we have carried the Tournelles and I shall bring an English prisoner along to help us finish up the fish."[95]

Saying this Joan mounted her horse and preceded by her page, her equerry and the town trumpeters, who at her orders blew the reveille and the call to arms, she crossed the whole city and rode towards the Bourgogne Gate where she was to be joined by Master John the cannonier, the representative of the carpenters named Champeaux, and the representative of the fishermen, named Poitevin, both of them intelligent and resolute men.

By traversing the town from one end to the other to the sound of trumpets, it was the Maid's purpose to call the townsmen up and out, and to announce to them that she was about to start on the assault; and thus to compel the captains to choose between seconding her in a combat upon which the final deliverance of Orleans depended, or else covering themselves with overwhelming shame and exposing themselves to be killed by an indignant people. Upon arriving at the Bourgogne Gate Joan found Master John together with Champeaux and Poitevin. She ordered the former to gather all the necessary workmen and quickly construct a drop-bridge to be thrown over the arches where the English had cut the bridge for the purpose of isolating the Tournelles from the boulevard of the town and thus turning the Loire into a natural moat for their fortification. The communication being thus re-established it would enable the captains who remained in town to advance with their men to the very foot of the fortress and assail it. The placing of the bridge and the eruption of the soldiers from that side were to be announced by the town belfry. At that signal Joan was to commence the assault from her side. The carpenter promised that all would be ready in two hours. The equerry Daulon was sent by Joan to inform the captains of her dispositions. Nevertheless, preparing against the contingency of the captains' failing to comply, she ordered Poitevin to fill two large barges with tarred and pitched fagots, and in case no attack was made by way of the improvised bridge, Poitevin, assisted by some other intrepid skippers, was to drive the burning barges against the Tournelles and fasten them there against the lower framework of the English fortress. The English were thus to be hemmed in between a conflagration and the lances and pikes of the French.

Obedient to the instructions he had received from Joan the previous evening, Master John carried during the night a large number of scaling ladders to the Augustinian Convent for the attack from that side; moreover, assisted by his two sturdy friends, Champeaux and Poitevin, and their workmen, he had established two pontoon bridges, one from the right bank of the Loire to the small island of St. Aignan, the second from that island to a path on the left bank of the river and almost opposite the ruins of the bastille of St. John-le-Blanc. By opening this path to the foot soldiers, to the cavalry and to the artillery, the Maid facilitated the passage of the troops and cannons of Master John, both of which could thus be easily brought to bear upon the Tournelles; if occasion should arise, the bridge alone offered a safe means of retreat.

Joan was about to step upon the pontoon bridge when she was joined by Dunois and Lahire. Yielding to the point of honor, no less than to the public outcry of the townspeople, who were notified of the departure of Joan to the assault, the two captains came at the head of their companies of troops to take part in the battle. Commander Gireme, Marshal St. Sever and other captains were, according to the Maid's orders, to attack the Tournelles from the side of the bridge. At a signal from the belfry the attack of the fortress was to commence upon both sides. Followed by Lahire and Dunois, the heroine arrived before the Augustinian Convent. Formed in battle line since early morning, the militiamen awaited impatiently the order to march upon the enemy. Loud were the cheers with which they received the Maid. While waiting for the signal for the general assault, she desired to inspect more closely the outer fortifications of the Tournelles, and she approached the fortress which she found protected by a wide moat on the other side of which rose a palisaded embankment, and beyond and above that a rampart equipped with artillery and flanked with frame turrets. The works presented a formidable appearance. Already the pieces of artillery of longest range were showering their projectiles at Master John and his cannoniers, who were training their cannons against the rampart to the end of knocking a breach through for the assault. Unconcerned at the bullets that at times buried themselves in the ground at the feet of her horse, the warrior maid attentively watched the work of Master John, and with a visual precision that threw the old cannonier into confusion and wonder, she pointed out to him more correct positions for several of his pieces. Master John recognized the justice of her opinion and followed her instructions. Suddenly the peals of the belfry reached the ears of Joan's troops. It was to be the signal for the general attack, but it turned out otherwise. Instead of beginning the action from their side, the captains wasted time with false manoeuvres, and left Joan to engage the English alone, in the hope that the latter, not being compelled to divide their forces as Joan had counted that they would, might easily crush her. Ignorant of this fresh act of treason on the part of the captains, the Maid gave Master John orders to open fire upon the ramparts in order to protect the descent of the troops into the moat.

The cannons roared. At their sound, and unable to support the idea of remaining nailed to her horse instead of taking an active part in this decisive combat, the warrior maid, despite the smarting wound of the previous day, jumped to the ground, and soon forgot the stinging pain in the effervescence of the struggle. Her standard in her hand, she marched to the assault.

The English were commanded by their most illustrious captains—Lord Talbot, the Earl of Suffolk, Gladescal and many more. Violent at their recent defeats, these warriors were bent upon wiping out the stain on their arms. This supreme day would decide the fate of Orleans, perchance also of the English domination of Gaul. It was necessary for the English to restore by a brilliant victory the drooping courage of their troops. The captains gathered their best men, veterans of scores of battles, reminded them of their past victories, pricked their national pride, fired their military ardor, and succeeded once more in overcoming the terror that the Maid filled them with. The French met with a furious and dogged resistance. Three times they mounted to the assault, here through the breach, yonder by means of their scaling ladders. Three times they were repelled and their ladders thrown down with all who were climbing them. A hailstorm of balls, bolts and arrows showered down upon the French. The bottom of the moat was covered with the dead and dying. The breach having been opened, Master John hastened to join the Maid and reached her side at the moment when she rushed at a ladder that her intrepid followers raised for the fourth time at the foot of one of the turrets. Master John followed the Maid. She had mounted several rungs when she was struck at the juncture of her gorget and cuirass by a "vireton," a long and sharp steel arrow, that was ejected with such force from a ballista that, piercing her armor, it entered near her right breast and partly issued under her shoulder.[96]

Thrown back by the force of the projectile, the Maid fell into the arms of the cannonier who followed close behind her, and who, with the aid of a few militiamen, carried her fainting beyond the moat. There they laid her on the grass near a tree that protected her from the enemy's fire. She felt, she said, as if she were dying, but still retaining her full presence of mind she deplored the slowness of the captains, who, not having attacked the Tournelles from the side of the town, endangered by their treason an otherwise certain victory. Informed of the wound received by Joan, her equerry Daulon hastened to her and realizing the seriousness of her condition informed her that in order to avoid being choked by the flowing blood, her cuirass had to be instantly unfastened and the dart extracted. At these words, Joan's pale face turned purple. Her modesty revolted at the thought of exposing her shoulder and bosom to the eyes of the men who surrounded her; and so painful was the thought that her tears—touching tears, not drawn by the physical pain that she was suffering from, welled up to her eyes and rolled down her cheeks.[97]

Master John, who also had considerable experience in wounds, confirmed the equerry's opinion—to allow the dart to remain longer in the wound was to expose the heroine's precious life. Indeed, feeling more and more suffocated, Joan believed her last hour had struck, still she did not wish as yet to die. Her mission was not yet fulfilled. She invoked her saints, gathered strength from the mental prayer and mustered up the necessary resolution to submit to a necessity that cruelly wounded her modesty. Before, however, allowing her wound to be attended, Joan ordered the assault to be suspended in order to give the troops some rest. She ordered Dunois, who ran to her, together with Lahire and Xaintrailles, to send one of their orderlies into Orleans on the spot, in order to ascertain the cause of the fatal inaction of the other chiefs, and to enjoin them to commence the attack from the side of the town within an hour, or else to order the barges with combustibles to be set on fire and pushed against the Tournelles. Again the belfry was to give the signal for a general attack. The trumpets sounded a retreat amidst the triumphant cheers of the English, who were intoxicated with their first triumph. Thanks, however, to the exaltation that the heroine had produced in her soldiers, they clamored to be allowed to return to the assault. A cordon of sentinels, placed at a little distance from the tree at whose base Joan had been laid, kept back the alarmed, trembling and desolate crowd of soldiers. Blushing with confusion, the warrior maid allowed her equerry to unfasten her cuirass, and with a steady hand herself extracted the dart from her breast, emitting, however, in doing so, a piercing cry of pain. Dunois and the other captains wished to have her transported to Orleans, where, said they, she would receive the best of care, and they proposed to adjourn the battle for the next day. Joan opposed both propositions, and maintained that, even then, if the captains would support her from the side of Orleans, success was certain.

"Let our people take some food," she said to Dunois; "we shall return to the assault; the Tournelles will be ours!"[98]

Once the dart was extracted from the wound, the warrior maid allowed herself to be tended. The mental tortures that she underwent at the moment by far exceeded her physical pain. When, her cuirass and padded jacket having been taken off, she felt her linen shirt, wet with blood and the sole cover on her shoulder and breast, respectfully removed by her equerry, a shudder ran through Joan's body and she involuntarily closed her eyes. She seemed to wish to close her eyes to the looks that she feared might be cast at her. But so sacred was the nation's virgin to all the troops that not even the shadow of an improper thought stained the purity of the pious offices of any of the men who saw the beautiful warrior maid thus semi-nude.[99]

Like all other professional equerries, Daulon was expert in surgery. He carried about him, in a leather case suspended from his shoulder, lint, bandages and a bottle of balm. With these he tended the wound which he pronounced so serious that he considered it highly imprudent for Joan to return to the combat. But on that point she remained inflexible. So great was the relief she speedily experienced, that she said she hardly felt the wound. Tightly laced, her armor would keep the bandage in position. All she wanted was a few mouthfuls of water to slake her burning thirst. Master John ran to a nearby streamlet, filled up full a pouch that was half full of wine and returned with it to the Maid. She drank and felt better, rose, put on her armor and took a few steps to test her strength. Her celestial face, grown pale with the loss of blood, speedily recovered its serene and resolute expression. She requested those near her to step aside for a moment, whereupon she knelt down near the old oak tree, joined her hands, prayed, thanked her good saints for having delivered her from a mortal danger, and besought them further to sustain and protect her. Immediately she heard the mysterious voices murmur in her ear:

"Go, daughter of God. Courage! Combat with your wonted audacity. Heaven will give you victory. By you Gaul will be delivered."

Inspired anew the heroine rose, put on her casque, seized her banner that had been placed against the tree, and cried out aloud:

"Now, to the assault! Ours will the Tournelles be, by the order of God! To arms! Be brave! Forward, victory to Gaul!"[100]

The cry was repeated from mouth to mouth with a tremor of impatient bravery. The quick peals from the belfry rent the air. The detonations of the artillery resounded from the side of the town, announcing the execution of the Maid's orders, however tardy. The Tournelles was assailed by the captains from the bridge at the moment when the Maid marched to the attack of the fortress in front. The happy plan redoubled the already exalted ardor of the assailants under the Maid. Led by her they resumed the assault with irresistible impetus. After a stubborn and bloody struggle that lasted until night the Tournelles was carried. As on the previous day, the sinking rays of the sun cast the gleam of their ruddy aureola upon the folds of Joan Darc's standard, planted by herself upon the battlements of the fortress. The enemy was vanquished again.

Gladescal, who had so outrageously insulted Joan, was killed during the combat, as also the Seigneurs of Moulin and Pommiers and the Bailiff of Trente, together with a great number of English noblemen. Almost all their men who were not killed were made prisoners, the rest were either burned or drowned in the attempt to flee when the assailants were upon them. They sought to escape by the improvised bridge under which Poitevin let his burning barges float. The bridge took fire and broke under the feet of the fleeing soldiers who thus perished either in the flames or the river.

As Joan had calculated, the garrisons of the other bastilles, to the number of from eight to ten thousand men, decamped in haste during the very first night that followed the capture of the Tournelles. They left in terror and consternation. At break of the next day, the warrior maid mounted her horse, assembled the town militiamen and a few companies of the captains' troops and marched out to offer battle to the English whom they supposed to be still there. But these were gone, they were beating a precipitate retreat towards Meung and Beaugency, fortified places held by the English.

On that day, Sunday, May 8, 1429, Joan re-entered Orleans at the head of the troops, and attended noon mass at the Church of St. Croix in the midst of an immense concourse of people, delirious with joy and gratitude to the warrior maid—the redeeming angel of Orleans.

Such was the "Week of Joan Darc." In eight days and with three battles she caused the raising of the siege that had lasted nearly a year. The deed achieved by the peasant girl of Domremy dealt a mortal blow to the rule of England in Gaul.

But not yet was Joan's secret martyrdom at an end; it increased from day to day with her glory. Charles VII, that poltroon and ingrate prince, unnerved and plunged in ignoble effeminacy, was yet to cause the shepherdess of Domremy to undergo all the tortures and all the disappointments that a soul inflamed with patriotism can not choose but undergo when it has devoted itself to a prince whose baseness is equal to his selfishness and cowardice.

CHAPTER X.

THE KING CROWNED.

Immediately upon the raising of the siege of Orleans, Joan hastened to the Castle of Loches. The fame of her triumphs ran ahead heralding her approach. The gates of the palace flew open before her. She was told the King was closeted in his private cabinet with his council. Thither Joan walked resolutely, knocked at the door and intrepidly addressed Charles VII:

"Sire, pray do not hold such long conferences with these seigneurs. The siege of Orleans is raised. The good town is now restored to you. You must now march boldly to Rheims and be consecrated. The consecration will crown you King of France in the eyes of the French. The English will then be impotent against you."

The sound sense and political acumen of Joan traced to Charles VII in these few words the only path that wisdom dictated. His consecration at Rheims, a divine attestation of his contested rights, would impart in the eyes of the ignorant and credulous mass a powerful prestige to a royalty thus reconstituted, rehabilitated, rejuvenated and breaking forth in renewed splendor. The step was moreover a bold challenge flung at the English, whose King claimed also to be King of France, and the challenge had the proper threatening ring coming swiftly upon the victory of Orleans. But Joan had counted without the pusillanimity of a prince who doted on his idleness, who was jealous of his pleasures, who hated the bare thought of physical exertion, and who considered only his personal comfort. In order to be consecrated at Rheims he would have to mount on horseback and place himself at the head of the army. It would be necessary to confront considerable danger seeing that from Orleans to Rheims the whole country still was in the hands of the English.

"Go to Rheims! Why, the project is insane, criminal!" cried La Tremouille and the Bishop of Chartres. "Does it not endanger the life, at least the health of the King?"

And the sorry King joined his council:

"I, risk myself out of my Castles of Loches and Chinon! And do so when the English still are in possession of Meung, Beaugency, Jargeau and other strongholds on the frontier of Touraine! Why, at the first step that I take out of my retreat they will gobble me up!" and to himself he cursed his luck and wished the possessed Maid to the devil, seeing her more interested than himself in the honor of the crown.

Disappointed and grieved Joan hardly repressed her indignation. The brave Maid answered that if Charles's departure for Rheims only depended upon the capture of the strongholds held in Touraine by the English, she would capture these fortresses and drive the enemy so far, so very far that they could not then inspire the King with the slightest fear.[101] She then appointed Gien for their rendezvous, implored the King to meet her there in a week, and promised him that he would then be able to undertake the journey to Rheims without danger. The Maid forthwith left the court and rejoined the army.

On the 12th of June, 1429, Joan took the fortified town of Meung; on the 17th of the same month she captured Jargeau, and the next day Beaugency. In all these assaults the Maid displayed the same bravery, the same military genius that distinguished her at the siege of Orleans. At the capture of Jargeau she came near being killed. This second series of triumphs was crowned by the battle of Patay, where all the English forces were assembled under the command of Warwick and their most illustrious captains, most of whom were taken prisoner. At this bloody and hotly contested battle Joan showed herself the peer of the most famous captains by the boldness of her manoeuvres, the quickness of her eye, the use that she put the artillery to, by the enthusiasm that she knew how to fire her soldiers with, and by her imperturbable good nature. Just before the battle she said to the Duke of Alençon with a cheerfulness and terseness worthy of the best passages of antiquity:

"Gallant sir, are your spurs good?"

"What?" asked the Duke in surprise. "Spurs? To flee?"

"No, sir—to pursue!" was the answer.[102]

Indeed, after their defeat, the enemy was pursued at the point of the lance for over three leagues. But these victories were won by the warrior maid not over the English merely, they were won also over the ill will of most of the French captains, whose envy of her increased in the same measure as her triumph. Accordingly she no longer doubted their secret animosity, and a vague presentiment told her she would be eventually betrayed by them to the enemy. The foreboding did not affect her conduct. Long before had she made a sacrifice of her life.

Considering that these last triumphs must have finally put an end to Charles's hesitancy, Joan returned to him, and said:

"Sire, Meung, Beaugency, Jargeau have all been carried by assault, is that enough? The English have been defeated in pitched battle at Patay, is that enough? Talbot, Warwick, Suffolk, are either captured or forced to flee, is that enough? Would you still hesitate to follow me to Rheims and be consecrated King by the command of God?"

The royal coward did not now hesitate, he declined point blank. The English had been driven out of Touraine, but still they held the provinces that had to be crossed in order to reach Rheims.

Joan was unable to overcome her disgust. No longer expecting anything from the coward, she was of a mind to give him up to his fate. In despair she took off her armor, left the court, and communicating her designs to none, she took to the woods where she wandered the whole day intending to return to Domremy. Towards evening, and noticing that she had lost her way, she asked for hospitality at a poor peasant house of Touraine.[103] Unarmed and in her male attire, Joan looked like a young page. She was received as such by the good people who gladly gave her shelter, treated her at their best and made room for her at their hearth. Joan sat down. The peaceful aspect of the rustic home recalled to her mind the happy days of her childhood spent in Domremy. The sweet recollections of the paternal home drew involuntary tears. Struck by her sadness, her hosts questioned her with timid and respectful interest.

"How can you cry in such happy days as these," they asked naïvely, "in these days of the deliverance of Gaul? They are happy days, especially for us peasants! For us who are now at last delivered from the English by the grace of the Lord and the bravery of Joan the Maid, our redeeming angel!"

In the enthusiasm of their gratitude, the peasant hosts showed the tenderly touched warrior maid a bit of parchment fastened to the wall above the hearth. On the parchment the name of "Joan" was inscribed, surmounted with a cross. In default of the image of their beloved liberatrix, these poor people had inscribed her name and thus gave token of the sincere reverence that they rendered the heroine. The questions were innumerable that they plied their young guest with regarding Joan. Perhaps he had seen her, seen that holy maid, the new Our Lady of the peasants who had suffered so grievously at the hands of the English before she drove them away. The questions were tantamount to a choir of benedictions mixed with passionate adoration of the Maid. More and more touched by these words, Joan began to reproach herself severely for her momentary weakness. To abandon Charles VII to his fate was to abandon France; it was above all to expose these poor peasants, the humble and industrious race of which she was herself born, to fall back under the yoke of the stranger; it was to re-deliver the poor wretches to all the horrors of a war which it was her mission to put an end to. These thoughts re-invigorated her; they inspired her with the resolve to struggle onward for the accomplishment of her projects, to struggle doggedly even against the King, against his councilors, against the captains who pursued her with their hatred and whom she perhaps stood in greater fear of than of the English. The latter fought in arms in the open; the former labored in the dark, and plotted treason. Absorbed in these meditations, Joan threw herself upon a bed of fresh cut grass, the only couch that her hosts could offer her. She invoked the support and the advice of her saints, and their dear voices speedily whispered in her ear:

"Go, daughter of God; no weakness; fulfil your mission; heaven will not forsake you!"

Early the next morning, the heroine left her hosts, who remained in ignorance that their humble roof had sheltered the country's savior. Resolved to conceal from the King the contempt she entertained for him and to see in him only an instrument for the welfare of Gaul, Joan returned to court. The Maid's disappearance had caused alarm, alarm among those whose every wish was for the termination of the English domination. Joan's project—the King's consecration at Rheims—spread abroad by the councilors in the hope of giving the widest publicity to its absurdity, met, on the contrary, with a large number of supporters, all of whom were impressed with the political grandeur and the audacity, withal, of the idea. The Maid's return was looked upon as providential, and so powerful did the popular outcry wax that the craven monarch finally resigned himself to the idea of departing at the head of his troops that were constantly swelling in numbers, thanks to the fame of the Maid. The march to Rheims was decided on and undertaken.

The journey to the royal town displayed the genius of the heroine from a side not before dreamed of. Matchlessly energetic and intrepid in her desperate combats with the foreign enemy of Gaul, she now showed herself endowed with an inexpressible power of persuasion. She undertook and succeeded in inducing the towns of the English or Burgundian party to become French again and to open their gates to Charles VII, from whom she had obtained, not without much trouble, a written promise of absolute amnesty for the dissidents. Without drawing her sword, Joan reconquered for the King all the fortified places on the route to Rheims. The heroine found in her soul, in her aversion to civil war, in her patriotism, such treasures of naïve eloquence that, coupled with her fame, her words penetrated the spirits of all, unarmed all hands, and won over all hearts to the cause of the miserable prince whom she protected, whom she covered with the splendor of her own plebeian glory, and whom she caused the people to love by speaking in his name.

Upon the arrival of the royal army before a fortified town, Joan would approach the barriers alone, her standard in her hand. She swore to God she did not wish to shed French blood; she besought and implored those who heard her to renounce the English domination that was so disgraceful and so fatal to the country, to recognize the sovereignty of Charles VII, if not out of loyalty to him at least out of hatred for the foreigner, out of love for the motherland that for so many years had bled and been dishonored by an atrocious yoke. The heroine's beauty, her emotion, her sweet and vibrant voice, the immense stir made by her victories, the irresistible charm of the virginal and martial being, all combined to operate prodigies. The old Gallic blood, cold for so long a time, boiled again in the veins of even the least valorous at the cry of national deliverance uttered by the maid of seventeen, whose sword was fleshed in the victory of so many battles. The barriers of the towns fell down at her voice.

Amazed and above all delighted at not having to incur danger, the royal coward made his triumphant entry into the good towns that acclaimed the Maid. One day, however, he had a great fright. A strong English garrison occupied the town of Troyes, whose councilmen were bitter partisans of Burgundy. The gates were barricaded, the ramparts manned, and the cannons opened fire upon the royal vanguard. Charles already spoke of plying his spurs, but was with difficulty restrained by Joan, who advanced unescorted towards the barrier and requested a parley with the councilmen. The English captains answered her with insults accompanied with a shower of missiles. The soldier who bore the heroine's banner was killed at her side. A few townsmen of Troyes belonging to the French party, who happened to be on the ramparts and heard Joan's request for a parley, spread the news among the townsmen, most of whom were tired and dissatisfied with the foreign rule, but were held under by the obstinate Burgundian councilmen. A great and increasing agitation manifested itself in the town. A few English companies attempted a sally against the royal vanguard commanded by Joan and were beaten back. Encouraged by the defeat, the French party within the walls gathered courage and ran to arms. Their numbers proved unexpectedly large. The Burgundian councilmen were overthrown, a new set of municipal magistrates was set up and they immediately took measures against the English who entrenched themselves in a fort that dominated the town. Frightened at the threatening attitude of the people, the English evacuated the citadel over night and drew away. The new councilmen asked for a parley with Joan, and in their turn they experienced the irresistible charm of her beauty, her mildness and her eloquence. Assured by her that none of the inhabitants would be troubled on the score of past acts, the magistrates placed the keys of the town in the hands of Joan, who took them to the King, and he thus resumed possession of one of the most important towns of his empire.

The King's march continued triumphal unto Rheims, thanks to the marvelous influence of Joan. At Chalons a delightful surprise was in store for the heroine's heart. She there met four peasants of Domremy. Informed by public rumor that Joan was to traverse Champagne, they boldly started out to see her at her passage. Among them was Urbain, the one-time general of the boys' army, that owed its famous victory over the boys of Maxey to Jeannette's bravery. These and many other memories of the village were exchanged between the heroine and the companions of her youth. During the conversation that they had a few words of sinister augury escaped from Joan's lips. Urbain had ingenuously asked her how she had the strength and the courage to face all the dangers of battle. A painful smile played around her lips, she remained pensive for a moment, and then as if moved by the presentiment of the evil days that were approaching for her through the machinations of the captains, she answered Urbain:

"I fear nothing—except—TREASON!"[104]

Poor girl of Domremy! Her apprehensions did not deceive her. But before climbing her Calvary to its summit, and there experiencing her martyrdom, she was first to accomplish the sacred mission that she had assumed—deal a fatal blow to English rule in Gaul by awakening the national spirit that had lain in a stupor for over fifty years, and having Charles VII consecrated King at Rheims. It was not the man, contemptible in her eyes, that Joan wished to consecrate in the face of the world; it was the living incarnation of France in the person of the sovereign, an incarnation visible to the eyes of the people.

The warrior maid fulfilled her promise. Charles VII was led to Rheims. He arrived there on July 16, 1429, thirty-five days after the siege of Orleans was raised—the signal for the long series of English routs that followed and that culminated with the breakdown of English rule. At Rheims Joan conceived the noble thought of putting an end to the civil strife—the furious strife that had raged between the Burgundians and the Armagnacs, and that for so many years had desolated and exhausted the land, and delivered it over to the foreigner. On the day of the consecration of Charles VII she dictated the following beautiful and touching letter addressed to the Duke of Burgundy, the chief of the party that bore his name:

HIGH AND REDOUBTABLE PRINCE, DUKE OF BURGUNDY:—I, Joan, call upon you, by orders of the King of heaven, my sovereign Lord, to make a good, firm and sincere peace with the King of France, a peace that shall last long. Pardon one another with a full heart and entirely, as all loyal Christians should. If you take pleasure in war, war against the Saracens.

Duke of Burgundy, I pray you and implore you, as humbly as I can implore, do no longer wage war against the holy kingdom of France! Do promptly order your men, who still hold several fortresses in the kingdom, to withdraw. The King of France is ready to accord you peace, without detriment to his honor! I notify you in the name of God that you will win no battle against the loyal French, none. So, then, do no longer wage war against us. Believe me, whatever the number of soldiers may be that you take to field, they will accomplish nothing. And it would be a great pity still to shed so much blood in fresh battles.

May God protect you and give us all peace!

Written at Rheims, before the consecration of King Charles, on the seventeenth day of July, 1429.

JOAN.[105]

This letter, to which, being unable to write, the warrior maid attached her "cross in God," as was her custom, was sent by a herald to Philip of Burgundy. Thereupon, putting on her white armor, mounting her fine white charger, and with her casque on her head, her sword at her side and her standard in her hand, the Maid rode on the right side of Charles VII at the head of the captains and splendidly accoutred courtiers to the ancient Cathedral of Rheims. The procession marched through a vast concourse of people who saw in the consecration of the King the end of the foreigner's rule and the termination of the misfortunes of France. The ceremony was performed with all the pomp of the Catholic Church. By the light of thousands of wax candles, across the clouds from gold censers, in front of the high altar that was resplendent with candles and where Charles VII knelt down, the Bishop of Rheims consecrated him King to the ringing of bells, the sounding of trumpets and the booming of cannon.

A witness to the imposing spectacle, the young peasant girl of Domremy stood in the choir of the basilica; pensively as she leaned on the staff of her standard, her recollections wandered four years back. A tear dropped from her eyes in memory of her god-mother Sybille, and the passage of Merlin's prophecy, now fulfilled, recurred to her mind:

> "For the martial maid the steed and the armor!
> But for whom the royal crown?
> The angel with wings of azure holds it in his hands.
> The blood has ceased to run in torrents,
> The thunder to peal, the lightning to flash.—
> I see a serene sky; the banners float;
> The clarions sound; the bells ring.
> Cries of joy! Chants of victory!
> The martial virgin receives the royal crown
> From the hands of the angel of light; a man,
> Wearing a long mantle of ermine
> Is crowned by the warrior virgin.—
>
> "It matters little what may happen—

What must be, shall be.
Gaul, lost by a woman,
Is saved by a virgin
From the borders of Lorraine and a forest of oaks!—"

PART IV.

ROUEN; OR, THE MYSTERY OF THE PASSION OF JOAN DARC

CHAPTER I.

BISHOP AND CANON.

In these my days, so-called "mysteries"—dialogued recitals between men and women who figure as historic personages—are frequently written and performed. These "mysteries" are imitations of the dramatic works of antiquity, such as were also the so-called "plays" of the Thirteenth Century, of which my ancestor Mylio the Trouvere left a sample behind. Therefore, I, Jocelyn the Champion, who write this chronicle of Joan Darc, have decided to conclude it in the form of these "mysteries," now so much in vogue. I shall therein trace the "Passion" of the plebeian heroine—for Joan, like Christ, also underwent her "Passion," crowned with martyrdom.

The first scene is placed in a hall of the palace of the Archbishop of Rouen, an ancient building where, eight centuries and more ago, King Charles the Simple married his daughter Ghisèle to old Rolf, and relinquished one of his best provinces to the Northman pirates. These bandits later invaded the country of England under William the Conqueror and there raised the breed of English captains who for so many years have been ravaging and enslaving Gaul. Normandy thus became a province of England. The Duke of Bedford, Regent, occupies Rouen. The archbishop's palace of the town serves as the residence of Peter Cauchon, Bishop of Beauvais, sold, body and soul, mitre and crosier, to the English party. The month of February, 1431, approaches its end. Daintily wadded in a robe of violet silk, Peter Cauchon is seated in an arm-chair near an open fire-place whence both heat and light radiate into the sumptuously furnished apartment. Cheerful reflections play upon the Oriental rug on the floor and the painted and gilded roof-beams overhead. A table, covered with parchment scrolls, and placed near the sculptured chimney, is lighted by a candelabrum of massive silver furnished with burning wax candles. A chair, vacant at the moment, and on the back of which lies a black furred cloak, faces on the other side of the table the seat occupied by the Bishop. Peter Cauchon's face, at once striking and repulsive, betokens a mixture of audacity, wile and extraordinary stubbornness. His small light blue eyes, that sparkle with craftiness and occasionally glisten with ferocity, almost disappear under the folds of his fat red cheeks and heavy eyebrows, grey like his hair that is almost wholly covered under his violet skull cap. His forehead is furrowed with purplish veins. His flat nose, bored with large and hairy nostrils, helps to set off the singular prominence of his chin and jaws. When he laughs, his cruel laughter exposes two broken rows of uneven and yellowish teeth. At times he leans over the table, reads a parchment covered with a fine and close writing and rubs his hirsute hands with manifest pleasure; other times he looks impatiently towards the door as if he would hasten with his wishes the return of some absent personage. The door finally opens and another prelate appears. He is a canon of the name of Nicolas Loyseleur. His face is long and worn; his eyes are covered like a reptile's. His red eyelids are stripped of their lashes. A colorless fissure barely indicates the location of his lips whose smile bears the imprint of hypocrisy. It is at once the face of a hypocrite and a gallows-bird.

BISHOP PETER CAUCHON (half rising and with deep interest)—"What news? What news? Good or bad?"

CANON LOYSELEUR—"The messenger sent by Captain Morris left the Maid in the prison of Breville."

BISHOP CAUCHON—"What is the man's errand?"

CANON LOYSELEUR—"He came by orders of Captain Morris to request the Earl of Warwick to have the dungeon of the old tower prepared to receive Joan Darc, who is to arrive at Rouen under a strong escort to-morrow morning at the latest."

BISHOP CAUCHON—"Did Captain Morris follow my instructions accurately?"

CANON LOYSELEUR—"From point to point, monseigneur. The captive travels in a closed litter, with irons on her feet and hands. When a town has to be crossed, the said Joan is gagged. No one has been able to approach her. The guards of the escort informed all inquirers that they were taking to Rouen an old witch who throttled little children to accomplish her evil deeds."

BISHOP CAUCHON (laughing)—"And the good people forthwith crossed themselves and gave the litter a wide berth? Stupid plebs!"

CANON LOYSELEUR—"It was just as you say. That notwithstanding, at Dieppe, the exasperation of the mob at what they really took for a witch became so violent that the people sought to tear her from our hands and trample her to death."

BISHOP CAUCHON—"The idiots! What would have been left for us?"

CANON LOYSELEUR—"This incident excepted, the journey went smooth. No one along the route thought for a moment that the prisoner was Joan the Maid."

BISHOP CAUCHON—"That was of the highest importance. The girl's renown is such in Gaul at present, even in the provinces that are subject to our English friends, that if it had been learned that she was being taken in chains, the town and country plebs would have been greatly agitated, they might even have taken the she-devil away from her keepers. Well, at any rate, we got her now!"

CANON LOYSELEUR (pointing to the parchments)—"Shall we now proceed with the reading of the condensed acts of the Maid?"

BISHOP CAUCHON (taking up a parchment on which he has made a large number of notes)—"Yes; these facts and acts are to be the basis of the process. While you, canon, read, I shall mark down the acts upon which the said Joan is to be particularly interrogated. This report, which my brother in God the Bishop of Chartres secretly sent me by orders of the Sire of La Tremouille, is very full and accurate. It is attributed to one Percival of Cagny, equerry of the Duke of Alençon[106] and a partisan of the Maid, or to be more accurate, he does her justice. The justice done to her in the report does not trouble me. Her acts have been witnessed by such a large number of people, that it would be tactless to deny or alter the truth on that head, all the more seeing that the very acts carry with them their own condemnation. Where did we break off in our reading?"

CANON LOYSELEUR—"At the departure from Rheims after the consecration."

BISHOP CAUCHON—"Continue." (He dips his pen in the ink-horn and makes ready to take notes.)

CANON LOYSELEUR (reading)—"'After being consecrated, the King remained at Rheims until the following Thursday. He left Rheims bound for the Abbey of St. Marcoul where he took supper and slept over night. The keys of Laon were there brought to him. On Saturday, July 23, 1429, the King went to dine and sleep at Soissons. He was very well received, the Maid having preceded him and harangued the people at the barrier of the town, conjuring them to renounce the English party and become again French. Her words were received with enthusiasm. Several women who were about to go to child bed, or whose children had not yet been baptized, prayed the Maid to choose their baptismal names, which, said they, would be to them a pledge of divine protection—'"

BISHOP CAUCHON (writing rapidly)—"This must be noted—very important—excellent! *Excellentissime!*"

CANON LOYSELEUR (continuing to read)—"'On Friday, July 29, the King presented himself before Chateau-Thierry. The Maid ordered the banners to be unfurled, spoke to the people, and the town opened its gates. The King remained there until the following Monday, August 1. That day he slept at Montmirail in Brie. On Tuesday, August 2, the King made his entry into Provins, where he was received no less well than in the other towns. He remained there until Friday the 5th. On Sunday, the 7th of August, he slept at Coulommiers; on Wednesday, the 10th, at Ferté-Milon; on Thursday at Crespy in Valois; on Friday, the 12th, in Lagny-le-sec. In this town a woman in tears pressed through the crowd that surrounded the Maid and implored her to come to a little dying child, whom, the mother said, the Maid could with one word recall to life. In her naïve admiration for the Maid, the poor mother attributed to her divine powers comparable to those of Jesus of Nazareth—'"

BISHOP CAUCHON (writing with ghoulish glee)—"I would not sell that fact for a hundred gold sous! (Inflating his wide and hairy nostrils) Oh! What a delectable smell of fagots and roast flesh I begin to scent. Proceed, canon. The process is taking shape."

CANON LOYSELEUR (reading)—"'On Saturday, August 13, being instructed by her forerunners that the enemy was only at a little distance, the Maid, with her wonted promptness, drew up the army in order of battle in the plain of Dammartin-in-Gouelle, assigned his post to each, and issued her orders with the consummate skill of a captain. But frightened at the attitude of the royal army the English did not dare to give battle, although much stronger in numbers—'"

BISHOP CAUCHON (in a hollow voice)—"Oh, in order to save the honor of our friends from the other side of the water, it will be absolutely necessary to attribute their cowardice to Joan's witchery."

CANON LOYSELEUR (reading)—"'Sunday, August 14, 1429, the Maid, the Duke of Alençon, the Count of Vendome and other captains, accompanied by six or seven thousand soldiers, encamped near Montepilloy, two leagues from Senlis. The Duke of Bedford with eight or nine thousand soldiers defended the approaches of Senlis. They were posted half a league in front of the town, having before them the little River of Nonette and to their right a village of the name of Notre Dame de la Victoire. Both sides skirmished. When night fell both retired to their camps to the great displeasure of the Maid, who, contrary to the opinion of the King and his captains, wished to enter into a general engagement. The English profited by the delay. They threw up earthworks during the night, dug moats and set up palisades, and utilized even their carts to cover themselves. At break of day, and despite the opposition of the captains, the Maid marched at the head of a few determined companies that always obeyed her and pushed up to the foot of the enemy's entrenchments. Arrived there she learned that the English had decamped over night, given up Senlis, and withdrawn to Paris, the earthworks they had thrown up being intended merely to delay their pursuit—'"

BISHOP CAUCHON—"Witchcraft! Devil's work! The girl is possessed!"

CANON LOYSELEUR (reading)—"'On Wednesday, August 17, the keys of Compiegne were brought to the King, and on Thursday he made his entry into the town amidst the acclamations of the people who cried frantically: "Blessings on the daughter of God!"—'"

BISHOP CAUCHON (writing)—"'Daughter of God!' You have rather imprudent fanatics among your admirers, my little girl!"

CANON LOYSELEUR (reading)—"'When the King left Crespy, he ordered Marshals Boussac and Retz to summon the inhabitants of Senlis to surrender. They answered that they would surrender, not to the King, but to the Maid, whom they considered sent by God and to be a sister of the angels-'"

BISHOP CAUCHON (writing)—"'Sister of the angels!' 'Sent by God!' Well, the scamps will have contributed their fagots to the pyre."

CANON LOYSELEUR (reading)—"'Much to the annoyance of the Maid, the King wished to stop at Senlis instead of pushing forward. He seemed satisfied with the success he had so far had, and to wish for nothing more. His council was of his opinion; the Maid, however, held that it would be enough for the King to show himself before Paris for the town to open its gates to its sovereign. "Fear not," Joan said to the King; "I shall speak so sweetly to the Parisians that they will prefer to become French again rather than to remain English"—'"

BISHOP CAUCHON—"What an impudence on the part of the she cowherd. She is certain of everything. Well, she shall pay dearly for her infernal vanity!"

CANON LOYSELEUR (reading)—"'On Tuesday, August 23, despite the opposition of the King and his council, the Maid left Compiegne together with the Duke of Alençon, leaving the prince behind with the bulk of the army. The following Friday, August 26, without striking a blow, the Maid entered St Denis, which declared itself royalist. At this news, the King decided, not without considerable hesitation to proceed to that town, where he arrived in safety. The King's council now opposed the Maid more doggedly than ever before. Joan, however, affirmed that if she was listened to she would render the Parisians to the King by the command of God, and without shedding a drop of blood—'"

BISHOP CAUCHON (in a rage)—"The execrable hypocrite! To hear her speak she is all honey—and yet at her homicidal voice the French have been turned into the butchers of the English! (writing) We must not forget above all to designate her as a furious monster of carnage."

CANON LOYSELEUR (reading)—"'Learning of the capture of Senlis and of the Maid's march upon Paris, the Duke of Bedford reinforced his garrison, and took vigorous measures against those of the Armagnac or royalist party who wished to surrender the town. The Duke picked out only Englishmen and bitter Burgundians to guard the gates, men who were expected to be able to resist the charm of the Maid's sweet words. Several times she advanced alone on horseback near the barriers of the town, imploring all those who were French like herself no longer to tolerate the rule of the English, who had inflicted so much damage upon the poor people of France. But the men of the Burgundian party and the English answered her with insults and threatened to fire at her although she came for a parley. She would then return weeping over the hard-heartedness or the blindness of men, who, although French, wished to remain English. This notwithstanding, she every day heard "her voices" assure her that Gaul would not be saved until all the English were driven from her soil, or were exterminated—'"

BISHOP CAUCHON (writing)—"Again 'her voices.' Let us note that important fact. It is capital in the framing of the process."

CANON LOYSELEUR (reading)—"'Seeing that the King continued to refuse to draw nearer to Paris and to present himself before the gates, as the Maid desired, she declared to the Duke of Alençon, who placed great confidence in her, that St. Marguerite and St. Catherine, having again appeared before her, ordered her to demand of the King that he put forth all his efforts to regain the good town of Paris by coming in person and by promises of his clemency and a general amnesty—'"

BISHOP CAUCHON (writing)—"Again St. Marguerite and St. Catherine. Let us jot down the fact. It is no less capital than the one about the 'voices.' Ah, you double-dyed witch! You see visions! Apparitions! (laughing) You will have to roast for it, my daughter!"

CANON LOYSELEUR (reading)—"'Yielding to the wishes of the Maid, the Duke of Alençon returned to the King, who promised him that on August 27 he would proceed to Chapelle-St. Denis and march from there to Paris. But he did not keep his promise. The Duke of Alençon returned to him on Monday, September 5. Thanks to the pressure that he exercised, after long hesitating and against the advice of his council, the King came to Chapelle-St. Denis on September 7 to the great joy of the Maid. Everybody in the army said: "The Maid will restore Paris to the King, if he but consents to show himself before the gates." On Thursday, the 8th of September, the Duke of Alençon together with a few captains whom the Maid carried away with her persuasion, started from Chapelle-St. Denis towards eight in the morning with flying colors but leaving behind the King, who did not wish to accompany them. The Maid advanced toward the St. Honoré Gate, which was defended by a body of English soldiers, because, said she, she had a horror of seeing Frenchmen fighting Frenchmen. She took her standard in her hand and boldly leaped at the head of all into the moat, near the swine market. The assault was long and bloody; the English defended themselves bravely; the Maid was wounded by an arrow that ran through her thigh; she fell, but in falling cried out that the attack had to be kept up with all the greater vigor. But despite her feeble efforts, the Sire of Gaucourt and others carried her to a place of safety seeing that she was losing much blood. She was placed on a cart and taken back to Chapelle-St Denis—'"

BISHOP CAUCHON (writing)—"Let us underscore once more the bloodthirsty nature of the she-devil, who against the advice of all insists upon fighting. We must emphasize her thirst for carnage. She recommends the extermination of the English."

CANON LOYSELEUR (reading)—"'On Monday, September 12, and still hardly able to keep herself in the saddle, the Maid wished to ride out towards St. Denis in order to assure herself that a bridge over the Seine, the construction of which she had ordered in order to facilitate the passage of the troops, had been properly built. The bridge had been built, but was afterwards cut by orders of the King, who had decided to make no further attempts against Paris. On Tuesday, the 13th of September, 1429, and with the advice of his council, the King left St. Denis after dinner, intending to retreat towards the Loire. In despair at the King's departure the Maid wept bitterly, and carried away by the first impulse of her grief she decided to renounce his service. She took off her armor and deposited it *ex voto* before the statue of Our Lady in the basilica of St. Denis—'"

BISHOP CAUCHON (rubs his hands and writes)—"Excellent! Very excellent! Idolatry! Sacrilege! In her infernal pride, she offers her armor to the adoration of the simple-minded!"

CANON LOYSELEUR (reading)—"'In her despair, the Maid wished to return to her own country of Lorraine, to her family, and forever renounce war. But the King ordered her to follow him to Gien, where, said he, he would need her services. They arrived in that town on September 29. The Maid offered the Duke of Alençon to aid him in reconquering his duchy of Normandy. The Duke communicated the project to the King. He refused his consent. He wished to keep the Maid near him in Touraine to defend the province in case the English should return to attack it. The Maid took several fortified towns in the neighborhood of Charité-on-the-Loire and then laid siege to that place. But as the royal council sent neither provisions nor money to the Maid for the soldiers, she was, much to her sorrow, forced to give up the attack, and on March 7, 1430, she went to the Castle of Sully, the property of the Sire of La Tremouille, where the King was sojourning. The Maid expressed in the presence of the prince her unqualified indignation against the royal councilors and the captains, and bitterly reproached them with traitorously putting obstacles in the way of the complete recovery of the realm. Fully aware of the uselessness of her further services to the King, but still hoping to serve France, she left Charles VII forever, and without taking leave of him she departed under the pretext of exercising outside of the castle a company of determined men attached to her fortunes. She went with them to Crespy in Valois. There she was soon called for by the Sire of Flavy who wished her aid in Compiegne, a town that the Duke of Burgundy and the Count of Arundel had jointly besieged. The Maid was not a little perplexed what to do in the matter. She was not ignorant of the proverbial perfidy and ferocity of the Sire of Flavy. But the inhabitants of the place that he commanded had, at the time of her first visit to the town, received Joan with so much affection, that, overcoming her apprehensions, she decided to go to the aid of the good people. On the 23rd of May, 1430, Joan departed from Crespy at the head of her company, two or three hundred men strong. Thanks to the darkness and to the skilful precautions in which she wrapped her nocturnal march, her troops passed unperceived between the Burgundian and English camps and entered Compiegne with her before daylight. She immediately went to mass in the parish church of St. James. It was barely day, but a large number of the inhabitants had learned of the arrival of their emancipatrix and went to church to see her. After mass, Joan retired near one of the pillars of the nave, and addressing herself to several of the people who were gathered there together with their children, all anxious to see her, she said to them in sad accents: "My friends, I have been sold and betrayed, I shall soon be taken and put to death—my voices have for some time been warning me of the contemplated treason"—"'

BISHOP CAUCHON—"What a lucky thing it was for us that Joan did not hearken to these presentiments! The she-devil so often escaped the snares vainly laid for her by the captains, whose vindictive jealousy so well served our purposes and the purposes of the Sires of La Tremouille and of Gaucourt and of my companion in God, the Bishop of Chartres!"

CANON LOYSELEUR—"Indeed, the emissary whom Monseigneur the Bishop of Chartres sent here secretly and whom I visited in your name, informed me that it was in concert with the Sire of La Tremouille that the Sire of Flavy invited the Maid to Compiegne, meaning to deliver her to the English."

BISHOP CAUCHON (laughing)—"I shall give Flavy, whenever he wishes it, full absolution for all his crimes in return for the capture of Joan. Proceed, canon. I shall presently tell you more fully what my projects are."

CANON LOYSELEUR (reading)—"'When it was full daylight the Maid made preparations for a vigorous sally. The town of Compiegne is situated on the left bank of the Oise. On the right bank is a wide meadow about a quarter of a league in length and bounded by crags on the side of Picardy. This low meadow, which often is under water, is crossed by a road that starts at Compiegne and ends at the foot of the hill that bounds the horizon on that side of the town. Three villages border on the meadow: Margny, at the extreme end of the road; Clairoy about three-fourths of a league up the river at the confluence of the Aronde and the Oise; and Venette about half a league below on the road to Pont St. Maxence. The Burgundians had a camp at Margny and one at Clairoy. The English occupied Venette. The defences of Compiegne consisted of a redoubt raised at the head of the bridge and the boulevards. The redoubt was zigzagged and strongly palisaded. The Maid's plan of attack was first to carry the village of Margny, then that of Clairoy, and, mistress of the two positions, to await in the valley of the Aronde the troops of the Duke of Burgundy, who, so soon as he heard the noise of the action, would not fail to hasten to the help of the English. Foreseeing the movement and wishing to keep her retreat free, the Maid demanded of the Sire of Flavy to charge himself with keeping the Duke of Burgundy in check, should he turn into the valley before the capture of Margny and Clairoy, and also to keep a reserve of troops on the front and the flanks of the redoubt, ready to cover her retreat. Furthermore, covered barges, placed on the Oise, were to stand ready to receive the footmen in case of a reverse. Having given these orders, the Maid, despite her sinister forebodings, hastened to mount her horse, and, at the head of her company, marched straight upon the village of Margny, which, although vigorously defended, she swiftly carried. The English encamped at Clairoy rushed to the defence of their allies and were thrown back; but they thrice returned to the attack with maddening fury. This battle was fought in the low meadow and was dragging along. The Duke of Burgundy was not long in entering the valley of the Aronde with his men and he reached the jetty. It was in order to guard against such a move that Joan had charged Flavy to keep the Burgundians in check. Her order was not executed. The Burgundians entered the valley by the road. At the sight of these hostile reinforcements, some cowards or traitors cried: "Run for your lives! Run to the barges!" The Maid's auxiliary troops, commanded by Flavy's lieutenants, broke ranks and rushed to the barges that lay at the river's bank, leaving Joan and her small band to sustain alone the shock of the combined English and Burgundian forces. She sustained it bravely, and assailed by fresh presentiments at the sight of the rout of her auxiliaries, whose captains had failed to execute her orders, she decided to die rather than fall alive into the hands of the English. She drew her sword and rushed temerariously upon an enemy a hundred times more numerous than the handful of heroes who stood by her. After prodigies of valor, and seeing the battle lost, the latter wished to save the Maid's life at the cost of their own. Two of them seized her horse by the bit, and despite her prayers, despite even her resistance, sought to force her back to the city while their companions were to allow themselves to be cut down to the last man in order to cover her retreat. Already were they near a drawbridge, thrown over a moat that separated the redoubt from the road, when the bridge was raised by orders of the Sire of Flavy. Thus vilely betrayed and delivered to the enemy, the Maid and her soldiers fell upon the surging foe with the fury of despair. Struck by several simultaneous blows, Joan was thrown from her horse and was immediately surrounded by a mass of English and Burgundians who disputed with each other the possession of the glorious capture. Joan remained in the power of an archer, who was a banneret of the Bastard of Vendome, an equerry, a native of the county of Artois and lieutenant of Sire John of Luxembourg of the Burgundian party. Pinioned on the field of battle, the Maid was tied fast to a horse and taken to the Castle of Beaurevoir, belonging to the Sire of Luxembourg, the sovereign of the Bastard of Vendome, whose archer had made the capture. After remaining some time a prisoner in the castle, Joan learned that the Sire of Luxembourg had sold her as a prisoner of war to the English Regent for the sum of ten thousand gold sous. Despair seized her at the thought of being delivered to the English, and whether she hoped to escape, or whether she meant to put an end to her life, she threw herself out of one of the towers of the Castle of Beaurevoir. But the fall did not prove fatal. Picked up unconscious and severely hurt, Joan was thrown into a dungeon and soon thereupon was surrendered to the English captain who was commissioned to deliver to the Sire of Luxembourg the ten thousand gold sous—the price agreed upon for the blood of the Maid. She was taken under a strong escort to the Castle of Dugy near St. Riquier. Thus was Joan the Maid betrayed and sold, to the deep sorrow of the loyal French.'" (The canon lays down on the table the chronicle that he has just read to the end.)

BISHOP CAUCHON (with ferocious joy)—"And I shall add what that royalist chronicler could not know, to wit, that taken from the Castle of Dugy to that of Crotoy, the Maid was there embarked upon the Somme, on which she sailed as far as St. Valery. She was thence conveyed to the Castle of Eu, thence to Dieppe, and from Dieppe hither to Rouen, where she is to arrive this very night or to-morrow morning. So, then, the she-devil is in our hands! And, now, canon, I must make a very serious revelation to you. It is in your power to render a signal service to our friends from across the water, to the Cardinal of Winchester, to the Duke of Bedford the Regent, and to the whole English government. The remuneration will exceed your hopes, I swear that to you! As true as the archbishopric of Rouen has been promised to me by the Regent of England if Joan is duly brought to the pyre and burned, you will be royally rewarded."

CANON LOYSELEUR—"What must I do, monseigneur? I am ready to obey you."

BISHOP CAUCHON—"Before answering you, and although I am from experience acquainted with the keenness of your mind and the subtlety of your resources, I must succinctly and clearly inform you of the reason and object of the process that we are to start to-morrow against the said Joan."

CANON LOYSELEUR (impassively)—"I listen attentively."

BISHOP CAUCHON—"First of all let us sum up the situation in a few words and *ab ovo*.[107] Two years ago the whole of France was on the point of falling into the hands of the English and would have so fallen but for the help that the Maid brought Charles VII. In the teeth of that prince, in the teeth of the Sire of La Tremouille, in the teeth of the captains, the she-devil forced the siege of Orleans to be raised, won a number of other and no less brilliant victories, and finally had the King consecrated at Rheims—an act of incalculable importance in the eyes of the people, with whom the divine consecration is tantamount to sovereign power. Thus a large number of towns, that until then remained in the hands of the English, opened their gates to Charles VII upon his return from Rheims. Everywhere the national spirit awoke at the voice of the Maid, and the foreign rule, that had been accepted for over half a century, suddenly seemed unsupportable. On the other hand, and parallel with all this, the prodigious successes of Joan have spread consternation and terror in the ranks of the English army. Matters have reached such a pass in this line that the government in London has seen itself compelled to issue two decrees, whose titles are (the Bishop takes up two parchments from the table and reads:) 'A Decree against the Captains and Soldiers Who Refuse to Pass into France out of Fear of the Witcheries of the Maid,'[108] and, 'A Decree against Fugitives from the Army out of Fear of the Witcheries of the Maid.'[109] I shall do even better. I shall confidentially read to you a significant passage from a letter addressed by our Regent the Duke of Bedford, to the council of the King of England, Henry VI. Now listen, canon, and ponder. (The Bishop reads:) 'We succeeded in everything until the siege of Orleans. Since then the hand of God has struck our army with severe blows. The principal cause of the unfortunate turn of affairs is, as I think, the fatal opinion and fatal fear that our soldiers entertain for a disciple of the devil, a hound from hell, named "The Maid," who has used enchantments and witchery, and thereby caused us discomfitures that have not only greatly diminished the number of our soldiers, but have wondrously depressed the courage of those that are left us.'[110] (The Bishop places the parchment back upon the table, and turns again to the other prelate who continues impassive.) The charm of half a century of victories is broken, and the enthusiasm of the masses is now on the ascendant. If Charles VII were not the incarnation of indolence and cowardice; if by promising to the Sire of La Tremouille the sovereignty of Poitou and other great advantages to the Bishop of Chartres and to Gaucourt, the Regent had not secured for his side the secret support of these powerful dignitaries; finally, if the Maid had not been captured at Compiegne—France would have become French again! The labors of more than fifty years' struggles would be lost, and Henry VI would no longer hold the two most beautiful crowns in the world! But we must not indulge in delusions. Henry VI is King of France in name only. The provinces that he still holds in the heart of Gaul are about to slip from his hands. The victories of the she-devil, have awakened the sense of patriotism, that slumbered so long. Everywhere hope springs up. The people feel ashamed of what they call the foreign yoke, and they curse it. The continued rule of England in this country is gravely compromised. Now, then, to those of us who have become English, such a thing spells ruin, exile or the gallows, the moment the French party has vanquished. Such is the true state of things. If Charles VII triumphs we are all lost."

CANON LOYSELEUR—"Indeed, monseigneur, I was convinced myself of the truth of what you say when I had my last secret interview with the emissary of the Sire of La Tremouille. The seigneur, although he is the supreme councilor of Charles VII, is in the secret recesses of his soul as English as ourselves, and as desirous as we of seeing his master vanquished. He indulges in no illusions on the progress of the malady."

BISHOP CAUCHON—"As the malady exists, we must endeavor to cure it by ascertaining its cause. Now, then, what is the cause?"

CANON LOYSELEUR—"Joan! The bedeviled Maid—a veritable limb of Satan."

BISHOP CAUCHON—"We then understand each other. Now, then, the Sire of Flavy, having at the instigation of the Sire of La Tremouille drawn the Maid to Compiegne under the pretext of requesting her assistance in behalf of the good people of the town, pushed the fighting maid forward and then had the drawbridge raised behind her, so that, to make a long story short, she is taken. It is now for us to draw the largest possible advantage from our capture, for which we paid ten thousand shining gold sous to John of Luxembourg. Now let us sum up. The English soldiers are convinced that as long as Joan lives they will be beaten by the French. If this continues, the rule of England in Gaul will crumble down to nothing, and we will be buried under the ruins. In order to protect ourselves against such a misfortune, what is to be done? Restore confidence to the English by freeing them from their bogie—Joan! Accordingly, Joan must die. The Maid must be burned alive."

CANON LOYSELEUR—"Logic so orders. She must be tried, sentenced and burned."

BISHOP CAUCHON—"Certes. *Logice*, she must be roasted; but right there a serious difficulty arises. It is this: The English captains, proud and imbued with the principles of chivalry, would have considered it an act of cowardice simply and merely to kill a prisoner who had vanquished them by the force of military genius. They feared that if they had Joan killed in her prison they would incur the contempt of all who carry spurs and swords. In view of that, the Cardinal of Winchester and myself held to them the following language: 'You, captains, can not order the death of a warrior who has fallen into your hands by the accidents of war. But the Church can. More than that, the Church must, at the first call of the Holy Inquisition, proceed against a witch, an invoker of demons, must convict her of sorcery and heresy, and deliver her to the secular arm, which will then burn her, roast her to the greater glory of God.'"

CANON LOYSELEUR—"It is the right of the Church, our holy mother."

BISHOP CAUCHON—"And she will exercise the right. Then, as soon as the Maid shall be delivered to the executioner as a witch, the terror of the English soldiers will vanish, they will pick up courage, and the power of the English rule in Gaul, now tottering to its fall, will be reaffirmed. The Sire of La Tremouille continues to serve us in the hope of obtaining Poitou for his domain; the English army will reconquer all that it has recently lost, and will invade the remaining provinces; completely dispossessed and although consecrated at Rheims, Charles VII will go to live in London, like the good King John II, his great grandfather did; he will forget all about his kingdom of France; we will have nothing more to fear; and the archepiscopal see of Rouen will be mine. The question being thus clearly understood, the point now is, to have Joan roasted, in other words to have her convicted of heresy."

CANON LOYSELEUR—"It all depends upon that, monseigneur. We shall conduct the matter according to your wishes."

BISHOP CAUCHON—"Yes, all, absolutely everything, depends upon that. Now, let us look into the chances of the process that we are to institute against her. The first obstacle is this: A direct appeal of Charles VII to the Pope. That prince may possibly request the Holy Father to use his omnipotent influence against the Inquisition's pursuing its trial of the Maid for heresy. It is to her that Charles owes his crown. Before the consecration at Rheims he was quasi uncrowned. The most common gratitude, the least human regard would dictate the measure to him, even if he were certain of failing. But we know what the gratitude of kings amounts to."

CANON LOYSELEUR—"I received a formal assurance at my interview with the emissary of the Sire of La Tremouille and the Bishop of Chartres that such an application on the part of Charles VII will not be made. The process of heresy will be allowed to take its course peacefully. Besides, the Bishop of Chartres is commissioned to notify the notables of Rheims of the capture of the Maid, and to foreshadow the fate that awaits her. He expressed himself in the following terms which his emissary transmitted to me and which I wrote down. They are these: (he reads) 'The Bishop of Chartres hereby notifies the people of Rheims that the Maid has been captured before Compiegne, as a result of her disinclination to listen to any counsel, and wishing to act only at her own pleasure.' The Bishop adds: 'As to the rumor that is rife that the English will put the Maid to death, God has so willed it because she set herself up in pride, wore male attire, and did not obey the orders of God.'[111] So you see, monseigneur, after such a letter, written by a bishop, a member of the royal council, we may rest assured that Charles VII will neither directly nor indirectly attempt anything with the Holy Father in the matter of the process. She is dropped and renounced by the King."

BISHOP CAUCHON—"Furthermore, we have the certainty that Charles VII and his council are secretly as desirous as ourselves of having Joan burned. Accordingly, they will not intervene with the secular, seeing that they will not do so with the clerical, power. For the last six months the Maid has been dragged from prison to prison, and have Charles VII or his council made a shadow of a move with the King of England in favor of the prisoner? Could he not demand her either under bail or in exchange for English prisoners? Idle attempts, perhaps; but they would at least have been a sign of that self-respect that ingrates always feel it necessary to display."

CANON LOYSELEUR—"Nevertheless, monseigneur, allow me to put you a question. Joan was taken on May 24 of last year, 1430. Since then she has been a prisoner. Why this delay in starting the process? Why not taken, sentenced and executed?"

BISHOP CAUCHON—"I shall answer your question, and you will see that I was not to blame. The news of Joan's capture reached us on the morning of May 25. The very next day, the registrar of Paris, acting under my orders, addressed in the name and under the seal of the Inquisitor of France a summons to Monseigneur the Duke of Burgundy, who is the suzerain of John of Luxembourg, one of whose equerries was the captor of the Maid. The summons was to the effect that the said Joan be surrendered to the jurisdiction of the said Inquisitor, to the end that she may answer, in the words of the good formula 'to the good council, favor and aid of the good doctors and masters of the University of Paris.'"

CANON LOYSELEUR—"But, monseigneur, four or five months passed before the summons of the Inquisitor received an answer. The preliminaries of the process might have been shortened, and the Maid delivered to the executioner before this."

BISHOP CAUCHON—"Do you not know that the decisions of the University of Paris—an ecclesiastical body, that, however, has a hand in politics—have a powerful influence not only upon the majority of the higher clergy which upholds the English rule, but also upon the bishops who have remained faithful to the royalist party? Now, then, did not the latter, yielding to popular clamor, declare through the medium of the clerics gathered at Poitiers two years ago for the purpose of interrogating Joan, that 'she is neither a heretic nor a witch, and Charles VII may without endangering his salvation, avail himself of the aid that she brought him'? Very well, then. That opinion found partisans, even in the bosom of the University of Paris, which is an enlightened body and little inclined to believe in witches. The University was at first recalcitrant to my project of itself undertaking the process of heresy against Joan. It took me a long time, many negotiations and not a little money, to convince the objectors that from a political point of view it was of the highest importance to seem to believe in the witchery of Joan, and thus to deliver her to the flames, without which her influence would continue to assert itself, despite her captivity, and that such an influence, disastrous to the English, beneficent to the French, might, as it came very near doing, make Charles VII master of Paris. What would then happen? The University would be shorn of its power, its members would be proscribed and stripped of their privileges. In order to escape such a danger, it was imperative to break the instrument that threatened it, in other words, have Joan burned as a witch. (Laughing) It is a fact, we must always go back to the fagot. The pyre is our supreme argument."

CANON LOYSELEUR—"And finally, monseigneur, did the University start the process?"

BISHOP CAUCHON—"Yes; but that was only a slight success. The opposition that I had to overcome with many of the members of the University caused me to fear for the issue if it depended wholly upon them. I wished to have the process started by the University, and then continued before an ecclesiastical tribunal devoted to myself. After sedulous endeavors to reach the desired end I hit upon the right means. It is quite ingenious and worthy of us, whose mission it is to lead men by the nose. You may judge for yourself. Where was the Maid captured?"

CANON LOYSELEUR—"In Compiegne."

BISHOP CAUCHON—"To what diocese does Compiegne belong? Follow my reasoning closely."

CANON LOYSELEUR—"To the diocese of Beauvais."

BISHOP CAUCHON—"Who is Bishop of Beauvais by the grace of intrigues, the intervention of pretty courtesans and divine consent?"

CANON LOYSELEUR—"You, monseigneur; you are in possession of the bishopric."

BISHOP CAUCHON (rubbing his hands)—"So, there you have it! The Maid, taken on the territory of my diocese, falls within my jurisdiction. I am her judge. The University started the process, but will conduct it before an ecclesiastical tribunal chosen by myself. I have appointed to that tribunal the canons of the chapter of Rouen and the priests of the University of Paris who are faithful to me. I have above all placed in the tribunal a number of Norman beneficiaries whose interests place body and soul on the side of the English. I have also convoked a few young laureates of the college, but only such as are little versed in affairs. My choice of them flatters their pride and assures me their blind support. Among these I may name William Erard, Nicole Midi, Thomas of Courcelles, rising luminaries of theology and canon law. The tribunal is entirely my creature. It can begin operations to-morrow, according to inquisitorial laws. That subject, dear canon, brings me to the matter that concerns you personally. I mean the great service that you can render England. The Duke will not show his gratitude to you in the manner that Charles VII did to Joan. You will have honors and wealth."

CANON LOYSELEUR—"What must I do, monseigneur?"

BISHOP CAUCHON—"You are acquainted with the inquisitorial law. Its proceedings are simple, and go straight to the point. The sixteenth decretal formally sets forth: 'The judges of heretics have the faculty to proceed in a simplified manner, direct, without the noise of advocates, or form of judgment.'"

CANON LOYSELEUR—"*Simpliciter et de plano, absque advocatorum ac judiciorum strepitu et figura*—The text is formal."

BISHOP CAUCHON—"Whence it follows that myself and the inquisitor John Lemaitre will constitute a sufficient authority to apply to Joan the law against heretics. But in order to do that she must give us proofs of her heresy. There is where we run up against a grave difficulty, which it will be for you to remove."

CANON LOYSELEUR—"How, monseigneur? What must I do?"

BISHOP CAUCHON—"However devoted to me the judges of the tribunal may be, they will require some proofs in order to condemn Joan and protect the dignity of the Church. Now, then, the she-devil has a reputation for craftiness. I have read her answers to the interrogatories at Poitiers. She more than once astounded and embarrassed the judges by her quick wit or by the loftiness of her answers. It must not go at Rouen as it did at Poitiers. This is the summary course that I would stamp upon the process, to the end that Joan may not escape. To obtain from herself condemnatory admissions, and pronounce her guilty upon them. And then after her sentence to find means of causing her to make a public recantation and to admit her to penitence."

CANON LOYSELEUR (stupefied)—"But if she renounces her errors, then she is not condemned, monseigneur! If she is admitted to penitence, then she can not be burned!"

BISHOP CAUCHON—"Patience, listen. If Joan abjures her errors, she is admitted to penitence. We shall have given a proof of our gentleness and indulgence. At any rate the fools will think so."

CANON LOYSELEUR—"If Joan escapes the fagot your end is not reached."

BISHOP CAUCHON—"For one day. Immediately after she must be led by some skilful method to relapse into her previous heretical conduct. We may even get her to maintain that her abjuration was the result of a snare, a surprise. We can thus lead her to persevere in her damnable errors. The criminal relapse then gives us the right to condemn the penitent as 'relapsed.' We abandon her to the secular arm, and by it she is delivered to the executioner. Thus, the appearances of ecclesiastical charity being saved, the full burden will fall upon Joan herself."

CANON LOYSELEUR—"The proposal is excellent. But how to carry it out?"

BISHOP CAUCHON—"I shall come to that presently. Let us first consider what flagrant proofs of heresy we must find in Joan's answers. One example will explain my thoughts to you. The girl pretends to have seen saints and angels and to have heard supernatural voices. Now, then, in the eye of the Church and its holy canons Joan has not the *sufficient and recognized, quality to converse and hold commerce with the blessed beings of paradise.* In the eye of the canon law, the visions and apparitions of the said Joan, so far from proceeding from God, and emanating from celestial beings—"

CANON LOYSELEUR—"Proceed directly from Satan. A flagrant proof that Joan is an invoker of devils, hence a witch, hence deserving of the fagot."

BISHOP CAUCHON—"One moment—a stone lies there in our way. It will have to be removed."

CANON LOYSELEUR—"What stone, monseigneur? I do not see the said stone."

BISHOP CAUCHON—"Our canon law admits a qualification in avowals concerning supernatural matters. Thus the tribunal would find itself prevented from passing sentence upon the Maid, if by some mishap, instead of her declaring affirmatively: 'I have heard the voices,' she were to say: 'I believe I heard the voices.' The doubtful form would cause the principal charge to fall. Now, then, I fear that whether guided by the instinct of self-preservation, or whether properly indoctrinated in advance, Joan may give her answers such a form as to perfidiously raise an unsurmountable obstacle in our way. Do you understand me?"

CANON LOYSELEUR—"Perfectly, monseigneur. But how shall we manage it that instead of saying: 'I believe I heard the voices,' Joan shall say: 'I have heard the voices'?"

BISHOP CAUCHON—"Nothing is simpler. All we need is to have a councilor, in whom Joan may have full confidence, dictate to her certain answers that will be certain to lead to her condemnation."

CANON LOYSELEUR—"Monseigneur, the girl is of extraordinary intelligence and is gifted with exceptional sound judgment. That is her reputation. How can we expect her to repose blind confidence in an unknown adviser?"

BISHOP CAUCHON—"My son in Christ, what is your name?"

CANON LOYSELEUR—"My name is Nicolas Loyseleur."[112]

BISHOP CAUCHON—"I believe the name is truly predestined."

CANON LOYSELEUR—"Predestined?"

BISHOP CAUCHON (laughing)—"Without a doubt. What is the way that the skilful fowler practices the piping of birds in order to attract the mistrusting partridge? He skilfully imitates the bird's chirping, and the latter believing one of his kind near, flies in the direction of the deceitful voice and falls into the snare. Now, then, my worthy canon, the apostle St. Peter was a fisher of men, you shall be a decoyer of women—to the greater glory of our order."

CANON LOYSELEUR (after a moment's reflection)—"I vaguely perceive your thought, monseigneur."

BISHOP CAUCHON—"The Maid will arrive towards morning in Rouen. Her cell, her irons are ready. Well, then, it is necessary that when she enters her cell in the morning, she find you there. You must be a companion in her misery, and presently her confidant."

CANON LOYSELEUR—"I, monseigneur! Such a mission for me!"

BISHOP CAUCHON—"You—in chains, hands and feet. You will moan. You will sigh at the cruelty of the English, at the severity with which I, a bishop, allow a poor priest to be treated whose only crime is that he remained faithful to the King of France. That is the outline of your role."

CANON LOYSELEUR (smiling)—"Our divine master said: 'Render unto Caesar what is Caesar's, and unto God what is God's.'"

BISHOP CAUCHON—"What is the application of that quotation! It is out of all connection."

CANON LOYSELEUR—"Let us render to the Inquisition what belongs to the Inquisition. The method that you propose is skilful, I admit. But it has been practiced before upon the great Albigensian heretics as is attested by the following seventh decretal of the inquisitorial law: 'Let none approach the heretic, except, from time to time, one or two faithful persons, who cautiously, and as if greatly moved by pity for him, shall give him advice,' etc., etc."[113]

BISHOP CAUCHON—"Well! Just because the method has often been successfully put in practice by the Inquisition it is sure to succeed again! I do not mean to plume myself upon having invented it. It goes without saying that being Joan's fowler you are also to be among her judges. To the end that you may enjoy the results of your skilful chirping, I reserved a place for you on the tribunal. You will sit in your robes with your cowl wholly over your head; it will conceal your face. Joan will not be able to recognize you. Informer and judge—it is agreed."

CANON LOYSELEUR—"It will be all the more necessary, seeing that, thanks to my quality of priest, it will be easy for me to induce the girl to confess. In that case, you realize the tremendous advantage that may be gained over her, through her sincerely made avowals before the sacred tribunal of penitence."

BISHOP CAUCHON (transported with joy)—"Canon! Canon! The Regent of England and the Cardinal of Winchester will worthily reward your zeal. You shall be bishop; I, archbishop."

CANON LOYSELEUR—"My reward is in myself, monseigneur. What I do, I do, as you said, to the greater glory of our Church, and above all to its great profit. I feel outraged at the sight of a stupid mob attributing supernatural powers and divine relations to this peasant girl, who, according to canonical law, has none of the qualities for such celestial commerce. I feel for Joan the hatred, vigorous and legitimate, that the captains, her rivals, pursue her with. 'What is the use,' they justly said, 'of being born noble? What is the use of growing old in the harness, if it is enough for a cowherdess to come and our illustrious houses are eclipsed?' You tax Charles VII with ingratitude, monseigneur. You are wrong. By showing himself ungrateful, he asserts his royal dignity. His conduct is politic when he repudiates the services of the Maid. Charles VII could not intervene in Joan's behalf without thereby making the admission, disgraceful to his Majesty—'A vassal has rendered the crown to a descendant of the Frankish Kings.' England, the Church, the knighthood of France, Charles VII and his council—all are interested in having the Maid burned alive. And she shall be roasted, even if I should myself have to light the pyre!"

BISHOP CAUCHON (laughing)—"That is too much zeal, canon! In her infinite mercy, our holy mother the Church sends people to the pyre but never herself burns them with her maternal hands. Execution is the province of the secular arm. Thanks to your spiritual aid, it will be done that way with Joan. She shall be roasted as a relapsed heretic, and the Church will have shown herself full of clemency to the very end. Our triumph will have results of an importance that you do not dream of. Joan will become even in the eyes of her partisans the most despicable of creatures. We shall burn her body and we shall stain her name and fame for now and evermore."

CANON LOYSELEUR—"How, monseigneur? I do not quite grasp your meaning."

BISHOP CAUCHON—"I shall prove to you to-morrow what I am now saying. In the meantime we must also see what advantage we can draw from the otherwise annoying chastity of the she-devil. Because, may God pardon me, she is still a virgin. But it is growing late. Go and take a few hours of rest. To-morrow early you must be all sorrow, moans and sighs, with irons to your hands and feet and lying upon straw in the cell of Joan."

The canon departs; the Bishop remains alone. He busies himself with the preparation of the process and the drawing up of a series of questions based upon the actions and words of Joan the Maid.

CHAPTER II.

IN THE DUNGEON.

It is still night. A lamp feebly lights a dark subterraneous cell in the old donjon of the Castle of Rouen. The cell is a semi-circular cave. Its greenish walls ooze with the moisture of winter. A narrow window, furnished with an enormous iron bar is cut in a stone wall six feet thick. Opposite the airhole and under a vaulted passage is a massive door studded with iron and pierced with a grated wicket always kept open. A wooden box filled with straw lies to the left of the door; a long chain that is soldered in the wall and the other end of which is fastened to a heavy iron belt, now open, lies on the straw. At one end of the box, that is to serve as a bed, rises a beam so contrived as to hold fast the feet of the girl prisoner that is soon to be conveyed thither. A trunk, a stool, a table, the sorrowful furniture of a prisoner's cell, are barely distinguishable by the light of the lamp. Opposite this straw bed is another, furnished exactly like the first. On it lies Canon Loyseleur, in chains. He has just said a few words to the jailer John, an English soldier in burly middle age, who wears an old fur coat, and whose low and savage face is bloated by excessive indulgence in wine and strong liquors. His thick long beard, unkempt like his hair, falls down upon his chest. A cutlass hangs at his side. Presently another man of hang-dog looks pushes open the door and says to John:

"Come, quick. Here is the witch!"

The jailer goes out precipitately, makes a sign of intelligence to the canon and carries the lamp out. The canon stretches himself on the straw and pretends to sleep. The door is double locked on the outside. The weak light of approaching dawn, so pale in those winter days, filters through the airhole of the cell, yet leaves the interior in substantial darkness. The bed occupied by the canon lies completely in the shadow. The scene is about to begin.

Again the heavy door grates on its hinges. Joan Darc enters preceded by John. He casts a savage look upon her. Two other jailers, also armed, follow their chief. One of them has a hammer and shears in his hands, the other carries on his shoulder a small box containing some clothes that belong to the prisoner. Joan is hardly recognizable. Since her prolonged sojourn in a succession of prisons, the fresh color of the child of the fields or of the martial maid always living in the open has disappeared. Her beautiful face, now furrowed with suffering and worn with sorrow, is of a sickly hue. A bitter smile contracts her lips. Her appearance is sad yet proud. Her black eyes seem enlarged through the hollowness of her cheeks. She wears a woman's felt hat, a brown tunic and tight hose fastened with hooks to her shirt. The laces of her leather shoes are hidden under two large iron rings held together by a chain that is hardly long enough to allow her to walk. Close manacles hold her hands together. Her clothes, worn out and tattered by her journey, are ripped at the elbows and allow glimpses of a coarse shirt. The English soldiers charged to guard the heroine have received orders not to lose sight of her night or day, and to sleep in her room during the few halts that were made. As her chastity would not allow her to undress in their presence, she has not removed her clothes for a whole month.

John orders his aides to unchain the prisoner and to fasten her firmly to the straw bed. They approach her with an insolence that is not unmixed with fear. In their eyes she is a witch. They are always in fear of some sorcery. Nevertheless they first place around her waist the heavy iron belt, lock it, and give the key to John. The length of the chain, that is fastened at the other end to the wall, barely allows her to sit down or stretch herself out upon the litter. Being thus secured to her new fastenings, one of the jailers begins to remove her traveling irons. With a hammer he strikes a chisel which he applied to the jointure of the manacles and these drop from Joan's sore wrists. With a sigh of relief she stretches out her aching and swollen arms. Her feet are then unchained, to be immediately secured in the rings at the end of the chain that is fastened to the beam at the foot of the litter, on which, worn out with fatigue and broken with sadness, the martial maid drops in a sitting posture and covers her face with her hands.

John orders his men out and casts a knowing look at Canon Loyseleur. The latter has not yet been noticed by the prisoner, as he crouches in a corner that lies wholly in the dark. The jailer goes out and locks the door. Through the wicket the iron casques of the two sentinels, posted on the outside, are seen passing and repassing. Invisible in the thick darkness, which the feeble light that filters through the airhole is unable to dispel, the canon holds his breath and observes Joan. With her face in her hands, she remains profoundly absorbed in her own thoughts—painful, heartrending thoughts. She indulges in no false hopes. Charles VII has abandoned her to her executioners. For some time she had known the egotism, cowardice and ingratitude of the prince. Twice she had wished to leave him to his fate, indignant and shocked at his cowardice. But out of patriotism she had resigned herself to cover him with her glory, knowing that in the eyes of the people France was personified in the King. This notwithstanding, the heroine at first expected that the prince would endeavor to save her. He owed everything to her, only from him could she expect some degree of pity. Enlightened by so many evidences on the envy and hatred that the captains pursued her with, she in no way counted with help from that quarter; after so many attempts at infamous treason, they had finally succeeded in delivering her to the English before Compiegne. For a moment, in the innocence of her heart, she expected aid from the charity of the clergy, the bishops who at Poitiers declared that Charles VII could with a safe conscience accept the unexpected aid that she brought him in the name of God. She hoped for the intervention of the ecclesiastics who were so anxious to admit her, to communion and to confession, who sang her praises, and who, with all the pomp of the church, celebrated the feast of the 8th of May, a commemorative anniversary of the raising of the siege of Orleans, a religious solemnity ordered by the bishop of the diocese, which comprised an imposing procession of the clergy, who marched at the head of the councilmen, holding wax candles in their hands, and made its pious stations at the several spots that had been the theater of the glorious deeds of the Maid.

But Joan now no longer indulged in false hopes. The clergy, like the King, abandoned her to her executioners. Other priests of Christ would judge and condemn her. The English who brought her in chains often told her on the route: "You are going to be burned, witch! We have priests in Rouen who will send you to the pyre!"

Convinced by these words that she need expect neither mercy nor justice from the ecclesiastical tribunal before which she was about to be arraigned, and overpowered by the bitter disillusionment, the recollections of which stabbed her heart without souring her angelic spirit, Joan asked herself in a perplexity of doubt, why did the Lord forsake her, her the instrument of His divine will? Her who was ever obedient to the saintly voices that she heard so distinctly, and that since her captivity still repeated to her: "Go, daughter of God! Fear not—submit meekly to your martyrdom. You have fulfilled your duty—heaven is with you!"

And yet heaven delivered her to the English, her implacable enemies!

And yet the priests of the Lord were impatient, it was told her on all hands, to sentence her to the flames!

These contradictions profoundly troubled the prisoner. Often she was overcome with sadness, whenever she thought of her uncompleted mission—the soil of Gaul was not yet completely delivered from the foreign rule!

Such are the thoughts of Joan at this hour when, with her face hidden in her hands, she sits on the straw of her cell, and is yet ignorant of the presence of Canon Loyseleur. Suddenly the girl trembles with surprise, almost fright. From the midst of the darkness at the opposite side she hears a compassionate voice addressing her, and the following dialogue ensues:

CANON LOYSELEUR—"Raise your head, virgin! The Lord will not forsake you! He watches over you!"

JOAN DARC—"Who is speaking to me?"

CANON LOYSELEUR (rising on the straw)—"Who speaks to you? A poor old priest—a good Christian and royalist—a victim to his loyalty, to his faith, and to his King—crimes that the English do not pardon. For more than a year have I lived chained in this dungeon, and have asked but one favor of my Creator—to be recalled to Him! Alack! I have suffered so much! But I forget my sufferings since I am permitted to behold the holy maid, the virgin inspired by heaven, vanquisher of the English, deliverer of Gaul! May her name be glorified!"

JOAN DARC (tenderly)—"Not so loud, my Father! You might be heard. I fear not for myself, but I fear for your sake the anger of the jailers."

CANON LOYSELEUR (with exaltation and a ringing voice)—"What can the English, whom I abhor, these enemies of our beloved country, do to me? I pray God to send me martyrdom, if He thinks me worthy of such a glorious aureola!"

JOHN (appearing at the wicket and affecting rage)—"If you keep on screaming like that, I shall have you whipped till you bleed!"

CANON LOYSELEUR (with greater exaltation)—"Hack my limbs to pieces! Tear my scalp from my skull, ferocious beast! Unto death shall I cry: 'Glory to God—Long live King Charles VII! Anathema upon the English!'"

JOHN (still at the wicket)—"The captain of the tower will soon be here. I shall notify him of the danger there is in leaving you in the same cell with that witch, with whom you might enter into wicked machinations, you tonsured devil! But if you continue to scream, your flesh will be flayed!" (He withdraws from the wicket.)

CANON LOYSELEUR (shaking his chains)—"Heathen! Criminal! Idolater! You will burn in hell!"

JOAN DARC (beseechingly)—"Good Father, calm yourself; do not irritate that man. He will remove you from me, if you do. Oh, in my distress, it would be a great consolation to me to hear the word of a priest of our Lord. Do not withdraw your support from me."

CANON LOYSELEUR (contritely)—"May God pardon me for having yielded to an impulse of anger! I would regret the act doubly if it were to cause these wicked men to separate me from you. (In a low voice and feigning to look toward the wicket with fear of being overheard) I have hoped to be useful to you—perhaps to save you—by my advice—"

JOAN DARC—"What say you, good Father?"

CANON LOYSELEUR (still in a low voice)—"I have hoped to be able to give you useful advice in the matter of the process that is to be instituted against you, and keep you from falling into the snares that those unworthy priests will surely spread before you. Those judges are simoniacal, they have been sold to the English. I hoped to be able to admit you to confession and to the ineffable happiness of communion, that you have probably been long deprived of."

JOAN DARC (sighing)—"Since my captivity I have not been able to approach the sacred table!"

CANON LOYSELEUR—"I have succeeded in concealing from the jailers some consecrated wafers. But so far from reserving the bread of the angels for myself alone, I wished to invite you to the celestial feast!"

JOAN DARC (clasping her hands in pious delight)—"Oh, Father! Good Father! How thankful I shall be to you!"

CANON LOYSELEUR (hurriedly, but in a still lower voice, and casting furtive glances hither and thither)—"Our moments are precious. I may be taken away from here any time. I know not whether I shall ever again see you, holy maid. Give me your full attention. Remember my advice. It may save you. You must know that to-morrow, perhaps to-day, you will be arraigned before an ecclesiastical tribunal on the charges of heresy and witchcraft."

JOAN DARC—"The English who brought me hither a prisoner have announced the tribunal to me. I am to be condemned."

CANON LOYSELEUR—"The threat is not idle. Yesterday my jailer said to me: 'You will soon have Joan the witch as your cell-mate; she is to be tried, sentenced and burned as a magician who sold herself to Satan, and as a heretic'!"

JOAN DARC (trembling)—"My God!"

CANON LOYSELEUR—"What is the matter, my dear daughter? You seem to tremble!"

JOAN DARC (with a shiver)—"Oh, Father! May God stand by me! Thanks to Him, I never knew fear! (She covers her face with her hands in terror.) I, burned! Oh, Lord God! Burned! What a frightful death!"

CANON LOYSELEUR—"You are well justified in your fears. The purpose of the tribunal is to send you to the pyre."

JOAN DARC (in a smothered voice)—"And yet they are priests! What harm have I done them? Why do they persecute me?"

CANON LOYSELEUR—"Oh, my daughter, do not blaspheme that sacred name of priest by applying it to those tigers who thirst for blood."

JOAN DARC—"Pardon me, Father!"

CANON LOYSELEUR (in a voice of tender commiseration)—"Sweet and dear child, need you fear a word of blame from my mouth? No, no. It was but a generous impulse of indignation that carried me away against those new Pharisees who conspire to kill you, as their predecessors years ago conspired to kill Jesus our Redeemer! I am a clerk of theology. I know the manner in which such tribunals as you are about to face are wont to proceed. I know your life; the glorious voice of your fame has informed me of your noble deeds."

JOAN DARC (dejectedly)—"Oh, if I had only remained home sewing and spinning. I would not now be in imminent danger of death!"

CANON LOYSELEUR—"Come, daughter of God, no weakness! Did not the Lord tell you by the voice of two of His saints and of His archangel: 'Go, daughter of God! Go to the aid of the King. You will deliver Gaul'?"

JOAN DARC—"Yes, Father."

CANON LOYSELEUR—"As to those voices, did you hear them?"

JOAN DARC—"Yes, Father."

CANON LOYSELEUR (pressingly)—"You heard them, the sacred voices? With your bodily ears?"

JOAN DARC—"As clearly as I hear your voice at this moment."

CANON LOYSELEUR—"And you saw your saints? You saw them with your own eyes?"

JOAN DARC—"As I see you."

CANON LOYSELEUR (delighted)—"Oh, dear daughter! Hold that language before the ecclesiastical tribunal, and you are saved! You will then escape the snare that they will spread before you."

JOAN DARC—"Please explain what you mean, dear Father and protector."

CANON LOYSELEUR—"However perverse, however iniquitous these tribunals of blood may be, they are nevertheless composed of men who are clothed with a sacred character. These priests must save appearances towards one another and the public. Your judges will tell you with a confidential and benign air: 'Joan, you claim to have seen St. Marguerite, St. Catherine and St. Michael, the archangel; you claim to have heard their voices. Can it not have been an illusion of your senses? If so, the senses, due to their grossness, are liable to error. The Church will be slow to impute to you as a crime what may be only a carnal error.' Now, then, my poor child (the canon's features are screwed into an expression of anxious concern) if, misled by such insidious language, and thinking to see in it a means of escape, you were to answer: 'Indeed, I do not affirm that I saw the saints and the archangel, I do not affirm that I heard their voices, but I believe to have seen, I believe to have heard,' if you should say that, dear and holy child, you will be lost! (Joan makes a motion of terror) This is why: To recoil before the affirmation that you have actually seen and heard, to present the fact in the form of a doubt, would be to draw upon your head the charge of falsehood, blasphemy, and heresy in the highest degree. You would be charged (in an increasingly threatening voice) with having made sport of the most sacred things! You would be charged with having, thanks to such diabolical jugglery, deceived the people by holding yourself out as inspired by God, whom you would be outraging in a most infamous, abominable, impious manner! (In a frightful hollow voice) They would then pronounce upon you a terrible excommunication cutting you off from the Church as a gangrened, rotten, infected limb! You would thereupon be delivered to the secular arm, you would be taken to the pyre and burned alive for a heretic, an apostate, an idolater! The ashes of your body will be cast to the winds!"

Joan Darc, pale with fear, utters a piercing cry. She is terrified.

CANON LOYSELEUR (aside)—"The pyre frightens her. She is ours! (He joins his hands imploringly and points to the wicket where the face of John reappears.) Silence! Joan, my dear daughter, you will ruin us both!"

JOHN (roughly, through the wicket)—"You are still making a noise and screaming! Must I come in and make you behave?"

CANON LOYSELEUR (brusquely)—"The irons of my poor mate have wounded her. Pain drew from her an involuntary cry."

JOHN—"She has not yet reached the end! She will scream much louder on the pyre that awaits her, the miserable witch!"

CANON LOYSELEUR (seeming hardly able to contain his indignation)—"Jailer, have at least the charity of not insulting our distress. Have pity for the poor girl!"

John withdraws grumbling. Joan Darc, overwhelmed with terror, has fallen back upon the straw and represses her sobs. After the jailer's withdrawal she slightly regains courage, rises partly and the dialogue proceeds:

JOAN DARC—"Pardon my weakness, Father. Oh, the mere thought of such a horrible death—the thought of mounting a pyre!" (She does not finish the sentence, and sobs violently.)

CANON LOYSELEUR—"By placing before you the frightful fate reserved to you, in case you are snared, I wished to put you upon your guard against your enemies."

JOAN DARC (wiping her tears, and in an accent of profound gratitude)—"God will reward you, good Father, for the great pity you show me, a stranger to you."

CANON LOYSELEUR—"You are no stranger to me, Joan. I know you are one of the glories of France! The elect of the Lord! Now listen to the rest of what I have to say to you. I am in a hurry to complete my advice before I am dragged away from here. If, deceived by their perfidious suggestions, you should answer your judges that you believe you saw your saints appear before you, that you believe you heard their voices, instead of resolutely affirming that you saw them with your eyes and heard them with your ears, St. Catherine, St. Marguerite and the archangel St. Michael, sent to you by the Lord—"

JOAN DARC—"It is the truth, Father. I shall tell what I saw and heard. I have never lied."

CANON LOYSELEUR—"The truth must be boldly confessed, in the face of the judges. You must answer them: 'Yes, I have seen these supernatural beings with my eyes; yes, I have heard their marvelous voices with my ears.' Then, dear child, despite all its ill will, the tribunal, unable to catch the slightest hesitation in your words, will be forced to recognize that you are a sacred virgin, the elect, the inspired of heaven. And however perverse, however devoted to the English your judges may be, they will find themselves forced to absolve you and set you free."

JOAN DARC (yielding to hope)—"If all that is needed to be saved is to tell the truth, then my deliverance is certain. Thanks to God and to you, good Father. Thanks for your friendly advice!"

CANON LOYSELEUR—"If circumstantial details are asked for upon the form and shape of your apparitions, refuse to answer. They might be able to draw from your words some improper meaning. Limit yourself to the pure and simple affirmation of the reality of your visions and revelations."

Outside of the cell the noise of numerous steps is heard, together with the rattle of arms and the words: "To your posts! To your posts! Here is the captain of the tower!"

CANON LOYSELEUR (listens and says to Joan in great hurry)—"It is the captain. Perhaps the jailer will carry out his threat, and take me away from you, dear daughter. There is but one means for us to meet again. Demand of the captain permission to have me as your confessor. He will not dare to decline. I shall then be able to hold to your lips the sacred wafer, the bread of the angels."

The door opens with a great noise. A captain enters, followed by John and other keepers.

THE CAPTAIN (pointing to the canon)—"Take that tonsured old scamp to another cell, and keep him on a fast."

CANON LOYSELEUR—"Sir captain, I pray you, allow me to remain near Joan, my daughter in God."

THE CAPTAIN—"If the witch is your daughter, then you must be Satan in person."

CANON LOYSELEUR—"For pity's sake, do not separate us!"

THE CAPTAIN (to John)—"Take away this priest of Beelzebub!"

JOHN (brutally to the canon)—"Come, get up! Be quick about it!"

Canon Loyseleur rises painfully from his couch of straw, clanking his chains all he can and uttering lamentable sighs. Joan advances toward the captain as far as her chain will allow her, and says in a sweet and imploring voice:

JOAN DARC—"Sir, grant me a favor that never is denied to a prisoner. Allow me to take this holy man for my confessor."

THE CAPTAIN—"Your confessor shall be the executioner, strumpet!"

CANON LOYSELEUR (carrying his chained hands to his eyes)—"Oh, sir captain, you are merciless."

JOHN (rudely pushing the canon)—"March! March! You will have time enough to cry in your cell."

JOAN DARC—"Sir captain, do not spurn my prayer—allow the good priest to visit me occasionally as my confessor."

THE CAPTAIN (feigns to be mollified)—"I shall consult the Duke of Warwick upon that. For the present (to John), take the priest of Satan away and thrust him into some other cell."

CANON LOYSELEUR (following the jailer)—"Courage, noble Joan! Courage, my daughter! Remember what I told you! May the holy name of God be ever glorified." (He goes out.)

JOAN DARC (with tears in her eyes)—"May God guard me from forgetting your advice. May the Lord preserve you, good Father!" (She drops exhausted upon the straw.)

THE CAPTAIN (to John)—"Remove the irons from the prisoner. She is to be taken upstairs. The tribunal is in session."

JOAN DARC (rises and shivers involuntarily)—"So soon!"

THE CAPTAIN (with a savage laugh)—"At last I see you tremble, witch! Your bravery came from the devil!"

Joan Darc smiles disdainfully. John and another jailer approach her to remove the irons that hold her by the feet and by the waist. She trembles with disgust and becomes purple with shame at the touch of these men's hands while they remove the irons from her limbs and body. Wounded not in her vanity but in her dignity at the thought of appearing before her judges in torn garments she says to the captain:

JOAN DARC—"Sir, I have in that little trunk some linen and other clothes. Please order your men out for a few minutes in order that I may dress myself."

THE CAPTAIN (bursting out laughing)—"By the devil, your patron! If you want to change your clothes, change them before us, and instead of a few minutes, I shall let you have all the time that you may want for your toilet. I would even help you, if you wish it, my pretty witch!"

JOAN DARC (blushing with confusion, and with a firm voice)—"Let us be gone to the tribunal. May God help me. You are truly severe in refusing so slight a favor to a prisoner."

CHAPTER III.

THE INQUISITION.

The ecclesiastical tribunal before which Joan Darc is to appear is assembled in the ancient chapel of the old Castle of Rouen. The vaults overhead, the walls, the pillars, are blackened with age. It is eight in the morning. The pale light of this winter morn, chilly and foggy, penetrates to the vast nave through a single ogive window, cut into the thick wall behind the platform where the clerical judges are seated under the presidency of Bishop Peter Cauchon. To the left of the tribunal is a table at which the registrars are placed. Their duty is to keep the minutes of the questions and answers. Facing this table is the seat of Peter of Estivet, the institutor of the process. Nothing could be more sinister than the aspect of these men. In order to keep out the cold, they are clad in long furred robes with hoods down and almost completely covering their faces. Their backs are turned to the solitary window from which the only light, and that a weak one, enters the place. Thus they are wholly in the shade. A slight reflection of greyish light fringes the top of their black hoods and glides over their shoulders.

The judges have numerous substitutes to take their places when needed. The priests of the University of Paris are partly reserved for the other sessions. Here are the names of the infamous priests present at this first session. Their names should be inscribed in letters of blood and consigned to eternal execration:

Peter of Longueville, Abbot of the Holy Trinity of Fecamp; John Hulot of Chatillon, Archdeacon of Evreux; James Guesdon of the Order of Minor Friars; John Lefevre, Augustinian monk; Maurice of Quesnay, priest and professor of theology; William Leboucher, priest and doctor of canon law; William of Conti, Abbot of the Trinity of Mount St. Catherine; Bonnel, Abbot of Cormeilles; John Garin, Archdeacon of French Vexin; Richard of Gronchet, canon of the collegiate of Saussaye; Peter Minier, priest and bachelor of theology; Raoul Sauvage, of the Order of St. Dominic; Robert Barbier, canon of Rouen; Denis Gastinel, canon of Notre Dame-la-Ronde; John Ledoux, canon of Rouen; John Basset, canon of Rouen; John Brouillot, chanter of the Cathedral of Rouen; Aubert Morel, canon of Rouen; John Colombelle, canon of Rouen; Laurent Dubust, priest and licentiate of canon law; Raoul Auguy, canon of Rouen; Andre Marguerie, Archdeacon of Petit-Coux; John Alespee, canon of Rouen; Geoffroy of Crotoy, canon of Rouen; Gilles of Les Champs, canon of Rouen; John Lemaitre, vicar and Inquisitor of the faith; finally, Nicolas Loyseleur, canon of Rouen, who completely hides his face under his hood.

The registrars, Thomas of Courcelles, Manchon and Taquel Bois-Guillaume, are at their table ready to take down the proceedings. Canon Peter of Estivet, the institutor of the process, is in his seat. The other members of the ecclesiastical tribunal have taken their places.

BISHOP PETER CAUCHON (rising)—"My very dear brothers: Peter of Estivet, institutor of the process against Joan the Maid, will concisely state our petition. Listen attentively."

CANON PETER OF ESTIVET (rises, takes a parchment from the table and reads)—"We, Peter Cauchon, Bishop of Beauvais by the grace of God, metropolitan of the town and diocese of Rouen, have convoked you, our very dear brothers, in the name of the venerable and very reverend chapter of the cathedral to examine and judge the facts hereinafter set forth.

"'To the author and consummator of the faith, our Lord Jesus Christ, greeting.

"'A certain woman, commonly named Joan the Maid, has been taken and made a prisoner at Compiegne, within the jurisdiction of our diocese of Beauvais, by the soldiers of our very Christian and Serene Master Henry VI, King of England and of the French.

"'The said woman being strongly suspected by us of heresy, and our duty in the premises being to investigate her on her faith, we have requisitioned and demanded that the said woman be delivered and sent to us. We, Bishop, being informed by public rumor of the acts and deeds of the said Joan, acts and deeds that assail not only our faith but the faith of France and of all christendom, and wishing to proceed in this matter with all speed yet deliberately, have decreed that the said Joan shall be summoned to appear before us and be interrogated concerning her acts and deeds, as well as upon matters that concern the faith, and we have cited her to appear before us in the chapel of the Castle of Rouen, on this twentieth day of February, 1431, at eight o'clock in the morning, in order that she may answer the charges brought against her.'" (The institutor resumes his seat.)

BISHOP PETER CAUCHON—"Introduce the accused before the tribunal."

Two beadles in black gowns leave the chapel and speedily re-enter leading Joan. Once so resolute, so serene in those days of battle when, cased in her white armor and riding her charger, she dashed upon the enemy, her standard in her hand, the martial maid now shivers with fear at the sight of this tribunal of priests half hidden in the shadow of the chapel and their faces barely visible under their hoods—silent, motionless, like black phantoms. She recalls the words and the advice of Canon Loyseleur, whose presence among her judges she does not remotely suspect. The recollection of his words and advice at once give her heart and fill her with fear. By pretending to give her the means of escaping the snare spread for her, the canon had also informed her that the tribunal was predetermined to deliver her to the pyre. This thought upsets and frightens the prisoner, already weakened by so many sorrows and trials. She feels her knees shake at the first steps that she takes into the chapel, and forced to lean upon the arm of one of the beadles, she halts for a moment. At the sight of the young girl, now hardly nineteen, still so beautiful despite her pallor, thinness and tattered clothes, the ecclesiastical judges contemplate her with somber curiosity, but experience neither concern nor pity for the heroine of so many battles. From the political and religious viewpoint, she is to them an enemy. Their animosity towards her smothers all human sentiment in their breasts. Her great deeds, her genius, her glory irritate them all the more seeing they are conscious of the abominable crime in which they are about to share through ambition, orthodox fanaticism, cupidity and partisan hatred. Presently controlling her emotions, Joan Darc takes courage and advances between the two beadles. They lead her to the foot of the tribunal, and withdraw. She dares not raise her eyes to her judges, respectfully takes off her hat which she keeps in her hand, inclines herself slightly forward, and remains standing before the platform.

BISHOP CAUCHON (rising)—"Joan, approach (she draws nearer). Our duty as protectors and upholders of the Christian faith, with the aid of our Lord Jesus Christ, compels us to warn you in all charity that, in order to hasten your trial and the peace of your soul, you must tell the truth, the whole truth. In short, answer without subterfuge to our interrogatories. You are to swear on the Holy Scriptures to tell the truth. (To one of the beadles) Bring a missal."

The beadle brings a missal and presents it to Joan.

BISHOP CAUCHON—"Joan, down on your knees. Swear on that missal to tell the truth."

JOAN DARC (mistrustful)—"I know not what you mean to interrogate me upon, sir. You may put such questions to me that I may be unable to answer."

BISHOP CAUCHON—"You shall swear that you will sincerely answer the questions that we shall put to you concerning your faith—and other things."

JOAN DARC (kneels down and puts both her hands on the missal)—"I swear to tell the truth."

BISHOP CAUCHON—"What are your given names?"

JOAN DARC—"In Lorraine I was called Jeannette. Since my arrival in France I have been called Joan. That is my name."

BISHOP CAUCHON—"Where were you born?"

JOAN DARC—"In the village of Domremy, in the valley of Vaucouleurs."

BISHOP CAUCHON—"What are the names of your father and your mother?"

JOAN DARC (with deep emotion)—"My father is named James Darc, my mother Isabelle Romée. These are the names of my dear parents."

BISHOP CAUCHON—"In what place were you baptized?"

JOAN DARC—"In the church of Domremy."

BISHOP CAUCHON—"Who were your god-father and god-mother?"

JOAN DARC—"My god-father's name was John Linguet, my god-mother's Sybille." (At the recollections invoked by this name a tear rolls down her cheek.)

BISHOP CAUCHON—"This woman claimed to have seen fairies. Did she not pass in the region for a soothsayer and sorceress?"

JOAN DARC (with a firmer voice)—"My god-mother was a good and wise woman."

BISHOP CAUCHON—"What priest baptized you at your birth?"

JOAN DARC—"Master John Minet, our curate, a holy man."

BISHOP CAUCHON—"How old are you?"

JOAN DARC—"Nearly nineteen."

BISHOP CAUCHON—"Do you know your Pater Noster?"

JOAN DARC—"My mother taught it to me, and I recite it mornings and evenings." (She sighs.)

BISHOP CAUCHON—"Will you pledge yourself not to flee from the Castle of Rouen, under pain of passing for a heretic?"

JOAN DARC (remains silent for a moment and reflects; by degrees she regains her self-assurance; she answers in a firm voice)—"I shall not take that pledge. I will not promise not to seek to flee, if the opportunity offers."

RAOUL SAUVAGE (threateningly)—"Your chains will then be doubled, to keep you from escaping."

JOAN DARC—"It is allowed to all prisoners to escape from their prison."

BISHOP CAUCHON (with severity, after consulting in a low voice with several of the judges sitting near him)—"The rebellious words of the said Joan having been heard, we shall particularly commit her to the keeping of the noble John Le Gris, a guardsman of our Sire, the King of England and

France, and join to John Le Gris the equerries Berwick and Talbot, English men-at-arms. All the three are hereby charged to keep the prisoner, and we recommend to them not to allow anyone to approach her or to speak with her without our permission. (Addressing himself to the tribunal) Those of our very dear brothers who have any question to put to the accused, are now free to do so."

A JUDGE—"Joan, do you swear to tell the whole truth? I await your answer."

JOAN DARC (with dignity)—"I have sworn; that is enough. I never lie."

THE SAME JUDGE—"Did you in your infancy learn to work like the other girls of the fields?"

JOAN DARC—"My mother taught me to sew and to spin, and also the labors of the field."

ANOTHER JUDGE—"Did you have a confessor?"

JOAN DARC—"Yes, the curate of our parish is my confessor and spiritual guide."

THE SAME JUDGE—"Did you confess your revelations to your curate or to any other man of the church?"

JOAN DARC—"No, I said nothing upon that."

The priests exchange meaning glances and a few words in a low voice.

THE SAME JUDGE—"Why that secrecy towards your curate?"

JOAN DARC—"Had I spoken about my apparitions my father and mother would have opposed my undertaking."

ANOTHER JUDGE—"Do you think you committed a sin in leaving your father and your mother, contrary to the precept of the Scriptures—'Thou shalt honor thy father and mother'?"

JOAN DARC—"I never disobeyed them before I left them. But I wrote to them; they pardoned me."

THE SAME JUDGE—"Accordingly, you think you can violate without sin the commandments of the church?"

JOAN DARC—"God commanded me to go to the aid of Orleans. I would not have been the King's servant had I not departed."

BISHOP CAUCHON (with a significant look at the judges)—"You claim, Joan, to have had revelations, visions—at what age did that happen to you?"

JOAN DARC—"I was then thirteen and a half years old. It was noon, in summer. I had fasted the previous day. I heard the voice, that seemed to proceed from the church. At the same time I saw a great light that dazzled me."

BISHOP CAUCHON (slowly and weighing every word)—"You say you heard voices—are you quite certain?"

JOAN DARC (to herself: Here is the snare that the good priest warned me against—I shall escape it by telling the truth)—"I heard the voices as clearly as I hear yours, Sir Bishop."

BISHOP CAUCHON—"Do you affirm that?"

JOAN DARC—"Yes, sir; because it is the truth."

BISHOP CAUCHON (lets his eyes travel triumphantly over the tribunal; his gesture is understood; a momentary silence ensues; then to the registrars)—"Have you taken down textually the prisoner's answer?"

A REGISTRAR—"Yes, monseigneur."

A JUDGE—"And in France, Joan, did you there also hear those voices?"

JOAN DARC—"Yes, sir."

ANOTHER JUDGE—"Whence do you suppose came those voices?"

JOAN DARC (with an accent of profound conviction)—"The voices came from God."

ANOTHER JUDGE—"What do you know about that?"

ANOTHER JUDGE—"What were the circumstances under which you were captured at Compiegne?"

ANOTHER JUDGE—"Who dictated the letter that you addressed to the English?"

These unrelated and cross questions followed close upon one another for the purpose of confusing Joan.

JOAN DARC (after a moment's silence)—"If you all question me at once, sirs, I shall be unable to answer any of you."

BISHOP CAUCHON—"Well, what makes you believe that the voices you speak about were divine?"

JOAN DARC—"They told me to behave like an honest girl, and that with the aid of God I would save France."

A JUDGE—"Was it revealed to you that if you lost your virginity you would forfeit your luck in war?"

JOAN DARC (blushing)—"That was not revealed to me."

THE SAME JUDGE—"Was it to the archangel St. Michael that you promised to remain a virgin?"

JOAN DARC (with chaste impatience)—"I made my vow to my good saints, St. Marguerite and St. Catherine."

ANOTHER JUDGE—"And so the voices of your saints ordered you to come to France?"

JOAN DARC—"Yes, for my own and the King's safety, and to deliver Gaul from the foreign yoke."

BISHOP CAUCHON—"Did you not at that epoch see the apparition of St. Marguerite and St. Catherine, to whom you attribute the voices, those divine voices according to you?"

JOAN DARC—"Yes, sir."

BISHOP CAUCHON (deliberately)—"You are certain of having seen the apparition?"

JOAN DARC—"I saw my dear saints as clearly as I see you, sir."

BISHOP CAUCHON—"You affirm that?"

JOAN DARC—"I affirm it upon my salvation."

Renewed and profound silence among the judges; several of them take notes; others exchange a few words in a low voice.

A JUDGE—"By what sign did you recognize those whom you call St. Catherine and St. Marguerite to have been saints?"

JOAN DARC—"By their saintliness."

BISHOP CAUCHON—"And the archangel St. Michael appeared before you?"

JOAN DARC—"Yes, sir; several times."

A JUDGE—"How is he clad?"

JOAN DARC (recollecting the advice of Canon Loyseleur)—"I do not know."

THE SAME JUDGE—"You refuse to answer? Was the angel perhaps quite nude?"

JOAN DARC (blushing)—"Do you imagine God has not the wherewithal to clothe him?"

BISHOP CAUCHON—"Your language is quite bold. Do you consider yourself under the protection of God?"

JOAN DARC—"If I am not, may God place me there. If I am, may He keep me there. (In a loud and strong voice:) But remember this: You are my judges, you assume a grave responsibility in accusing me. As to myself, the burden is light."

These noble words, pronounced by the martial maid in the conviction of her innocence, and indicative of her mistrust of her judges, announce a change in her spirit, a fortitude not there when the interrogatory commenced. She had secretly invoked her "voices" and they had answered—"Go on; fear not; answer the wicked priests boldly; you have nothing to reproach yourself with; God is with you; He will not forsake you." Strengthened by these thoughts and hope, the heroine raises her head; her pale and handsome face is now slightly colored; her large black eyes fix themselves boldly upon the Bishop; she realizes that he is her mortal enemy. The ecclesiastical judges remark the increasing assurance of the accused, who but a moment before was so timid and so dejected. The transformation augurs well for their projects. In the pride of her exaltation, Joan Darc may, and is bound to, drop admissions that she would have kept secret had she remained reserved, timid and mistrustful. Despite his wickedness, the Bishop feels rebuked by the eyes of Joan. He drops his hypocritical face, turns away his eyes and continues the interrogatory in a faltering voice.

BISHOP CAUCHON—"So, then, Joan, it was by order of your voices that you went to Vaucouleurs in search of a certain captain named Robert of Baudricourt, who furnished you with an escort to take you to the King, to whom you promised to raise the siege of Orleans?"

JOAN DARC—"Yes, sir, you speak truly."

BISHOP CAUCHON—"Do you admit having dictated a letter addressed to the Duke of Bedford, Regent of England, and other illustrious captains?"

JOAN DARC—"I dictated the letter at Poitiers, sir."

BISHOP CAUCHON—"In that letter you threatened the English with death?"

JOAN DARC—"Yes; if they did not return to their own country, and if they persisted in heaping trials upon trials on the poor people of France, in ravaging the country, in burning the villages."

BISHOP CAUCHON—"Was not that letter written by you under the invocation of our Lord Jesus Christ and of His immaculate Mother, the holy Virgin?"

JOAN DARC—"I ordered the words 'Jesus and Mary' to be placed in the form of a prayer at the head of the letters that I dictated. Was that wrong?"

BISHOP CAUCHON (does not answer; looks askance at the judges; several of these enter on their tablets the last answer of the accused, an answer that seems to be of extreme gravity judging from their hurry to note it)—"How did you sign the letters that you dictated?"

JOAN DARC—"I do not know how to write. I placed my cross in God as a signature at the foot of the parchment."

This second answer, no less dangerous than the first, is likewise noted down with great zest by the priests. A profound silence follows. The Bishop seems to interrogate the registrars with his looks, and to ask them whether they have finished writing down the words of the accused.

BISHOP CAUCHON—"After several battles you forced the English to raise the siege of Orleans?"

JOAN DARC—"My voices advised me. I fought—and God gave us the victory."

A JUDGE—"If those voices are of St. Marguerite and St. Catherine, these saints must hate the English."

JOAN DARC—"What God hates they hate; what He loves they love."

ANOTHER JUDGE—"Come, now; God loves the English, seeing He has so long rendered them victorious and they conquered a part of France."

JOAN DARC—"He undoubtedly left them to the punishment of their cruelty."

ANOTHER JUDGE—"Why should God have chosen a girl of your station rather than some other person to vanquish them?"

JOAN DARC—"Because it pleased the Lord to have the English routed by a poor girl like myself."

THE SAME JUDGE—"How much money did your King pay you to serve him?"

JOAN DARC (proudly)—"I never asked aught of the King but good arms, good horses, and the payment of my soldiers."

BISHOP CAUCHON—"When your King put you to the work of war, you ordered a standard to be made for you. What was its material?"

JOAN DARC—"It was of white satin." (She drops her head sadly at the recollection of the past glories of her banner, that was so terrible a device to the English, whose prisoner she now is. She smothers a sob.)

BISHOP CAUCHON—"What figures were painted on it?"

JOAN DARC—"Two angels holding a lily stalk. Two symbols; God and the King."

These words are likewise noted down with great zest by the members of the tribunal.

A JUDGE—"Was your standard frequently renewed?"

JOAN DARC—"It was renewed as often as its staff was broken in battle. That happened frequently."

ANOTHER JUDGE—"Did not some of those who followed you have standards made similar to yours?"

JOAN DARC—"Some did; others did not."

THE SAME JUDGE—"Were those who bore a standard similar to yours lucky in war? Did they rout the English?"

JOAN DARC—"Yes, if they were brave, they then triumphed over the English."

ANOTHER JUDGE—"Did your people follow you to battle because they considered you inspired?"

JOAN DARC—"I said to them: 'Let us fall bravely upon the English!' I was the first to fall to—they followed me."

THE JUDGE—"In short, your people took you to be inspired of God?"

JOAN DARC—"Whether they believed me to be inspired or not, they trusted in my courage."

BISHOP CAUCHON—"Did you not, when your King was consecrated at Rheims, proudly wave your banner over the prince's head?"

JOAN DARC—"No; but alone of all the captains, I accompanied the King into the cathedral with my standard in my hand."

A JUDGE (angrily)—"Accordingly, while the other captains did not bring their standards to the solemnity, you brought yours!"

JOAN DARC—"It had been at the pain—it was entitled to be at the honor."

This sublime answer, of such legitimate and touching pride and bearing the stamp of antique simplicity, strikes the assembled ecclesiastical executioners with admiration. They pause despite their bitter malice towards their victim. These were heroic and scathing words. They told of the price of perils and above all of disenchantment that Joan had paid for her triumph. Aye, she and her glorious standard had been cruelly in pain, poor martyr that she was. Her virginal body was broken by the rude trials of war. She had shed her generous blood on the fields of battle. She had struggled with admirable stubbornness, with mortal anxieties born of the most sacred patriotism, against the treasonable plots of the captains who finally brought on her downfall. She had struggled against the sloth of Charles VII, the poltroon whom with so much pain she dragged from victory to victory as far as Rheims, where she had him consecrated King. Her only recompense was to see her standard "at the honor" of that solemn consecration, from which she expected the salvation of Gaul. Her standard had been at the pain—it was entitled to be at the honor. The astonishment of the ecclesiastics at these sublime words is profound. Deep silence ensues. Bishop Cauchon is the first to break it. Addressing himself to the accused in measured words, an ordinary symptom with him of some lurking perfidy, he asks:

BISHOP CAUCHON—"Joan, when you entered a town, did not the inhabitants kiss your hands, your feet, your clothes?"

JOAN DARC—"Many wished to; and when poor people, women and children, came to me, I feared to grieve them if I repelled them."

This answer is to be used against her; several of the judges note it down, while a sinister smile plays around the lips of Bishop Cauchon; he proceeds:

BISHOP CAUCHON—"Did you ever hold a child at the baptismal font?"

JOAN DARC—"Yes; I held a child at the holy font of Soissons, and two others at St. Denis. These are the only ones to whom I have been godmother."

BISHOP CAUCHON—"What names did you give them?"

JOAN DARC—"To the boy the name of Charles, in honor of the King of France; to the girls the name of Joan, because the mothers so wished it."

These words, that charmingly depict the enthusiasm which the martial maid inspired among the people, and the generosity that she showed towards Charles, are to be a further charge against her. Several judges note them down.

BISHOP CAUCHON—"A mother at Lagny asked you to visit her dying child, did she not?"

JOAN DARC—"Yes, but the child had been brought to the Church of Notre-Dame. Young girls of the town were on their knees at the door and prayed for the child. I knelt down among them, and I also prayed to God for His blessing upon the child."

CANON LOYSELEUR (from under his completely lowered hood and disguising his voice)—"Which of the two Popes is the real Pope?"

JOAN DARC (stupefied)—"Are there, then, two Popes, sir? I did not know that."

BISHOP CAUCHON—"You claim to be inspired by God. He must have instructed you as to which of the two Popes you should render obedience to."

JOAN DARC—"I know nothing about that. It is for the Pope to know whether he obeys God, and for me to obey him who submits to God."

BISHOP CAUCHON (to Canon Loyseleur with a significant accent)—"My very dear brother, we shall reserve for another session the grave question that you have broached touching the Church triumphant and the Church militant. Let us now proceed with other matters. (Turning to Joan with an inflection of his voice that announces the gravity of the question.) When you left Vaucouleurs you put on male attire. Was that done at the request of Robert of Baudricourt, or of your own free will? Answer categorically."

JOAN DARC—"Of my own free will."

A JUDGE—"Did your voices order you to give up the garb of your sex?"

JOAN DARC—"Whatever good I have done I did by the advice of my voices. Whenever I understood them well, my saints and the archangel have guided me well."

ANOTHER JUDGE—"So, then, you do not think you are committing a sin in wearing the man's clothes that you are covered with?"

JOAN DARC (with a sigh of regret)—"Oh, for the happiness of France and the misfortune of England, why am I not free in man's clothes with my horse and my armor! I would still vanquish our enemies."

ANOTHER JUDGE—"Would you like to hear mass?"

JOAN DARC (thrilling with hope)—"Oh, with all my heart!"

THE SAME JUDGE—"You can not hear it in those clothes that are not of your sex."

JOAN DARC (reflects a moment; she recalls the obscene language of her jailers and fears to be outraged by them; in man's clothes she feels greater protection than in the habits of her sex; she answers)—"Do you promise me that if I resume my woman's clothes I shall be allowed to attend mass?"

THE SAME JUDGE—"Yes, Joan, I promise you that."

The Bishop makes a gesture of impatience and withers the judge who had last spoken with a look of condemnation.

JOAN DARC—"Let me, then, be provided with a long dress; I shall put it on to go to chapel. But when I return to my prison I shall resume my man's clothes."

The judge consults the Bishop with his eye to ascertain whether the request of the accused shall be granted; the prelate answers with a negative sign of his head, and turns to Joan.

BISHOP CAUCHON—"So, then, you persist in keeping your masculine dress?"

JOAN DARC—"I am guarded by men; such dress is safer."

THE INQUISITOR OF THE FAITH—"Do you now wear and have you worn masculine garb voluntarily, absolutely of your own free will?"

JOAN DARC—"Yes; and I shall continue to do so."

Again silence ensues. The ecclesiastical judges feel triumphant over the answer made so categorically by the accused, a grave answer seeing that Bishop Cauchon says to the registrars:

BISHOP CAUCHON—"Have you entered the words of the said Joan?"

A REGISTRAR—"Yes, monseigneur."

BISHOP CAUCHON (to the accused)—"You have often spoken of St. Michael. In what did you recognize that the form that appeared before you was that of the blessed archangel? Could not Satan assume the form of a good angel to lead you to evil?"

JOAN DARC—"I recognized St. Michael by the advice he gave me. It was the advice of an angel and not of Satan; it came from heaven, not from hell."

A JUDGE—"What advice did he give?"

JOAN DARC—"His advice was that I conduct myself as a pious and honest girl; he said to me God would then inspire me, and would aid me to deliver France."

THE INQUISITOR OF THE FAITH—"So that you claim not only to have seen a supernatural apparition under the form of St. Michael with your bodily eyes, but you furthermore claim that the figure was actually that of that holy personage?"

JOAN DARC—"I affirm it, seeing that I heard it with my ears, seeing that I saw it with my eyes. There is no doubt in my mind concerning the archangel."

BISHOP CAUCHON (to the registrars)—"Enter that answer without omitting a syllable."

A REGISTRAR—"Yes, monseigneur."

Canon Loyseleur, whose face is carefully concealed under his hood, and who for greater security holds a handkerchief to the lower part of his countenance, rises and whispers in the ear of the Bishop; the latter strikes his forehead as if reminded by his accomplice that he had overlooked a matter of grave importance; the canon returns to his seat in the rear.

BISHOP CAUCHON—"Joan, when, after you were captured at Compiegne, you were taken to the Castle of Beaurevoir, you threw yourself out of one of the lower towers, did you not?"

JOAN DARC—"It is true."

BISHOP CAUCHON—"What was the reason of your action?"

JOAN DARC—"I heard it said in my prison that I had been sold to the English. I preferred the risk of killing myself to falling into their hands. I endeavored to escape by jumping down from the tower."

THE INQUISITOR—"Did you act by the advice of your voices?"

JOAN DARC—"No. They advised me to the contrary, saying: 'Take courage; God will come to your help; it is cowardly to flee danger.' But my fear of the English was stronger than the advice of my saints."

A JUDGE—"When you jumped out of the tower, had you the intention of killing yourself?"

JOAN DARC—"I wished to escape. When I jumped I commended my soul to God, hoping with His help to escape from the English."

THE INQUISITOR—"After your fall, did you renounce the Lord and His saints?"

JOAN DARC—"I never renounced either God or His saints."

A JUDGE—"Did you, at the moment of jumping down from the tower, invoke your saints?"

JOAN DARC—"Yes, I invoked them. Despite their having advised me against the move, I invoked through them the protection of God for Gaul, my own deliverance, and the salvation of my soul."

THE INQUISITOR—"Since you have been a prisoner in Rouen, have your voices promised you your deliverance?"

JOAN DARC—"Only an instant ago, they said to me: 'Accept everything meekly, bravely undergo your martyrdom. Have courage and patience. You will gain paradise!'"

THE INQUISITOR—"And do you expect to gain paradise?"

JOAN DARC (radiantly)—"I believe it as firmly as if I were there now. God keeps my place."

BISHOP CAUCHON (excitedly, and looking at the judges)—"Here is an answer of much weight. Pride! Presumption!"

JOAN DARC (with a celestial smile)—"Indeed, I hold my belief in paradise as a great treasure. Hence my strength."

The radiancy of Joan's face illumines her beautiful features and imparts to them a divine expression. Her black eyes, shining with the spark of inspiration, are raised heavenward. She looks through the window, contemplates the sky whose azure is for a moment visible through a rift in the clouds, and in the expansion of her celestial ravishment she seems detached from earth. But, alack! a puerile incident speedily recalls the poor prisoner to reality. A little bird flutters cheerily by the window and lightly touches the glass with its wing. At the sight of the little creature, free in space, the heroine, instantaneously yielding to the painful feeling of awakened reality, drops headlong from the height of her radiantly towering hopes. She sighs, lowers her head, and tears roll from her eyes. These rapidly succeeding emotions prevent Joan from observing the joy of the ecclesiastical judges, busily entering on their tablets the last two enormities, which, coupled with so many others, are certain to take her to the pyre. The entries were: "The said Joan voluntarily risked suicide by throwing herself down from the tower of Beaurevoir"; "The said Joan has the sacrilegious audacity of saying and believing that she is as sure of paradise as if she were there now." But the task of the criminal ecclesiastics is not yet complete. The heroine is suddenly drawn from her own painful thoughts by the voice of the Bishop.

BISHOP CAUCHON—"Do you believe you are in mortal sin?"

JOAN DARC—"I refer all my actions to God."

THE INQUISITOR—"You, then, think it useless to confess, even if you are in a state of mortal sin?"

JOAN DARC—"I never have committed a mortal sin, at least not that I know of."

A JUDGE—"What do you know about it?"

JOAN DARC—"My voices would have reproached me for the sin. My saints would have abandoned me. Still, if I could, I would confess. One's conscience can not be too clear."

BISHOP CAUCHON—"And is it not a mortal sin to accept ransom for a man and yet have him executed?"

JOAN DARC (stupefied)—"Who has done that?"

BISHOP CAUCHON—"You!"

JOAN DARC (indignantly)—"Never!"

THE INQUISITOR—"What about Franquet of Arras?"

JOAN DARC (consults her memory for a moment)—"Franquet of Arras was a captain of Burgundian marauders. I took him prisoner in battle. He confessed to being a traitor, a thief and a murderer. His trial consumed fifteen days before the judges of Senlis. I asked mercy for the man, hoping to exchange him for a worthy bourgeois of Paris who was a prisoner of the English. But learning that the bourgeois died in prison, I said to the bailiff of Senlis: 'The prisoner whose exchange I wished to obtain has died. You may, if you think fit, execute justice upon Franquet of Arras, traitor, thief and murderer.'"

A JUDGE—"Did you give money to the one who helped you capture Franquet of Arras?"

JOAN DARC (shrugging her shoulders)—"I am neither minister nor treasurer of France, to order money to be paid out."

BISHOP CAUCHON—"You placed your arms *ex voto* in the basilica of St. Denis. What did you mean by that?"

JOAN DARC (remains silent for an instant, absorbed in painful recollections. Seriously wounded under the walls of Paris, she had upon recovery offered her armor to the Virgin Mary as a pious homage, and did so also through an impulse of indignation, that was provoked by the cowardice of Charles VII, who, after the prodigies of the Maid's victorious campaign, had returned to Touraine to join his mistresses. Vainly had Joan said to him: "Face the English, who almost alone defend the walls of Paris; present yourself bravely at the gates of the town promising to the Parisians oblivion for the past and harmony for the future; it is almost certain that you will thus conquer your capital!" But the royal poltroon had recoiled before the danger connected with such a step. In utter despair, Joan had decided to renounce war, she gave up her armor, and offered it up *ex voto*. Joan can not make such an admission to the priests. Guided by the generosity of her soul and instructed by her sound judgment, she would prefer to die rather than accuse

Charles VII and cover him with ignominy in the eyes of his enemies. She sees France in the royalty. The King's shame would fall indelibly upon the country itself. Her answer is accordingly so framed as to save the honor of Charles VII)—"I was wounded under the walls of Poitiers; I offered my armor at the altar of the Holy Virgin in thankfulness that my wound was not mortal."

THE INQUISITOR (seeming to remember something that he had forgotten)—"Did you, during the time that you were making war in battle harness and man's attire, take the Eucharist?"

The stir among the priests and the silence that falls upon the tribunal indicates the gravity of the question put to the accused.

JOAN DARC—"I partook of communion as often as I could, and not as often as I would have wished."

BISHOP CAUCHON (excitedly)—"Registrars, did you enter that?"

A REGISTRAR—"Yes, monseigneur."

BISHOP CAUCHON—"Whence did you come the last time you went to Compiegne?"

JOAN DARC (shivers at the painful recollection)—"I came from Crespy, in Valois."

BISHOP CAUCHON—"Did your voices order the sally at which you were taken?"

JOAN DARC—"During the last week of the Easter holidays my voices often warned me that I was soon to be betrayed and delivered—but that it was so decreed—not to be surprised, and to accept everything meekly, and that God would come to my aid."

A JUDGE—"Thus your voices, the voices of your saints, told you you would be captured?"

JOAN DARC (sighing)—"Yes, they told me so a long time. I requested my saints to let me die the moment I was taken so as not to prolong my sufferings—"

THE INQUISITOR—"Did your voices tell you exactly the day on which you would be captured?"

JOAN DARC—"No, not exactly; they only announced to me that I was soon to be betrayed and delivered. I said so to the good people of Compiegne on the day of the sally."

A JUDGE—"If your voices had ordered you to deliver battle before Compiegne while warning you that you would be taken prisoner on that day, would you still have obeyed them?"

JOAN DARC—"I would have obeyed with regrets; but I would have obeyed, whatever was to happen."

A JUDGE—"Did you cross the bridge in order to make the sally from Compiegne?"

JOAN DARC (more and more cruelly affected by these remembrances)—"Does that belong to the process?"

BISHOP CAUCHON—"Answer."

JOAN DARC (rapidly in short sentences)—"I crossed the bridge. I attacked with my company the Burgundians of the Sire of Luxembourg. I threw them back twice as far as their own trenches, the third time only half way. The English then came up. They cut off my retreat. Several of my soldiers wished to force me back into Compiegne. But the bridge had been raised. We were betrayed. I was captured." (She shudders.)

BISHOP CAUCHON—"Joan, your interrogatory is closed for to-day. Pray to the Lord that He may enlighten your soul and guide you to the path of eternal salvation. May God help you, and come to your assistance." (He makes the sign of the cross.)

ALL THE OTHER PRIESTS (rising)—"Amen."

BISHOP CAUCHON—"Conduct Joan the Maid back to her prison."

The two beadles approach Joan. Each takes her by an arm; they lead her out of the chapel and deliver her to a platoon of English soldiers, who conduct her back to her dungeon.

CHAPTER IV.

THE TEMPTATION.

Livid, haggard, broken with exhaustion after her final interrogatory, Joan Darc reclines upon the straw of her cell; her male attire is still more dilapidated than when she first appeared before her judges. She is chained by the waist and feet as before. She has wound some rags around the heavy iron rings at her ankles. Their pressure made her flesh sore, and in spots broke it to the quick, creating painful wounds. Besides, one of the wounds received in battle opened anew and added to her physical suffering. But the look of profound distress upon the martial maid's face proceeds from other than these causes. One of the jailers, noticing that the prisoner barely touched the gross food furnished to her, had said that in order to restore her appetite Bishop Cauchon was to send her a dish prepared in his own palace. The following day she partook of a fish that the prelate sent her. Almost immediately after she was seized with convulsive retchings and had fallen into a swoon. The jailers thought she was upon the point of death and ran for a physician. The latter immediately discovered the symptoms of poison and succeeded in recalling her to life, but not to health. Since then the prisoner remained in a languishing state, downcast and weak.

Joan Darc is not alone in her cell. Canon Loyseleur is seated on a stool near the kind of coffin filled with straw on which she lies. Believing herself in danger of death, she has just confessed to Loyseleur, a solemnity at which she opened her soul to him and narrated her whole life. So far from remotely suspecting the infamous treason of the prelate, she drew vague hopes and religious consolation from the tokens of kindness which he seemed to bestow upon her. The canon had frequently visited the prisoner since their first interview. He obtained, said he, with much difficulty permission to leave his cell in order to offer her spiritual consolation. She reported to him what happened at her first and subsequent interrogatories. The canon congratulated her upon having asserted the reality of her apparitions and revelations, and warned her against another snare, a more dangerous one that he claimed to perceive. One of the judges having asked her which of the then two Popes should be obeyed, he advised her that, if further pressed for an answer thereon, and asked whether she would accept absolutely and blindly the opinion of her judges, she should refuse and appeal from them to God alone. A stranger to theological subtleties, Joan Darc placed confidence in Loyseleur's words. The snare thereby spread by the Bishop and his accomplice was extremely adroit.

On this day the canon had gone to Joan's cell under the pretext of fortifying her in her good resolutions, and after having taken Joan's general confession, and bestowed paternal and consoling words upon her, he went to the wicket to call John to let him out. The jailer quickly appeared, grumbled a few words in affected anger, opened the door, hurled the canon out with a great display of force and locked the door after him. Joan was left alone.

In making her general confession to the canon, in narrating to him her whole, life, Joan had yielded not merely to a religious habit, but also to the desire of once more evoking the memories of her whole past existence, and of scrupulously interrogating herself upon all her actions. The threatening present induced the desire. She wished to ascertain with inexorable severity towards herself whether any of her actions were blameworthy. The mere thought of the threatened punishment, to be burned alive, prostrated her mind. The reasons for her terror were various. First of all she shrank before the shame of being publicly dragged to death like a criminal; the atrocious torment of feeling the flames devouring her flesh threw her into further agonies; finally the chaste girl was distracted by the fear of being taken half naked to the pyre. She had questioned the canon several times upon that head, and had learned from him that "heretics, male and female, are taken to death without any other clothing than a shirt, and on their heads a large pasteboard mitre inscribed with the heretic's special crimes." At the thought of appearing in public in an almost nude condition the maid's dignity and modesty revolted. The despair that such thoughts threw her into made her ready to submit to any declaration that her judges might demand of her, if it only could save her from such ignominy. In vain did her voices whisper to her: "Submit bravely to your martyrdom, not the shadow of a wrongful act stains the luster of your life. Yield not to vain shame, the shamefulness of it must fall upon your murderers. Face without a blush the looks of men—glory covers you with a celestial aureola—be strong of heart!"

In these moments of despair, the heroine became again the timid young girl whose intense modesty had caused her even to renounce the sacred joys of wifehood, and who had taken the vow of virginity to her saints. Thus, despite the encouragement of her voices, her strength failed her, especially at the thought of being led to the pyre in a mere shirt. After her recent spell of sickness that, snapping the springs of her energetic and tender nature, slowly undermined her will power, Joan fell with increasing frequency under the dominion of weakness. At intervals her wonted courage and resoluteness resumed the ascendancy. Her voices said to her: "Do not yield to those false priests, who pretend to judge you and are but your butchers. Uphold truth bravely! Pride yourself in having saved France with the aid of heaven. Defy death! They may burn your body, but your fame will live imperishable as your immortal soul, that will radiantly rejoin its Creator! Noble victim of priests' hypocrisy and of the wickedness of man, quit this sad world and enter paradise!"

Such were, after her last interrogatory and the suffering produced by her illness, the spells of resoluteness and faint-heartedness that wrestled with each other and alternately exalted and again cast the heroine down. On this day, however, Joan Darc feels herself so exhausted that she feels certain she will speedily expire in her cell and escape the ordeal of the pyre. Suddenly the noise of approaching steps is heard outside and she recognizes the voice of the Bishop saying to the jailers:

"Open to us the door of Joan's prison; open it to the justice of God!"

The door is opened, and the prelate appears, accompanied by seven of the ecclesiastical judges—William Boucher, Jacob of Tours, Maurice of Quesnay, Nicolas Midi, William Adelin, Gerard Feuillet, and Haiton—and the inquisitor John Lemaitre.

The members of the holy tribunal are accompanied by two registrars. One of these carries a large lighted wax taper, the other a book of parchments and other writing material. The Bishop is clad in his sacerdotal robes, his accomplices wear their priestly or their monastic gowns. They silently range themselves in a semi-circle near the straw couch on which the chained prisoner is lying. The Bishop steps towards her; one of the registrars sits down at the table he has carried in, on which he lays his parchments; the other remains standing near his companion lighting the desk with his candle, whose reddish glamor falls upon the faces of the ecclesiastics, motionless as specters, and, rather than illuminating, imparts a somber aspect to the scene. Surprised at the unexpected visit, the object of which she is ignorant of, Joan Darc rises painfully and casts a frightened and wondering look around her.

BISHOP CAUCHON (in accents of hypocritic compassion)—"These reverend priests, doctors of theology, and myself, have come to visit you in your prison, out of which you are at present unable to move. We come to bring you words of consolation. You have been questioned by the most learned clerks of canonical law. Your answers, I must tell you paternally, have so far borne the stamp of most damnable error, and if you persist in these errors, errors so prejudicial to the salvation of your soul and the safety of your body, we shall see ourselves compelled to give you over to the secular arm."

JOAN DARC (in a feeble voice)—"I feel so ill and so weak, that it seems to me I am about to die. If it must be so by the will of God I request communion before death, and sacred soil for my body after death."

A JUDGE—"Submit yourself to the Church. The more you stand in fear of death, all the more should you mend your ways."

JOAN DARC—"If my body dies in prison, I request of you a sacred sepulchre for it. If you refuse that to me, I shall appeal to God. May His will be done."

BISHOP CAUCHON—"These are grave words. You appeal to God. But between you and God stands His Church."

JOAN DARC—"Is it not all one—God and His Church?"

BISHOP CAUCHON—"Learn, my dear daughter, that there is a *Church triumphant* where God is with His saints, His angels and the saved souls; there is, besides, the *Church militant* composed of our Holy Father the Pope, vicar of God on earth, the cardinals, the prelates, the priests and all good Catholics, the which Church is infallible, in other words, can never err, can never be mistaken, guided as it is by the divine light. That, Joan, is the Church militant. Will you submit to its judgment? Will you, yes or no, acknowledge us as your judges, us, members of the Church militant?"

JOAN DARC (recalls the advice of the canon; there can be no doubt, she thinks, that a snare is being laid for her; her mistrust being in accord with her naïve faith, she answers with all the firmness that her weakness allows)—"I went to the King for the sake of the salvation of France, sent to him by God and His saints. To that Church (making a sublime gesture), to that Church on high, do I submit in all my acts and words!"

BISHOP CAUCHON (with difficulty restraining his joy)—"You will not, then, accept the judgment of the Church militant upon your acts and words?"

JOAN DARC—"I shall submit to this Church if it does not demand the impossible from me."

THE INQUISITOR—"What do you understand by that?"

JOAN DARC—"To deny or repudiate the visions that I have had from God. For nothing in the world shall I deny or repudiate them. I shall not consent to save my life by a falsehood."

BISHOP CAUCHON (in a blandishing voice)—"If the Church militant were to declare those visions and apparitions illusory and diabolical, would you still refuse to submit to its judgment?"

JOAN DARC—"I submit only to God, who has ever inspired me. I neither accept nor shall I accept the judgment of any man, all men being liable to error."

BISHOP CAUCHON (addressing the registrar)—"Write down that answer, registrar; write it down without any omission."

THE REGISTRAR—"Yes, monseigneur."

THE INQUISITOR—"You do not, then, hold yourself subject to the Church militant, that is to say to our Pope, our seigneurs the cardinals, archbishops, bishops and other holy ministers of God?"

JOAN DARC (interrupting him)—"I recognize myself their subject—God being first served."

The admirable answer disconcerts the prelates. The ingenuous and pure soul that they expected to entangle in the perfidious net of their theological subtleties, slipped from them with one stroke of its wings.

BISHOP CAUCHON (is the first to recover, he addresses Joan with severity)—"You answer us like an idolater. You are exposing your body and your soul to a grave peril."

JOAN DARC—"I could not answer otherwise, monseigneur."

A JUDGE (harshly)—"You will then have to die an apostate."

JOAN DARC (with touching pride)—"I received baptism; I am a good Christian; I shall die a Christian."

BISHOP CAUCHON—"Do you desire to receive the body of the Savior?"

JOAN DARC—"Oh, I wish it with all my soul!"

BISHOP CAUCHON—"You will then have to submit to the Church militant."

JOAN DARC—"I serve God to the best of my ability—from Him I expect everything—nothing from the bishops, nothing from the priests, nothing from anybody."

THE INQUISITOR—"If you refuse submission to the holy Roman Catholic and Apostolic Church you will be given up for a heretic, and condemned to be burned."

JOAN DARC (in a high degree of exaltation springing from her convictions and the disgust that the ecclesiastics inspire her)—"Even if the pyre stood ready I would answer no otherwise!"

BISHOP CAUCHON—"Joan, my dear daughter, your stiff-neckedness is execrable. Do you mean to say that if you stood before a council composed of our Holy Father, the cardinals and bishops, and they called upon you to submit to their decision—"

JOAN DARC (interrupting him with pained impatience)—"Neither Pope, nor cardinals, nor bishops will draw from me other statements than those that I have made. Pray have mercy upon a poor creature! I am dying!" (She drops back upon the straw in a swoon.)

BISHOP CAUCHON—"Will you submit to the successor of St. Peter, our Holy Father? Answer categorically."

JOAN DARC (after a long pause and recovering)—"Have me taken to him, I shall ask him for his blessing."

BISHOP CAUCHON—"What you say is insensate. Do you persist in keeping your male attire, a most blameworthy conduct?"

JOAN DARC—"I would put on female clothes to go to church, if I could, in order to receive the body of my Savior. But back in my prison, I shall resume my male attire out of fear of being outraged by your people, as they have tried before now."

THE INQUISITOR—"Once more and for the last time, and be careful: if you persist in your damnable error our holy mother the Church will be forced, despite her infinite mercy, to deliver you over to the secular arm, and it will then be all over with your body and soul."

JOAN DARC—"It would then be all over with your own souls—with the souls of yourselves who will have condemned me unjustly. Reflect upon that."

BISHOP CAUCHON—"Joan, I must charitably declare to you that if you stubbornly persist in your ways, there are torturers near who will put you to the rack.(He points to the door, Joan shivers.) There are torturers near—they are waiting—they will put you to cruel torments, for the sole purpose of drawing less damnable answers from you."

JOAN DARC (yields at first to the terror of the thought of being tortured; the momentary weakness is, however, speedily overcome; she draws superhuman strength from the conviction of her innocence; sits up; casts a withering look upon the prelates and cries in an accent of indomitable resolution)—"Have my limbs torn one from the other! Have my soul leap out of my body! You shall be no further! And if the pain of the torture should draw from my distracted body aught that is contrary to what I have so far said, I take God for my witness, it will be pain alone that will have made me speak contrary to the truth!"[114]

BISHOP CAUCHON—"Joan, your transport singularly aggravates your position."

JOAN DARC—"Listen, Oh, ye priests of Christ; listen, Oh, ye seigneurs of the Church; you are bent upon my death. If in order to make me die, if in order to execute me my clothes are to be taken off, I ask of you but a woman's shirt to march in to the pyre."

BISHOP CAUCHON (affecting astonishment)—"You pretend that you wear a man's shirt and clothes by the command of God; why should you want a woman's shirt to go to death in? This is a singular inconsistency."

JOAN DARC—"Because it is longer."

The infamous ecclesiastics are determined to inflict upon the wretched young woman of hardly nineteen years all the tortures, from the rack to the pyre. A tremor, nevertheless, runs through them at the sublime modesty of the virgin, who requests of her butchers as a supreme act of mercy that she be allowed a woman's shirt to go to death in because such a shirt was longer, because it could better conceal her figure from the public gaze. Bishop Cauchon alone remains unaffected.

BISHOP CAUCHON (harshly addressing his accomplices)—"My very dear brothers, we shall assemble in a room of the tower in order to deliberate upon the torture that should be inflicted upon Joan."

The Bishop and his fellows depart from the cell, followed by the registrars.

CHAPTER V.

THE SENTENCE.

The full ecclesiastical tribunal is assembled in a low, somber and vaulted apartment. The registrar reads to the ecclesiastical judges the last interrogatory, at which they had not all been present. They are to consider whether the accused shall be put to the torture.

BISHOP CAUCHON—"My very dear brothers, you are again assembled in the name of our holy Church."

ALL THE JUDGES—"Amen."

BISHOP CAUCHON—"My very dear brothers, we Peter, Bishop of Beauvais by divine grace do, in view of the stubbornness of the said Joan, and in view of the pestilent heresy that her answers are poisoned with, consult with you, our very dear brothers, whether it is deemed expedient and urgent to submit the said Joan to the torture, to the end of obtaining from her answers and avowals that may save her poor soul from the eternal and her body from the temporal flames. Please give your opinion in the order of precedence."

NICOLAS OF VENDERESSE—"It does not seem to me, at present, opportune to put the said Joan to the torture."

ANDRE MARGUERIE—"I consider the torture superfluous. The answers of the accused are sufficient to condemn her upon. I am against the torture."

WILLIAM ERARD—"It is, indeed, unnecessary to obtain new avowals from the said Joan. Those that she has made call for the chastisement of the temporal arm. Let us not go beyond that."

ROBERT BARBIER—"I share the views of my very dear brother."

DENIS GASTINEL—"I am of the opinion that we should forego the torture. It is useless in the case at bar."

AUBERT MOREL—"I am of the opinion that the torture should be forthwith applied to the said Joan in order to ascertain whether the errors that she persists in are sincere or fraudulent."

THOMAS OF COURCELLES—"I hold that it would be well to put the said Joan to the torture."

NICOLAS OF COUPEQUESNE—"I do not think it expedient to submit Joan to bodily torture. But she should be admonished once more, in order to compel her to submit to the Church militant."

JOHN LEDOUX—"I think so, too. No torture."

ISAMBARD OF LA PIERRE—"That is my opinion."

NICOLAS LOYSELEUR—"I think it is necessary as a medicine to the soul of the said Joan that she be put to the torture.[115] For the rest I shall adhere to the opinion of my very dear brothers. The question must be decided."

WILLIAM HAITON—"I consider the torture useless. I pronounce against its application."

The result of the deliberation is that a majority of the ecclesiastics is against applying the torture to Joan Darc, not so much through a sentiment of humanity as because the admissions made by the accused sufficiently justify her condemnation, as Canon Andre Marguerie naïvely put it. Nevertheless, Bishop Cauchon, who panted for the torture like a wolf at the smell of blood, seems greatly displeased with the evangelical mildness of his very dear brothers in Jesus Christ, who seem so charitably disposed as to think that the burning of Joan Darc would be glory enough to the Church of Rome, without previously lacerating her flesh or cracking her bones. Moreover, these more clement ecclesiastics consider that, weak and ailing as Joan is, the girl may expire under the torture. They aim at a striking death for their victim.

BISHOP CAUCHON (ill disguising his displeasure)—"The majority of our very dear brothers have pronounced against submitting the said Joan to the torture. That means of obtaining her sincere avowals being discarded, I demand that before we now adjourn she be brought hither to the end that she may hear the verdict that is pronounced against her by our very dear brother Maurice, canon of the very reverend chapter of the Cathedral of Rouen."

The ecclesiastical judges bow approval. Nicolas Loyseleur goes out to issue the orders for the carrying in of Joan before the tribunal. He, however, does not resume his seat at the session, fearing to be recognized by the prisoner. The traitor trembles before his victim.

Too feeble to walk, Joan Darc is brought in upon a chair by two jailers with her feet chained. They deposit the chair a few paces before the ecclesiastical judges. Resolved to uphold the truth until death, Joan asks herself what crimes she could have committed. She has maintained the reality of the visions that she had; she has conscientiously submitted all the acts of her life to the judgment of her sovereign master—God. Convinced though she is of the bias and perfidy of the ecclesiastical tribunal, she is still unable to believe her condemnation possible, or rather she racks her mind to fathom its motive. A feverish hue has slightly colored her pale face. She partially rises from her seat, supporting herself on its arms. Her large black eyes are anxiously fixed upon her judges. She waits in the midst of the profound silence that falls upon the assembly at her entrance.

Dressed in his canonical robes, Canon Maurice holds in his hands a parchment on which the sentence that he is about to read is written.

The virgin warrior, defending her country's soil, had proved herself the peer of the most illustrious captains.

The Christian maid had usually kept her sword in its scabbard, and even in the heat of the most stubbornly contested battles never used it against men. She contented herself with guiding her soldiers with it and with her standard. Every day, when at all possible, she knelt in the temple and held communion with the angels. In the letters that she addressed to the foreign captains and the chiefs of the civil factions, she conjured the English in the name of the God of charity, of concord and of justice to abandon a country that they held contrary to right and that they ruled with violence, and she promised to them mercy and peace if they renounced the iniquitous conquest that rapine and massacre had rendered still more odious. When she addressed herself to the Frenchmen in arms against the French she ever reminded them that they were of France, and conjured them to join against the common enemy.

As a woman, Joan Darc ever gave the example of the most generous and most angelic virtues. Her chastity inspired her with sublime words that will remain the admiration of the centuries.

How could the ecclesiastical judges formulate against the warrior, the Christian and the virgin a single accusation that does not cause common judgment to revolt? an accusation that is not a heinous outrage, a despicable insult, a sacrilegious challenge cast at all that ever has been and ever will be the object of man's admiration?

These infamous ecclesiastics, these bishops sold to the English, ransacked the canons of the Church and the decretals of the Inquisition, and with the aid of these found twelve capital charges against the warrior, the Christian and the virgin.

Twelve capital charges! And what is still more abominable, in the eyes of the orthodox judges, the charges are well founded and legitimate. They are the "complete, absolute, irrevocable and infallible" expression of the Roman Church. They flow in point of right, from the legal application of the jurisdiction of a church that is infallible, eternal and divine—one as God; infallible as God; divine as God; eternal as God!—according to the claims of the ecclesiastics!

The sentence of Joan is supposed to be the summary of the life of the Maid, now present before her judges, and though broken and feverish, yet with a soul full of faith and of energy.

The session is re-opened.

BISHOP CAUCHON (addressing the accused in a grave voice)—"Joan, our very dear brother Maurice will read to you the sentence that has been pronounced upon you." (The Bishop devoutly crosses himself.)

ALL THE JUDGES (crossing themselves)—"Amen."

CANON MAURICE (reading in a sepulchral and threatening voice)—"'First: You said, Joan, that at thirteen years you had revelations and apparitions of angels and saints to whom you give the name of St. Michael, of St. Marguerite and of St. Catherine. You said you frequently saw them with the eyes of your body. You said that you frequently conversed with them.

"'Upon this point, and considering the aim and final object of these revelations and apparitions, the nature of the matters revealed, and the quality of your person, the Church pronounces your revelations and visions to be fraudulent, seductive, pernicious, and proceeding from the evil spirit of the devil.'"

Canon Maurice stops for a moment in order that the gravity of the first charge be properly weighed and appreciated by Joan Darc. But the words that she has just heard carry her back to the days of her childhood, days of peace that flowed in the midst of the sweet enjoyments of her family. She forgets the present and becomes absorbed in the recollection of her infancy, a recollection at once sweet and bitter to her.

CANON MAURICE (proceeds to read)—"'Secondly: Joan, you said that your King, having recognized you by your signs as truly sent by God, gave you men of arms to do battle with. You said that St. Marguerite and St. Catherine accompanied you to Chinon and other places, where they guided you with their advice.

"'The Church pronounces this declaration mendacious and derogatory to the dignity of the saints and the angels.

"'Thirdly: Joan, you said that you recognized the angels and the saints by the advice that they gave you. You said that you believed the apparitions to be good, and that you believe that as firmly as you do in the faith of our Lord Jesus Christ. This is an outrage to the Divinity.

"'The Church declares that those are not determining signs to recognize the saints by; that your belief is temerarious, your claim braggard, and that you err in the faith. You are outside of the pale of the communion of the faithful.'"

Recalled from her revery, Joan Darc listens to this new accusation without understanding it. In what did she brag? In what was she temerarious? In what did she lie? She recognized the saints by the wisdom of their counsel when they said to her: "Joan, be pious, behave as a wise girl; heaven will support you in driving the foreigners from Gaul." The promise of her saints is verified. She has won brilliant victories over the enemy of France. Where is the lie, the temerariousness, the bragging?

CANON MAURICE (reads)—"'Fourthly: Joan, you said you were endowed with the faculty of knowing certain things that lay in the future, and that you recognized your King without ever having seen him before.

"'The Church pronounces you convicted of presumption, arrogance and witchcraft.'"

Without concerning herself about the imputation of witchcraft, that seems to her senseless, Joan Darc sighs at the recollection of her first interview at Chinon with "the gentle Dauphin of France," when, drawn towards him out of commiseration for his misfortunes and devoted to the royalty, Charles VII received her with a miserable buffoonery, thereupon imposed upon her, upon so chaste a girl, an infamous examination, and then sent her to a council of ecclesiastics assembled in Poitiers, who, struck by the sincerity of her responses, declared her divinely inspired. And, now, here is another set of priests, speaking in the name of the same Church, and treating her as a witch!

CANON MAURICE (reads)—"'Fifthly: Joan, you said that by the advice of God you wore and continue to wear male attire—a short jacket, hose fastened with hooks, cap, and hair cut short down to your ears—preserving nothing that denotes your sex except what nature itself betrays. Before being taken prisoner, you frequently partook of the holy Eucharist in manly costume; and despite all our efforts to induce you to renounce such a costume, you obstinately persevere in keeping it, pretending to act by the advice of God.

"'The Church pronounces you upon that head a blasphemer of God, a contemner of its sacraments, a transgressor of divine law, of Holy Writ and of canonical sanction. The Church pronounces you astray and errant in the faith, and idolatrous after the fashion of the gentiles.'"

With her mind upon the chaste motives that had decided her to assume male attire so long as her divine mission compelled her to live in camps near soldiers; remembering also with what zeal priests had admitted her to communion when, clad in her martial outfit, she came to thank God for having granted her victory, Joan Darc asks herself by what mental aberration another set of priests of Christ can see in her a blasphemer and an idolatress after the fashion of the gentiles!

CANON MAURICE (reads)—"'Sixthly: Joan, you said that often you caused the divine names of Jesus and Mary to be placed at the head of the letters, which you addressed to captains and others, and that afterwards, at the bottom of the said letters, you drew the revered sign of the cross. In those homicidal letters, you boasted that you would cause the death of those who should dare resist your insolent orders. You affirmed that you spoke and acted thus by divine inspiration and suggestion.

"'The Church pronounces you a traitor, mendacious, cruel, desirous of shedding human blood, seditious, a provoker of tyranny and a blasphemer of God in His holy commandments and revelations.'"

At this stupid and iniquitous accusation, Joan Darc is unable to resist a tremor of indignation. They accuse her of cruelty, of causing the shedding of human blood—her who on the very day of her triumphal entry into Orleans, seeing an English prisoner fall under the blows of a brutal mercenary, was so moved with pity that she precipitated herself from her horse and knelt down beside the wounded soldier, whose head she raised, and for whom she implored help! She, desirous of the effusion of human blood! She who on many occasions saved English prisoners from massacre and set them free! She who, under the invocation of Christ, wrote so many letters making ardent pleas for peace! She who dictated the touching missive to the Duke of Burgundy imploring him to put an end to the disasters of civil war! She who ever marched into battle, confronting death with no weapon in her hand other than her banner of white satin! She whose own blood ran on the field of battle and who never shed the blood of any!

CANON MAURICE (reads)—"'Seventhly: Joan, you said that, as a result of your revelations, you left the paternal roof at the age of seventeen years, against the will of your parents, who were plunged by your departure into a sorrow that verged upon distraction; that you then went to a captain named Robert of Baudricourt, who had you escorted to Chinon to your King, to whom you said that you came in the name of God to drive away the English and restore him his crown.

"'The Church pronounces you impious towards your parents; a transgressor of the commandment of God—"Thou shalt honor thy father and mother;" a blasphemer of the Lord; erring in your faith; and the maker of presumptuous and temerarious promises in defiance of our mother the Church.'"

This accusation is as unjust as the preceding ones. What heartrending agonies did not Joan undergo when, beset by her voices that daily said to her:

"March to the deliverance of France!" she felt compelled to resign herself to the idea of leaving her dearly beloved and revered parents! How many times, overcoming the intoxication of her victories, has she not felt and declared: "I would prefer to be sewing and spinning near my dear mother!" And when, become the arbiter of the destiny of France, she received a letter from her father who whelmed her with blessings and pardoned her departure, did she not cry out, less delighted at her triumphs than at the paternal clemency, "My father has pardoned me!" And yet, despite the saintly absolution, these ecclesiastics accuse her of trampling under foot the commandments of God!

CANON MAURICE (reads)—"'Eighthly: Joan, you said that you jumped down out of the tower of the Castle of Beaurevoir because you preferred death to falling into the hands of the English; and that, despite the advice of the archangel St. Michael and your saints, who ordered you not to attempt to escape or kill yourself, you persevered in your project.

"'The Church pronounces you guilty of yielding to despair, of having contemplated homicide upon yourself, and of having criminally interpreted the law of human freedom of action.'"

Joan Darc smiles disdainfully at hearing these ecclesiastics condemn her for having endeavored to escape her enemies who sold her for ten thousand gold sous to the English.

CANON MAURICE (reads)—"'Ninthly: Joan, you said your saints promised paradise to you if you preserved your virginity and devoted yourself to God, and that you were as certain of paradise as if you were now in the enjoyment of the bliss of the blessed. You said you did not consider yourself in mortal sin because you ever heard the voice of your saints.

"'The Church pronounces you presumptuous and headstrong in assertions that are mendacious and pernicious, and that exhale a pestilential odor.'"

Joan raises to the vaulted roof of the apartment her face beaming with faith and hope, and she hears her voices whisper to her: "Courage, holy daughter, what need you care for the vain words of these men? God has adjudged you worthy of His paradise."

CANON MAURICE (reads)—"'Tenthly: Joan, you said that the archangel St. Michael and your saints, speaking to you in the language of Gaul, informed you that they were enemies of the English and friends of your King.

"'The Church pronounces you superstitious, a sorceress, a blasphemer of the archangel St. Michael and of Saints Marguerite and Catherine, and a contemner of love for your neighbor.

"'Eleventhly: Joan, you said that if the evil spirit had appeared under the form of St. Michael you would have been able to discover and discern the fact.

"'The Church pronounces you idolatrous, an invoker of devils and guilty of illicit judgment.'"

Joan Darc believes she is dreaming when she hears the accusation of sorcery and demoniacal invocations. A sorceress because she affirmed she saw what she did see! A sorceress because she affirmed she heard what she did hear! A sorceress and invoker of demons because those visions appeared before her, visions that she neither invoked nor desired, and that, frightening her at first, she prayed God to keep away from her!

CANON MAURICE (reads)—"'Twelfthly: Joan, you said that if the Church would demand from you an admission contrary to the inspirations that you pretend to have received from God, you would absolutely refuse obedience, and that in all such matters you do recognize neither the judgment of the Church nor of any man on earth. You said the answer proceeded not from yourself but from God, and you persisted, although frequently reminded of the article of faith, *Unam Ecclesiam Catholicam*, and although it was proven to you that every Catholic must submit his actions and words to the Church militant, represented by the Pope and his ministers.

"'The Church pronounces you a schismatic, an enemy of its unity and authority. It pronounces you, besides, stiff-necked in the errors of your apostate faith.—Amen!'"

ALL THE JUDGES (in chorus, and crossing themselves)—"Amen!"

If in her loyalty, in the habitual meekness of her spirit Joan Darc admitted some of the accusations against her, she would bow before the judgment of these ecclesiastics. But after hearing the charges, the Maid remains all the more convinced of their iniquity, and resolves more strongly than ever to spurn such judges and to appeal from them to God.

The reading of the indictment being ended, Bishop Peter Cauchon approaches the Maid's seat.

BISHOP CAUCHON—"And now, Joan, you know what terrible accusations weigh upon you. The trial is hereby ended. It is now time to reflect well upon what you have heard. If after having been so often admonished by me, as well as by my other very dear brothers, the vicar of the Inquisition and other learned prelates, you should, alack! in contumely of God, in defiance of the faith and the law of our Lord Jesus Christ, and in contempt of the safety and security of Catholic conscience, still persist in your errors; should you persist in standing out as an object of horrible scandal, of infectious and disgusting pestilence, it will be, dear daughter, a great injury to your soul and your body. In the name of your soul that is imperishable, but that may be damned, in the name of your perishable body, I exhort you once more and for the last time, to re-enter the bosom of our sacred mother the Roman Catholic and Apostolic Church, and to submit yourself to her judgment. If not, and I charitably warn you now a last time, your soul will be damned, damned to all eternity and delivered to Satan, and your body will be destroyed by fire—a thing that with my joined hands (he prostrates and crosses himself, and clasps his hands) I fervently pray our Lord to preserve you from."

JOAN DARC (makes a superhuman effort to rise and keep her feet; she succeeds by steadying her chained and shaking limbs against her seat. She then raises her right hand and cries in a firm voice and an accent of profound and heroic conviction)—"I take heaven for my witness! I shall be condemned, I shall see the fagots, the executioner ready to set them on fire; and yet I shall unto death repeat: Yes, I have said the truth. Yes, God has inspired me. Yes, from Him I expect everything, nothing from anybody else. Yes, God is my sole judge, my sole master."

Exhausted by this last effort, Joan Darc falls back upon her seat in the midst of profound silence. The ecclesiastics gather in a group with Bishop Cauchon in the center. They consult in a low voice. The prelate then approaches Joan Darc.

BISHOP CAUCHON (in a ringing voice and a gesture of malediction)—"The sentence is pronounced: We, Peter, Bishop of Beauvais by the grace of God, pronounce you a blasphemer and sacrilegious woman, an invoker of demons, an apostate and a heretic! We smite you with the sentence of the major and minor excommunication; we pronounce you forever cut off from the body of our holy mother the Church; and we leave you to the secular arm which will to-morrow burn your body and cast your ashes to the wind! Amen."

ALL THE ECCLESIASTICAL JUDGES (in chorus and making the sign of the cross)—"Amen."

JOAN DARC (sublimely inspired)—"That is your judgment. I confidently await the judgment of God!"

The jailers carry the prisoner back to her cell.

CHAPTER VI.

PHYSICAL COLLAPSE.

On the 24th of May, 1431, a great mass of people is crowding at about eight in the morning and under a brilliant springtide sun towards the cemetery of St. Audoin at Rouen. A low wall surrounds the place of burial. Within, and near the entrance of the cemetery, there rises on this morning a high scaffold with a wide platform on which a number of seats decked with violet coverings are placed. English soldiers, casqued and cuirassed, and lance in hand, form a cordon that keeps the crowd at a distance. All seem to expect a great event.

The people are waiting to see Joan Darc, who is to mount the scaffold, kneel down at the feet of Bishop Cauchon and with her arms crossed on her breast abjure her past errors, deny her visions and renounce her revelations, her faith, her glory and her patriotism; in short, to make her humble, contrite and repentful submission to the sovereign judgment of the Bishop and the ecclesiastics.

Only yesterday, despite the feebleness of her body, so proud and so resolute in her answers to her accusers, Joan had cried: "Let the fagots be there, let the executioner stand ready, and yet I shall repeat unto death: Yes, God has inspired me. Yes, God is my sole judge, my sole master!"

What inconceivable change has taken place in this soul, once so firm and so full of conviction? Human weakness!

After the sentence pronounced upon her the day before by Bishop Cauchon, the heroine was transported back to her cell. The feverish exaltation that upheld her in the presence of her judges was followed by a reaction of profound dejection. Still she was resigned to suffer death. Under these circumstances, and pretending to have obtained from the captain of the tower permission to administer to her the last consolations, Canon Loyseleur visited Joan. She received the priest with thankful joy. Instructed by Joan on the last events, the canon broke down in tears, moans and laments, and dwelled with affected horror upon the frightful details of Joan's pending execution—shocking details: Joan was to be taken in a shirt, not a woman's shirt as she had begged for on the ground of its being longer, but in a man's shirt; nor was that all. The English chiefs had decided that before delivering Joan to the flames, she was to be stripped wholly naked, and fastened in that state to the stake.

From the moment Joan learned that she was to be taken to the pyre in a man's shirt, and was then to be bound by the executioner in full view wholly naked to the stake, Joan's mind began to wander. She collected whatever strength was left her, and although chained by the feet, hands and waist, she stood upon her straw bed and flinging herself forward, violently struck her head twice against the wall of the dungeon in a frantic attempt to break her skull and die. But the impact of the poor creature, weak, exhausted and fainting as she was, was not strong enough to produce mortal, or even dangerous results. She fell down backward upon her couch where the canon charitably held her down. He sobbed; he implored his dear daughter in Christ not to yield to blind despair. True enough, it was an abominable ordeal for so pure a soul, so chaste a body, to be exposed at first half naked, and then wholly so, absolutely naked, to the lascivious looks and obscene jeers of the soldiery and mob! No doubt the ordeal would last an hour, perhaps longer; the English would take a delight in prolonging the period of the Maid's nudity. But, alack! how was the abomination to be avoided! There was only one way, and no doubtful one, a sure way of escaping, not the shame only, but even the pyre, aye, of escaping from the hands of the English. Thanks to that means, Joan might regain her freedom, return to her family at Domremy, and enjoy a restoring rest after so many trials. And then, when she should have recovered her health, the martial maid could again don her armor, call her valiant followers to arms, and marching at their head, complete her work of driving the English out of France.

Joan Darc believed herself in a dream as she listened to the canon. His age, his tears, his moaning, the constant interest that he had taken in her since she was brought to her present dungeon—everything contributed to remove from her spirit all thought of suspicion. In a semi-stupor she questioned the canon on the means that he had in mind, from which he promised such certain deliverance.

The tempter pursued his dark scheme with infernal skill. He began by asking the heroine whether in her soul and conscience she did not look upon her judges as monsters of iniquity? She readily assented. Could she, consequently, feel herself bound by any promises that she might make to the butchers, she a prisoner, under duress? She, sold for the price of gold? No, concluded the canon, a promise made to these butchers for the purpose of escaping abominable ignominy and the horrors of burning, could never be binding upon an innocent victim. Such engagements were null.

Joan asked what the promises would be. The canon answered that it was merely a matter of renouncing *in appearance* the errors that the tribunal charged her with; in short, to submit *in appearance* to the judgment of the Church.

Joan's conscience revolted at the lie; to renounce the truth was to renounce God.

"Yes, but with your lips, with your lips only, and not with your heart!" pursued the tempter. "It is simply yielding to force; it is speaking for a moment the language of the butchers, a fallacious and perfidious language, true enough; but, thanks to such a legitimate fraud, to escape from them, thus to preserve His elect to God, and to France her liberator! It is simply a mouth-renunciation, while the soul will continue to glorify all the acts inspired by heaven."

"But to promise to abjure under condition of being set free, is to bind oneself to abjure," answered Joan, disconcerted by the canon's sophism.

"And what would that matter?" argued the tempter. "What would it matter to make even a public abjuration, even kneeling at the Bishop's feet, saying to him with the lips: 'My apparitions and my visions were illusions; I have sinned in assuming man's habits; I have sinned in waging war; I have sinned in refusing to submit to the judgment of the Church. I now make my submission and regret my sins.' What would such vain words matter? Did they proceed from the interior tribunal, the sacred refuge of truth with the oppressed? Would perchance, the Lord, who reads our secret thoughts, fail to read in your soul, at the very moment when you would be pretending to abjure: 'My God, You before whom nothing is hidden, I internally glorify these visions and apparitions, the revered signs of Your omnipotence! I proclaim You my only judge, Oh, my divine Master! And in Your infinite mercy You will pardon me these few idle words, drawn from me by the desire of continuing to be the instrument of Your supreme will, and by the desire of, with Your aid, driving the stranger from the sacred soil of the fatherland.' Would God fail to read these sentiments?"

Joan succumbed before the infernal tempter. Vainly did she hear her voices warn her:

"To deny the truth is to deny God! You are about to lie in the face of heaven and of men, more out of a chaste shame than out of fear to burn. You are about to lie in the hope of regaining your freedom to finish your divine mission. Such a fraud is cowardly and criminal."

But weakened by her sufferings, exhausted in the physical and mental struggle that she had undergone, above all frightened out of her wits at the thought of her virginal body being exposed naked by the executioner to the eyes of men, and finally tempted by the prospect of freedom, of again seeing her family and perchance achieving her work of liberation, Joan shut her ears to the inflexible voice of her honor, of her faith, of her conscience, and promised Canon Loyseleur to make a public abjuration and submission to the Church, under the condition of a pledge from the Bishop that she would be set at liberty immediately after her abjuration. The canon charitably offered his services to the prisoner; he expressed his certainty of successfully conducting the negotiation, and of being able to overcome the resistance of the savage captain of the tower and secure permission to call upon the Bishop without delay.

As may be believed, Loyseleur readily obtained the permission. Towards midnight he returned with the institutor of the process and a physician. The latter induced the captive to take a mixture that was to serve at once as a tonic and a soporific. The mixture would enable her to sleep restfully until morning, and would give her strength for the expiatory ceremony. Joan Darc submitted to everything, saying to herself: "I shall be free to-morrow, and shall have escaped an ignominy that is worse than death."

The scaffold raised within the precincts of the cemetery of the Abbey of St. Audoin is the immediate result of Canon Loyseleur's machinations in Joan's cell. On the scaffold's spacious platform Joan is to appear, surrounded by the ecclesiastics, and make a public abjuration.

The impatient crowd awaits the arrival of the cortege. More than half a century under the yoke of English rule, most of the people of Rouen are of the Burgundian party, and see in Joan Darc only an enemy. Nevertheless, the astounding renown of the martial maid, her youth, her beauty, her misfortune, her glory, awaken a profound sentiment of pity for her among all, and the feeling is strongest among those who have remained French at heart and are of the Armagnac party. The purpose of Joan's public and solemn appearance is still unknown to the mass. Some say that a public exposure is to precede the death penalty, to which she is doubtlessly condemned; others, ignorant of the course of the trial, believe she is to be publicly interrogated. William Poole, the Earl of Warwick, and other English captains and prominent personages are grouped in a reserved space inside the cemetery and near the scaffold.

Presently a distant and increasing noise announces the approach of the train. The crowd presses and becomes more compact outside the cemetery. The procession draws near, escorted by English archers. At its head march the Cardinal of Winchester in the Roman purple, and the Bishop of Beauvais with a gold mitre on his head, a gold crosier in his hand and over his shoulders the chasuble of violet silk, resplendent in embroidery. Behind them and in his monk's frock comes the inquisitor John Lemaitre, together with Peter of Estivet, the official institutor of the process, William Erard and two registrars, carrying parchments and writing portfolios.

A few steps behind them, and sustained by two penitents whose grey robes, covering them from head to foot, are pierced with two holes at the elevation of their eyes, Joan advances slowly. Her weakness is extreme, and although her eyes are wide open she does not seem to be wholly awake; she still seems under the effect of the soporific and tonic of the night before. She seems to look without seeing, and to hear with indifference the hisses of the mob that, incited by the example of the English soldiers, makes hostile demonstrations against the victim. On Joan's head is a high mitre of black pasteboard which bears in large letters the following words: "Heretic," "Idolater," "Apostate." A long robe of coarse black wool envelops her from the neck down to her bare feet. She halts for a moment before the scaffold, while the Cardinal, the Bishop and other prelates take their seats upon it. At a signal from one of the registrars, the two penitents, holding Joan under the arms, help her to ascend the stairs of the scaffold. The sky is this day of an admirable clearness; the sun shines brilliantly; the pleasant warmth of its rays penetrates and gradually warms Joan Darc, who still shivers from the dampness of the subterraneous dungeon in which she has so long lain buried night and day. She inhales the bracing and pure air with delight, and in full draughts. The atmosphere of her cell was so heavy, so fetid! She seems to revive; her chilled and clogged blood courses anew with the delight of life; she experiences an indescribable sense of happiness at the contemplation of that azure sky bathed in light, and at the sight of the green grass of the cemetery, studded here and there with spring flowers. At a little distance stands a clump of trees, near the abbey. The birds chirp in their foliage, the insects hum—everything seems to sing and express delight on that sweet May morning. The sight of nature that Joan has so long been deprived of—she who was from early infancy accustomed to live on the meadows and in the woods—transports her into a sort of ecstasy. She forgets her sufferings, her martyrdom, her sentence and even the abjuration that she is about to pronounce. If her thoughts at all fall upon these topics, the only effect is the pleasurable reminder that she is soon to be free. Oh, free! to be free! To see her village again! the oak forest, the Fountain of the Fairies, the smiling and shady banks of the Meuse! To see again her family, her friends, and, renouncing the bitter illusions of glory, escaping the royal ingratitude, the hypocrisy, the hatred and the envy of men, quietly spend her days in Domremy at her rustic labors as in the happy days of yore! And that, all that at the price of a few words pronounced before her butcher-judges, those monsters of iniquity! Oh, at this moment of physical exaltation Joan would sign her abjuration with her own blood. Her heart-beats, pulsating with hope, smother within her the austere voices of her honor and her faith. In vain do these whisper to her: "Be not faint-hearted! Bravely uphold the truth in the teeth of those false priests, and you will be delivered from your trials, not for a day, but for all eternity!" These voices are not now listened to; her physical delight is too vast. Suddenly she is recalled to her condition by the voice of Bishop Cauchon who severely says to her:

"Joan, down on your knees; bow your head!"

Joan Darc kneels down without removing her eyes from the beautiful blue of the sky, from the radiant light of the sun from which she seeks to draw the strength necessary to persevere in her resolution of abjuring. A profound silence falls upon the crowd, the front ranks of which can hear the words uttered on the scaffold, and Bishop Cauchon, crossing himself, proceeds:

"My very dear brothers, the Lord said it to his apostle St. John, the palm tree cannot of itself produce fruit if it does not live. Thus, my very dear brothers, you must persevere in the true life of our holy mother the Roman Catholic and Apostolic Church, which our Lord Jesus Christ built with his right hand. But, alack! there are perverse souls, abominable and idolatrous (he points at Joan Darc) filled with heretical crimes, who rise with an audacity that is truly infernal against the unity of our holy Church, to the great scandal and to the painful horror of all good believers. (To Joan Darc with a menacing voice:) There you are now upon a scaffold, in the face of heaven and of men. Is the light to enter at last your haughty and diabolical soul? Will you at last submit in all humbleness your words and acts to the Church militant, the enormities of your acts! your monstrous words! according to the infallible judgment of the priests of the Lord? Reflect and answer! If not, the Church will abandon you to the secular arm and your body will go up in the flames of the pyre."

These words produce a deep commotion among the crowd. The majority of those present are hostile to Joan Darc. A small number feel sincere pity for her. These various sentiments find expression in cries, imprecations and charitable utterances:

"She has not yet been condemned, the witch! Death to the abominable idolater!"

"A door of safety is being held open to her. Death to the heretic!"

"By St. George! Upon the word of an English archer, I shall set the Bishop's house on fire if the strumpet is not brought to the pyre at once!"

"Mercy will be extended to her! And yet with her sorceries she has exterminated our invincible army!"

"Her partisans want to save her!"

"I hope they may succeed! Poor girl! She has suffered so much! Mercy for her!"

"How pale and thin she is! She looks like a ghost! Take pity upon the poor creature!"

"She fought for France. And after all, we are French!"

"Speak not so loud, my friend, the English soldiers may overhear you!"

"Jesus! My God! To burn her! Her who was so brave and so pious! It would be an act of barbarism!"

"Is it her fault that God inspired her?"

"If saints appeared before her, and spoke to her, all the greater the honor!"

"How can a bishop of the good God dare to pronounce her a sorceress!"

"Death! Death to the witch!"

"Death! Death to the she-devil!"

"To the pyre with the strumpet of the Armagnacs!"

At these ferocious cries and infamous insults Joan Darc's terror redoubles. The ignominy that awaits her if she does not abjure rises before her. To abjure means to escape mortal shame; to abjure means to regain freedom! Joan Darc resigns herself. Still her loyalty and conscience revolt at that supreme moment, and instead of completely renouncing her errors, she mutters on her knees: "I have sincerely stated all my actions to my judges; I believed I acted under the command of God. I do not wish to accuse either my God or anybody. If I have sinned I alone am guilty. I rely upon God. I implore His mercy."

"Subterfuges!" cried Bishop Cauchon. "Subterfuges! Yes, or no; do you consider true what the priests, your only judges in matters of faith, declare concerning your actions and words—words and acts that have been pronounced fallacious, homicidal, sacrilegious, idolatrous, heretical and diabolical? Answer! (Joan is silent) I call upon you a second time to answer! (Joan is still silent) I ask you a third time to answer! You are silent? You are an abominable criminal!"

Yes, the heroine remains silent, racked by a supreme internal struggle. "Abjure!" whispered to her the instinct of self-preservation. "Do not abjure! Do not lie! Courage! Courage!" cries her conscience; "maintain the truth unto shame and death!" The wretched girl wrings her hands, and remains silent, a prey to distracting agonies.

"Alack!" exclaims Bishop Cauchon, addressing the people. "My very dear brothers! You see the stiff-neckedness of this unhappy woman! She spurns her tender mother the Church, that extends her arms to her with love and pardon! Alack! Alack! The evil spirit has taken a firm hold of her who might now have been Joan. Her, whose body shall have to be delivered to the burning flames of the pyre! Her, whose ashes will be cast to the winds! Her, who, deprived of the holy Eucharist at the moment of death, and loaded down with the decree of excommunication, is about to be cast into the bottom of hell for all eternity! Alack! Alack! Joan, you willed it so. We believed in your repentance, we consented not to deliver you to the secular arm. But you persist in your heresy. Then listen to your sentence!"

While the Bishop is recalling the formula of the sentence several English soldiers brandish their lances and cry: "Let an end be made of this!"

"Throw the witch quickly into the fire!"

"Death to the magician!"

At the same time other voices from the crowd cry:

"Poor, brave girl! Mercy for her!"

"Lord God! How can she deny her visions! Mercy! Mercy!"

"It would be a lie and cowardice on her part! Courage! Courage!"

Bishop Cauchon rises, terrible, and with his hands extended to heaven makes ready to utter the final curse upon the accused. "Joan!" he cries, "listen to your sentence. In the name of the Church, we, Peter, Bishop of Beauvais by the mercy of God, declare you—"

Joan Darc interrupts the approaching imprecation with a shriek of terror, clasps her hands, and collapses upon the scaffold, crying: "Mercy! Mercy!"

"Do you submit yourself to the judgment of the Church?" again asks Bishop Cauchon.

Livid and her teeth chattering with terror, Joan Darc answers: "Yes, I submit myself!"

"Do you renounce your apparitions and visions as false, sacrilegious, and diabolical?" the Bishop asks.

Wholly broken down, and in a gasping voice, Joan makes answer: "Yes—yes—I renounce them—seeing the priests consider them wicked things. I submit to their opinion—I shall submit to everything that the Church may order—Mercy! Have pity upon me!" and cowering upon herself, she hides her face in her hands amidst convulsive sobs.

"Oh, my very dear brothers!" exclaims Bishop Cauchon with an affectation of charity. "What a beautiful day! What a holy day! What a glorious day! that on which the Church in her maternal joy opens her arms to one of her children, repentful after having long wandered from the fold! Joan, your submission saves your body and your soul! Repeat after me the formula of abjuration." The Bishop beckons to one of the registrars, who brings to him a parchment containing the formula of abjuration.

Violent outcries break out from the crowd. The English soldiers and the people of the Burgundian party feel irritated at the prospect of the Maid's escaping death, and break out into imprecations against the judges. They charge the Bishop and the Cardinal with treason and threaten to burn down their houses. The English captains share the indignation of their men. One of the former, the Earl of Warwick, steps out of the group in which he stands, rushes up the stairs of the scaffold, and approaching the prelate says to him angrily, in a low voice: "Bishop, Bishop, is that what you promised us?" "Be patient!" answers the prelate, also in a low voice; "I shall keep my promise; but calm your men; they are quite capable of massacring us!"

Sufficiently acquainted with Peter Cauchon to know he can trust him, the Earl of Warwick again descends from the platform, joins his companions in arms, and communicates the Bishop's answer to them. The latter hasten to distribute themselves among the ranks of the soldiers, whose anger they appease with assurances that the witch will be burned despite her abjuration. But while one part of the mob is enraged at the Maid's abjuration and the Bishop's pardon, another, consisting of the people who pity Joan, is thrown into consternation. This feeling soon makes way for indignation. She denies her visions; then they were false pretences; she lied when she claimed to be sent by God. And if her visions were true, she is now disgracing herself by a shameful act of cowardice. Coward or liar—such is the judgment they now pass upon Joan Darc. The infernal ecclesiastical plot is skilfully hatched; through it the sympathy once felt for the heroine is extinguished in the hearts of her partisans themselves. On her knees upon the scaffold, cowering down, and her face covered by her hands, Joan Darc seems a stranger to what passes around her. Overcome by so many conflicting emotions, her mind again begins to wander, she seems to have but one fixed idea—to escape the disgrace of the stake.

Silence being finally restored, Peter Cauchon rises with the parchment in his hands and says: "Joan, you shall now repeat with your heart and your lips, the following formula of abjuration, in the measure that I pronounce it. Listen!" and he proceeds to read in a voice that is heard by the remotest ranks of the pressing crowd: "'Any person who has erred in the Catholic faith, and who thereafter by the grace of God has returned to the light of truth and to the bosom of our holy mother the Church, must be careful not to allow himself to be provoked by the evil spirit into a relapse. For this reason, I, Joan, commonly named the Maid, a miserable sinner, recognizing that I was fettered by the chains of error, and wishing to return to the bosom of our holy mother the Roman Catholic and Apostolic Church, I, Joan, to the end of proving that I have returned to my tender mother, not in false appearance, but with my heart, do hereby confess, first, that I gravely sinned by falsely causing others to believe that I had apparitions and revelations of God in the forms of St. Marguerite and St. Catherine and of St. Michael the archangel.'"

Turning to Joan, the Bishop asks: "Do you confess having wickedly sinned in that, and of having been impious and sacrilegious?"

"I confess it!" comes from Joan Darc in a broken voice.

An outburst of cries from the indignant mob greets the confession of the penitent. Those now most furious are the ones who were before moved with tender pity for her.

"So, then, you lied!"

"You imposed upon the poor people, miserable hypocrite!"

"And I, who felt pity for her!"

"The Church is too indulgent!"

"Think of accepting the penitence of so infamous a cheat!"

"Upon my word, comrades, she is quite capable of being possessed of the devil as the English claimed! The strumpet and liar!"

"And yet her victories were none the less brilliant for all that!"

"Aye! through witchcraft! Are you going to show pity for the liar?"

"Fear of the fagot makes one admit many a thing!"

"Then she is a coward! She has not the courage to uphold the truth in the face of death! What faint-heartedness!"

Silence is restored only by degrees. Joan Darc hears the frightful accusations hurled at her. To return to her first declarations would be an admission of fear. Her mind wanders again.

Continuing to read from the formula of abjuration, Bishop Cauchon says: "'Secondly, I, Joan, confess to have grievously sinned by seducing people with superstitious divinations, by blaspheming the angels and the saints, and by despising the divine law of Holy Writ and the canonical laws.'" Addressing Joan the Bishop asks: "Do you confess it?'

"I confess it!" murmurs Joan.

Bishop Cauchon proceeds to read: "'Thirdly, I, Joan confess having grievously sinned by wearing a dissolute garb, deformed and dishonest, in violation of decency and nature; and by wearing my hair cut round, after the fashion of men, and contrary to modesty'—Do you confess that sin?"

"I confess it!"

"'Fourthly, I, Joan, confess having grievously sinned by boastfully carrying armor of war, and by cruelly desiring the shedding of human blood.'—Do you confess it?"

Joan Darc wrings her hands and exclaims: "My God! Can I affirm such things?"

"What! You hesitate!" exclaims Bishop Cauchon, and he adds, addressing her in a low voice: "Be careful, the fagots await you!"

"I confess it, Father," stammers Joan.

"Joan, do you confess having cruelly desired the effusion of human blood?" asks Bishop Cauchon in a thundering voice.

"I confess it!"

Loud cries of horror go up from the mob, while the English soldiers brandish their weapons at Joan. Some men pick up stones to stone the heroine to death. The imprecations against her redouble threateningly.

"The harpy waged war out of pure cruelty!"

"She merely wished to soak herself in blood!"

"And the Church pardons her!"

"At one time I felt great pity for the wretch. Now I say with the English, Death to the tigress who lived on blood!"

"You fools! Do you believe these priests? Do you think Joan went after battle to drink the blood of the slain?"

"You defend her?"

"Yes! Oh, why am I alone?"

"You are a traitor!"

"He is an Armagnac!"

"Death to the Armagnac!"

The mob beats Joan's defender to death. As to herself, her condition is now such that she no longer is aware of aught she hears or says. She has practically lost consciousness. She barely has enough strength to respond mechanically, "I confess it," each time she hears Bishop Cauchon ask her, "Do you confess it?" In the midst, however, of her weakness and the wandering of her mind, one thought she is fully conscious of, the thought that her agony cannot last long; within a short time she would be dead or free! Poor martyr!

Bishop Cauchon continues to read: "'Fifthly, I, Joan, confess that I grievously sinned in claiming that all my acts and all my words were inspired to me by God, His saints and His angels, while in truth I despised God and His sacraments and I constantly invoked evil spirits.'—Do you confess it?"

"I confess it!"

"She confesses that she is a witch!" cries a voice from the mob.

"By St. George, she has exterminated thousands of my countrymen by her sorceries! And shall she escape the fagots!"

"She will be burned later! Our captains have promised us!"

"They deceive us! We shall burn her ourselves, now!"

Bishop Cauchon reads: "'Sixthly, I, Joan, confess that I grievously sinned by being a schismatic.'—Do you confess it?"

"I confess it!"

Bishop Cauchon continues reading: "'All of which crimes and errors, I, Joan, having returned to the truth, by the grace of our Lord, and also by the grace of our holy and infallible doctrine, my good and reverend Fathers, I now renounce and abjure.'—Do you renounce, do you abjure these crimes and errors?"

"I renounce! I abjure!"

Bishop Cauchon reads on: "'In the faith and the belief of all of which, I declare that I shall submit to the punishment that the Church may inflict upon me, and I promise and swear to St. Peter, the prince of the apostles, and to our Holy Father the Pope of Rome, his vicar, and to his successors, and to you, my seigneurs, and to you, my reverend father in God, Monseigneur the Bishop of Beauvais, and to you religious person, Brother John Lemaitre, vicar of the Inquisition of the faith, I, Joan, swear to you, to all of you my judges, never again to relapse into the criminal errors that it has pleased the Lord to deliver me from! I swear ever to remain in the union of our holy mother the Church, and in obedience to our Holy Father the Pope!'—Do you swear?"

"I swear—and I am dying!"

Bishop Cauchon beckons to one of the registrars. The latter takes a pen out of his portfolio, dips it in ink, hands it to the prelate, and holds up his square cap for a desk. The prelate places the parchment on the cap, and continues to read from it in a loud voice:

"'I, Joan, affirm and confirm all that is said above; I swear to it and affirm it in the name of the living and all-powerful God and of the sacred gospels, in proof whereof, and not knowing how to write, I have signed this document with my mark,'" saying which he presents the pen to the kneeling Joan and pointing to the parchment on the registrar's cap, adds: "Now place your cross here, below, seeing you do not know how to write."

In an almost expiring condition Joan Darc endeavors to trace a cross at the bottom of the parchment. Her strength fails her. The registrar kneels down beside the Maid, and guiding her inert and icy hand, aids her to make her mark at the bottom of the document. This being done, he calls the two penitents dressed in long grey gowns who have remained at the foot of the scaffold, and delivers to them the almost insensible Joan Darc. They place themselves on either side of her and take her under the arms. Her head drops upon her shoulder; from between her half-closed eyelids her eyes appear fixed and glassy. The only sign that life has not yet fled is a slight tremor that from time to time runs over her frame.

Stepping forward, Bishop Cauchon addresses the crowd in a tremendous voice: "All pastors charged with the duty of lovingly guarding the flock of Christ must endeavor to keep far from their dear flock all causes of pestilence, infection and corruption, and must seek to lead back the sheep that has wandered off among the brambles. Wherefore, we, Peter, Bishop of Beauvais by the grace of God, assisted by John Lemaitre, Inquisitor of the faith, and other learned and reverend priests, all competent judges, having heard and considered your assertions and your admissions, do now declare to you, Joan the Maid: We pronounce you guilty of having falsely maintained that you have had divine visions and revelations; guilty of having seduced weak people and having stiff-neckedly held to your opinions; guilty of having despised the sacraments and the holy canons; guilty of having favored sedition against our sovereign and serene master the King of England and France; guilty of having cruelly shed human blood; guilty of having apostatized, schismatized, blasphemed, idolatrized and invoked the evil spirit. But seeing that by the grace of the All-Powerful you have at last returned to the pale of our holy and sweet mother the Church, and that, filled with sincere contrition and genuine faith, you have publicly and in a loud voice made abjuration of your criminal and heretical errors, we now suspend the punishment of excommunication and its consequences, upon the express condition that you sincerely return to our holy and merciful Church. And charitably wishing to aid you in accomplishing your salvation, we condemn you, Joan the Maid, to perpetual imprisonment where your food shall be the bread of pain, your drink the water of agony, to the end that, weeping throughout the rest of your life over your monstrous sins, you may never again incur them. This is your final and definite condemnation. You now see how the Church of our Lord shows herself a tender mother towards you. Do then forevermore abandon and deplore your culpable error! Renounce your male attire forever, a shame to your sex! And should you relapse into that or any other mortal and idolatrous sin, then will the Church with profound and maternal pain be forced to cut you off forever from her body, she will then deliver you to the secular arm, and you will be cast into the flames like a gangrened member, seized with incurable rottenness. Glory to God on high, Amen."

The mob, especially the English soldiers, receive the "merciful" sentence with a threatening clamor. The people make a move to force the gate of the cemetery, which is guarded by a platoon of archers. The latter, being no less exasperated, seem ready to join the discontented and attack the platform. The Earl of Warwick quickly ascends the scaffold and again angrily addresses the Bishop: "Bishop! Has not this comedy lasted long enough? We can no longer answer for our soldiers in their present state of exasperation if, despite her abjuration, the witch is not burned!"

Bishop Cauchon suppresses with difficulty a gesture of impatience. He whispers into the English captain's ear. The latter, seeming to be convinced by what he hears, answers with a gesture of approval. The prelate adds: "Rest assured of what I promise you. At present see to it that the gate of the cemetery is well guarded, and that the mob is not allowed to break in. We shall make our exit by the garden of the abbey, and the Maid will be taken the same way. She would otherwise be massacred by the good people. And that must not be. She has only fainted. She will be seen to in her prison."

The Earl of Warwick again descends from the platform. The Bishop issues his orders to the penitents who are supporting the wholly unconscious Joan in their arms. They raise her—one under the arms, the other by the feet, descend the stairs of the platform, and, bearing their burden, walk rapidly across the cemetery to the garden of the abbey, while the English soldiers, obedient to the orders of their captains, who promise to them the speedy execution of Joan, close their ranks before the gate of the cemetery and keep back the mob, that shouts for the death of the witch.

CHAPTER VII.

REMORSE.

After her formal abjuration Joan Darc is taken in an almost dying condition, not to her cell but to a room in the Castle of Rouen. By orders of the Bishop, two old women are appointed to nurse her. She is laid in a soft bed; her jaws, locked in convulsions, are forced open, and a calming beverage poured down her throat. Every day and night the physician visits her. On the second day after the abjuration, the patient is out of danger. When Joan Darc recovers consciousness, she finds herself in a spacious and neatly furnished room. The warm rays of the sun play upon the glass of the barred casement. The two old women, who have her in charge, are seated at the head of the patient's bed seeming to contemplate her with tender interest. Joan Darc first thinks that she dreams, but her next belief is that, agreeable to the promise made to her by the institutor in the name of the Bishop, she has secretly been set free. She believes that some charitable people have obtained from the Bishop permission to transport her to their own house. The first impression felt by Joan at these surmises is one of joy at being free, and no remorse assails her at having denied the truth. The bliss of having escaped the dreaded shame of exposure, the hope of soon recovering her health, the prospect of returning to Domremy and seeing her parents—all these pleasurable sentiments smother the reproaches of her voices. She asks the two old women where she is. They smile in answer, and mysteriously place their fingers on their lips. From these tokens Joan conjectures that they are not free to answer, but that she is in a safe and hospitable asylum. Preserving on this head the silence that seems to be recommended to her, Joan gives herself over without reserve to the joy of living, of looking through the window panels at the blue sky, at feeling her limbs, so long sore and even wounded by the weight of her chains, finally free from their cruel grip; above all she congratulates herself on being delivered from the presence of her jailers, whose revolting utterances and licentious looks have been a cause of unremitting torture to her. She accepts nourishment and even some generous wine mixed with water. Her strength returns. On the third day she is able to rise. Her nurses offer her a long woman's dress and a hat. No longer assailed by the chaste apprehension that her jailers inspired her with in her cell, Joan resumes without hesitation the garb of her sex. The door of the room that she occupies opens upon a terrace on which her nurses induce her to promenade. A board fence high enough to shut off the view surrounds the terrace.

Joan remains a long time upon the terrace, inhaling the spring air with delight. When night approaches, feeling herself slightly fatigued by her walk, she undresses, lies down upon her bed, and sleeps profoundly.

Subject to human weakness, and transported by the joy of being free after such a long, painful and rigid confinement, the poor martyr is not assailed by remorse until towards evening. Vague sentiments, the forerunners of the approaching awakening of her conscience having cast a shadow over her spirit, she seeks in sleep both further rest and oblivion. Her expectations prove false.

St. Marguerite and St. Catherine appear in the heroine's dream; they do not now smile and look down tenderly upon her. They are sad and threatening, and reproach her for having denied the truth out of fear and shame. Profoundly impressed by her dream, Joan wakes up, her face covered with tears, when, lo, she sees the two saints with their gold crowns on their heads and robed in white and blue, luminously, almost transparently floating in the darkness of the room, and calling her by her name.

With beating heart and clasped hands, Joan kneels down on her bed, sobs, and implores their forgiveness. Without answering her, the two saints point to heaven with a significant gesture. The apparition then gradually fades away, and darkness again reigns supreme.

Thus rudely awakened to a sense of her actual condition, the heroine forthwith feels the promptings of her own conscience, that has lain torpid since the abjuration. She traces back the solemnity in all its horrid details; she recalls the maledictions with which she was whelmed by those who just before commiserated her. The terrible, yet legitimate accusation pounds upon her ears:

"If Joan's visions are inventions and a fraud, she has deceived simple people—she has lied—she only deserves contempt."

"If her visions were genuine, if God inspired her, she covers herself with shame by abjuring out of fear of death!"

"*Coward* or *liar*!" her inexorable voices repeat to her; "coward, or liar!—such is the name that you will leave behind you!"

Indescribable are the tortures that the poor creature undergoes on that night of desperate remorse. The full lucidity of her mind, of her energy, of her character, have returned to her, but only to curse her. Her keen judgment points out to her the fatal consequences of her abjuration; the soldiers and the peoples who rose at her voice against the foreigner will soon learn of the perjury committed by her whom they believed inspired! Mistrust of themselves, dejection, even defeat may follow the victorious exaltation of the soldiers and the people. On the other hand, the memory of the martial maid, surviving her martyrdom, would have added fuel to their courage, it would have aroused an avenging hatred for the English, and the great work of the complete emancipation of Gaul would have been achieved in the name of the victim, and in execration of her butchers.

Finally, could Joan continue the war even after she regained her freedom? What confidence could she inspire in the masses, she who had been convicted of falsehood or cowardice?

The plot of the ecclesiastics was planned with diabolical craft. They foresaw and calculated the consequences of the heroine's apostasy; they realized that, taken to the pyre after she had confessed the divinity of her mission, Joan would have become a saint; if, however, she renounced her past actions, she was dishonored.

"Idle remorse!" thinks Joan. "How retract a public abjuration. Impossible! Who could believe in the sincerity of a creature who had once before renounced her faith and her honor!"

These mind and heartrending thoughts are tearing Joan Darc to pieces when morning dawns and a rap is heard at the door of her chamber. The old women rise and go to inquire who is there. It is their reverend father in God, Canon Loyseleur. He wishes to speak to Joan without delay. She hastily puts on her woman's clothes and prepares to receive the priest, towards whom she now experiences a secret aversion, seeing that she accuses him in her heart for having led her to abjure by superexciting her dread of the shame and fear of the fagots. She reflects, however, that after all, the priest might have actually believed in the wisdom of his advice, and that she alone is responsible for the cowardly apostasy. Joan receives the canon with her habitual sweetness of manners. She learns from him that she is still a prisoner in the Castle of Rouen, but that the Bishop will set her free. The prelate, adds the canon, has no interest in retaining her a prisoner, and is to allow her to escape at night in a day or two. Loyseleur pretends that, thanks to his own personal intercession with the captain of the tower, she has been transferred to that room; but the captain demands that, the prisoner being now almost well again, she be returned to her cell. His orders are to be carried out that very morning.

Joan Darc believes the priest's words and easily reconciles herself to the idea of returning to her cell, but she asks as a supreme favor that male attire be provided to her for the sake of protection against her jailers. Canon Loyseleur promises to carry her wishes to the captain of the tower. Suddenly one of the old women rushes into the room saying that the jailer and an escort of soldiers are coming to claim the prisoner. The canon assures Joan she is soon to be set free, and leaves the room at the moment that John enters, carrying manacles which he fastens on the wrists of the heroine, and then conducts her back to her cell. Upon entering, Joan notices that the male clothes which she left there have disappeared. She expects to see herself chained by the waist and feet as she was before; but, freeing her even of the manacles, John informs her that she is no longer to be chained, saying which he leaves, casting a strange look upon her. Hardly concerned at this leniency, Joan sits down upon her straw couch and remains motionless, occupied with her own thoughts.

CHAPTER VIII.

THE RELAPSE.

It has long been night. The little iron lamp lights the dungeon of Joan Darc, who lies upon her straw couch broken with remorse at the continuous reproaches of her voices, and racking her brain for the means to expiate her weakness. The captive bitterly regrets the disappearance of her masculine clothes. Agitated by vague presentiments, and apprehensive of dangers on which she hardly dares dwell, she has wrapped herself as closely as she can in her clothes, and fearing to yield to the sleepiness that is gaining upon her, she rises from her straw bed and sits down upon the floor with her back leaning against the wall. But pressed down by sleep, her eyelids close despite herself, by degrees her head droops forward, and finally drops upon her knees which she holds within her arms. She falls asleep.

A few minutes later the pale face of Canon Loyseleur appears at the wicket. He notices that Joan is asleep, and withdraws.

Shortly afterwards the heavy door of the dungeon turns noiselessly upon its hinges. It opens and recloses so silently that Joan Darc's slumber, is not interrupted either by the slight noise of the door or the steps of two men who creep into the cavernous precinct. The two men are Talbot and Berwick, the English captains, who are appointed by Bishop Cauchon as the additional keepers of Joan Darc. Both are men in the prime of life. They wear rich slashed jackets after the fashion of the time. The two noble officers have sought in the stimulus of wine the requisite courage to commit the unheard-of atrocity, the nameless crime that they are bent upon. Their cheeks are inflamed, their eyes glisten, a lewd smile contracts their vinous lips. At the sight of Joan asleep they stop a moment and take council. Presently the two rush upon their victim.

Awakened with a start, Joan Darc leaps up and struggles to free herself from the grasp of her assailants. Berwick seizes her by the waist, while Talbot, sliding behind, seizes her arms and approaches his mouth to the lips of Joan, who turns her head away and utters a piercing shriek. The two noblemen drag her to the straw couch. The heroine draws superhuman strength from her despair. A violent struggle ensues, horrible, nameless. The tipsy Talbot and Berwick, exasperated at the heroine's resistance, give a loose to the fury of unsatisfied lechery. They smite Joan Darc with their fists. Her face bleeds. Yet she resists, and calls for help.

At last the door opens and Canon Loyseleur appears at the entrance. He feigns indignation. He brings with him a little trunk containing Joan's male clothes, and addressing the captain of the tower who enters with him, says: "You see it with your own eyes! An infamous attempt is contemplated upon the unfortunate woman!" Perhaps not wholly dead to conscience, Berwick and Talbot allow Joan Darc to escape from their grasp, and leave the cell, followed by the captain. Distracted, her face black and blue and covered with blood, Joan Darc falls almost senseless upon her couch, near which the canon has deposited her man's attire. Before he has time to speak with the victim, he is called away by the jailer, who, shaking his fist at him, says roughly:

"Get out of here, you tonsured dotard, canon of Satan! The devil take the marplot!"

"Poor child!" cries the priest, walking out, "I brought you your clothes. Put them on despite the oath you took. You may perhaps be sentenced as a relapsed heretic. But death is preferable to outrage!"

The door of the cell closes behind the canon. Silence and darkness resume their empire in Joan's dungeon. The plot to cause Joan's condemnation, induce her abjuration and then provoke her relapse so as to justify her being publicly burned to death is being carried out to the letter.

CHAPTER IX.

THE WORM TURNS.

It is eight o'clock of the following morning. Joan Darc is again clad in her male attire. She is again chained. Her handsome face is bruised from the blows that she received in the nocturnal struggle. One thought only absorbs her mind—can she manage to confess aloud the truth of what she has denied? The heroine's expectations are met by the event. Instructed by his accomplice of the happenings of the day before, the Bishop has commissioned several judges to visit Joan in her cell. They are seven. Here are their names:

Nicolas of Venderesse, William Haiton, Thomas of Courcelles, Isambard of La Pierre, James Camus, Nicolas Bertin, Julien Floquet.

Considering her crime flagrant, Joan Darc feels a bitter joy at the sight of the priests. Her head erect, calm, resolute, she seems to challenge their questions. Out of modesty and dignity, however, and unwilling to run the risk of blushing before these men, she decides to be silent upon the attempt of the previous night. The judges range themselves around the couch of the enchained captive.

THOMAS OF COURCELLES (affecting astonishment)—"What, Joan, again in man's attire? And despite your oath to renounce such idolatrous garb forever?"

JOAN DARC (tersely)—"I have resumed these clothes because I was forced to."

NICOLAS OF VENDERESSE—"You have violated your oath."

JOAN DARC (indignant)—"It is you who have violated yours! Have the promises made to me been kept? Have I been allowed to attend mass? Have I been restored to freedom after my abjuration? You are knaves and hypocrites!"

JAMES CAMUS—"We had to conform to the ecclesiastical sentence which condemns you to perpetual imprisonment."

JOAN DARC—"I prefer to die rather than remain in this prison. (She shivers with horror at the thought of the previous night's attempt upon her.) Had I been allowed to attend mass, had I been left in a decent place, free from my chains, and kept by women, I would have continued to clothe myself in the garb of my sex. If there is any fault, it lies with you."

ISAMBARD OF LA PIERRE—"Have you heard your voices since your condemnation?"

JOAN DARC (with bitterness)—"Yes; I have heard them."

The priests look at one another and exchange meaning looks.

WILLIAM HAITON—"What did your voices say to you? We want to know."

JOAN DARC (with a firm voice)—"They told me I committed an act of cowardice by denying the truth."

JAMES CAMUS—"And before the abjuration, what did your voices say?"

JOAN DARC (intrepidly looking at her judges)—"My voices said to me it would be criminal to deny the divine inspiration that ever guided me. (Commotion among the judges.) Upon the scaffold my voices said to me: 'Answer that preacher boldly—he is a false priest!' Woe is me, I did not obey my voices!"

The judges remain silent for a moment, and exchange expressive looks.

THOMAS OF COURCELLES—"These words are as rash as they are criminal. After having abjured, you relapse into your damnable errors!"

JOAN DARC (in a ringing voice)—"The error lies in lying—by abjuring I lied! What is damnable is to damn one's soul, and I damned it by not maintaining that I obeyed the will of heaven! My voices have reproached me for having abjured."

JAMES CAMUS—"Thus, after resuming male attire, a capital crime, an unpardonable crime which makes you a relapsed one, *revolvistis ad vestrum vomitum*—you have returned to your vomit, you dare maintain that those alleged voices—"

JOAN DARC—"The voices of my saints—come from God."

THOMAS OF COURCELLES—"On the scaffold you confessed."

JOAN DARC—"On the scaffold I was a coward! I lied! I yielded to the feeling of terror!"

JAMES CAMUS—"At this hour, thinking you no longer need to fear death, you come back to your former declarations."

JOAN DARC—"At this hour I maintain that only fear forced me to abjure, to confess the contrary of the truth. I prefer to die, rather than remain in this prison. I have spoken. You shall have not another word from me."

JAMES CAMUS—"Be it so!"

The priests file out slowly and silently. Joan Darc remains alone, on her knees upon the straw. She raises her eyes to the vault of her prison with a radiant, inspired face, and with her hands joined, she thanks her saints for the courage they have given her to expiate and annul her apostasy by resolutely marching to death.

CHAPTER X.

TO THE FLAMES!

The scene changes. After the last interrogatory of Joan the priests proceed to Bishop Cauchon in order to inform him of the issue of their visit to the prisoner—a result that the prelate expects, so much so that he has convoked a sufficient number of judges to meet in the chapel of the Archbishop's palace at Rouen in order to proceed with the final sentence of the relapsed sinner. All the summoned prelates are assembled and in their seats in the chapel. Bishop Cauchon, seated in the center of the choir, presides, and orders silence with a gesture.

BISHOP CAUCHON—"My very dear brothers, Joan has fallen back into her damnable errors, and in contempt of her solemn abjuration, pronounced in the face of God and His Holy Writ, not only has she resumed her male attire, but she again stubbornly maintains that all that she has done and said was said and done by divine inspiration! I now call for your views, in the order of precedence, upon the fate of the said Joan who is now charged with having relapsed, reserving to myself the right of convoking you again, should I deem it necessary."

ARCHDEACON NICOLAS OF VENDERESSE—"The said Joan should be given over to the secular arm, to be burned alive as a relapsed sinner."

ABBOT AGIDIE—"Joan is a relapsed heretic, no doubt about it. Nevertheless, I am of the opinion that a second abjuration should be proposed to her, under pain of being delivered to the secular arm."

CANON JOHN PINCHON—"Joan has relapsed; I shall adhere to whatever plan of punishment my very dear brothers may decide upon."

CANON WILLIAM ERARD—"I pronounce the said Joan a relapsed sinner and deserving of the pyre."

CHAPLAIN ROBERT GILBERT—"Joan should be burned as a relapsed sinner and heretic."

ABBOT OF ST. AUDOIN—"The woman is a relapsed sinner. Let her abjure a second time or be condemned."

ARCHDEACON JOHN OF CASTILLONE—"Let the relapsed sinner be delivered to the secular arm."

CANON ERMANGARD—"I demand the exemplary death of Joan."

DEACON BOUCHER—"Joan should be sentenced as a relapsed one."

PRIOR OF LONGUEVILLE—"That is my opinion. She should be burned alive."

FATHER GIFFARD—"I think the relapsed sinner should be sentenced without delay."

FATHER HAITON—"I pronounce the said Joan a relapsed sinner. I am for her speedy punishment, provided, however, she refuses to abjure a second time."

CANON MARGUERIE—"Joan is a relapsed sinner. Let her be delivered up to secular justice."

CANON JOHN OF L'EPEE—"I am of my brother's opinion. She should be burned to death."

CANON GARIN—"I think so, too."

CANON GASTINEL—"Let us give up the relapsed sinner to the pyre."

CANON PASCAL—"That is my opinion. Let her be burned to death."

FATHER HOUDENC—"The ridiculous explanations of the woman are to me an ample proof that she has always been an idolatress and a heretic. Besides that, she is a relapsed sinner. I demand that she be delivered to the secular arm without delay."

MASTER JOHN OF NIBAT—"The said Joan is impenitent and a relapsed sinner. Let her undergo her punishment."

FATHER FABRE—"A heretic by habit, hardened in her errors, a rebel to the Church, the body of the said Joan should be delivered to the flames, and her ashes cast to the winds."

ABBOT OF MONTEMART—"I hold as my brother. Only I am of the opinion that she should be given a second chance to abjure."

FATHER GUELON—"That is my opinion."

CANON COUPEQUESNE—"Mine also."

CANON GUILLAUME—"Let the said Joan be offered a second chance to retract. If she refuses, then death."

CANON MAURICE—"I favor such a second summons, although I do not expect good results from it."

DOCTOR WILLIAM OF BANDIBOSC—"I side with my very dear brother."

DEACON NICOLAS CAVAL—"The relapsed sinner should be treated without pity, according to her deserts. She should be burned to death."

CANON LOYSELEUR—"The said Joan should be delivered to the temporal flames."

THOMAS OF COURCELLES—"The woman is a heretic and relapsed sinner. She may be summoned a second time, and told that if she persists in her errors, she has nothing to expect in this world."

FATHER JOHN LEDOUX—"Although such a second attempt seems to me idle, it might be tried so as to demonstrate the inexhaustible kindness of our mother the Church."

MASTER JOHN TIPHAINE—"I favor this second, though idle, attempt."

DEACON COLOMBELLE—"I am of the same opinion."

ISAMBARD OF LA PIERRE—"Secular justice will take its course if the said Joan refuses to abjure a second time."

From these opinions it transpires that some of the judges demand immediate death, while others, and these are a small majority, favor a second abjuration, although the opinion is general that the attempt is vain. The judges have learned from their accomplices that the heroine is now determined to seek in death the expiation of the confessions which only fear drew from her. More straightforward and frank in his projects, moreover, convinced of the success of his plan, the Bishop sums up the deliberation and absolutely opposes the idea of attempting a second abjuration. Do not most of those who favor the measure consider it idle? Why, then, try it? And even if it were certain that the relapsed sinner would abjure again, the performance would have a deplorable effect. Did not the soldiers and the people, exasperated at the clemency of the Church, cry "Treason!" and seem ready to riot at the time of the first abjuration? Is it wise to incur and provoke a terrible turmoil in the town? Has not the Church given evidence of her maternal charity by admitting Joan to penitence, despite her perverse heresy? How was this act of benevolence rewarded by her? It was rewarded with renewed and redoubled boastfulness, audacity and impiety! Bishop Cauchon closes, conjuring his very dear brothers in the name of the dignity of the Church, in the name of the peace of the town, in the name of their conscience, to declare without superfluous verbiage that the said Joan is a relapsed sinner, and, as such, is given over to the secular arm, in order to be led to death the next day, after being publicly excommunicated by the Church. The judges yield to the views of the prelate. The registrar enters the sentence of death, and the session rises.

Peter Cauchon is the first to leave the chapel. Outside he meets several English captains who are waiting for the issue of the deliberations. One of them, the Earl of Warwick, says to the prelate:

"Well, what has been decided shall be done with the witch?"

"*Farewell!* It is done!" answers the Bishop with glee.

"The Maid—".

"Shall be burned to-morrow—burned to death in public," interrupts Bishop Cauchon.

CHAPTER XI.

THE PYRE.

During the evening of May 29, 1431, the rumor spreads through Rouen that the relapsed sinner is to be burned to death on the following day. That same night carpenters raise the necessary scaffoldings while others build the pyre and plant the stake. Early the next morning companies of English archers form a cordon around the market-place, where Joan Darc is to be executed, and a double file extends into one of the streets that runs into the place. The two files of soldiers leave a wide space between them, connecting the street with the vacant area left around the scaffoldings. These are three in number, the highest of the three being at a little distance from the other two. On one of these, the one to the right, which is covered with purple cloth, rises a daised seat of crimson, ornamented with tufts of white feathers and fringed with gold. A row of seats equally decked extends on both sides of the central and daised throne, which is reached by several steps covered with rich tapestry. The scaffold to the left is of the same dimensions as the first, but it, as well as the benches thereon, is draped in black. The last of the three scaffolds consists of solid masonry about ten feet high, broad at the bottom, and ending in a narrow platform in the middle of which stands a stake furnished with iron chains and clamps. The platform is reached by a narrow set of stairs that is lost to sight in the midst of an enormous pile of fagots mixed with straw and saturated with bitumen and sulphur. The executioners have just heaped up the combustibles on the four sides of the pile of masonry. Tall poles, fastened in the ground close to the pyre bear banners on which the following legends are to be read in large white letters on a black ground:

"Joan, who had herself called the Maid, condemned to be burned alive."

"Falsifier, misleader, and deceiver of the people."

"Soothsayer, superstitious, blasphemer of God."

"Presumptuous, apostate from the faith of Jesus Christ, idolatress, cruel, dissolute."

"Invoker of devils."

"Schismatic, relapsed."[116]

At eight all the bells of Rouen begin tolling the funeral knell. Poor Joan, she loved the bells so well in her childhood! The May sun, that same sun that shone upon the first defeat of the English before Orleans, pure and luminous, floods the three scaffolds with its light. The crowd grows thicker around the space kept vacant by the archers; other spectators are grouped at the windows and on the balconies of the old frame houses with pointed gables that enclose the market place. Presently flags and plumes are seen waving, the steel of the casques, the gold and precious stones of the mitres and crosiers are seen shining between the two files of archers. The casqued and mitred gentry are the English captains and the prelates. Prominent among them is the Cardinal of Winchester, Clad in the Roman purple and followed by the Bishop of Boulogne and the Bishop of Beauvais, Peter Cauchon. Behind them come the Earl of Warwick and other noble captains. Slowly and majestically they ascend the stairs of the platform to the right of the pyre. The Cardinal takes his seat upon the dais, while the other dignitaries distribute themselves to his right and left. The other scaffold, that is draped in black, is occupied by the judges of the process, its institutor, its assessors and its registrars.

The appearance and arrival of these illustrious, learned or holy personages does not satisfy the gaping crowd; the condemned girl has not yet appeared. Menacing clamors begin to circulate. These are loudest among the soldiers and the Burgundian partisans, who say:

"Will the Bishop keep his promise this time? Woe to him if he trifles with us."

"Will the witch be burned at last?"

"The fagots are ready; the executioners are holding the lighted wicks."

"She ought to be burned twice over, the infamous relapsed sinner!"

"She had the brazenness to declare that she abjured under the pressure of force! She persists in declaring herself inspired!"

"What an insolent liar! By St. George! could she ever have vanquished us without the assistance of the devil, us the best archers in the world? I was at the battle of Patay, where the best men of England were mowed down. I saw whole legions of demons rush upon us at her command. We could be vanquished only by such witchery."

"Those demons, sir archer, were French soldiers!"

"Blood and death! Do you imagine plain soldiers are able to beat us? They were demons, by St. George! real horned and clawed demons, armed with flaming swords—they plunged over our heads and pelted us with stones and balls!"

"It might have been the furious projectiles from some artillery pieces that were masked behind some hedge, sir archer."

"Artillery pieces of Satan, yes; but of France, no!"

"As true as our Cardinal has his red hat on his head, if the strumpet of the Armagnacs is not burned this time, myself and the other archers of my company will roast Bishop Cauchon together with all his tonsured brethren."

"Ha, ha, ha, ha! That is well said, my Hercules! To roast Bishop Cauchon like a pig! That would be a funny spectacle!"

"They are taking long! Death to the witch!"

"Do they expect us to sleep here to-night?"

"To the fagots with the heretic!"

"Death to the relapsed sinner!"

"To the pyre with the invoker of demons! The strumpet! Death to Joan!"

"She cheated the people!"

"She denies the religion of Jesus Christ!"

"To the pyre with the idolatress! The apostate! To the pyre with her, quick and soon!"

Such are the clamors of the English and the partisans of Burgundy. The royalists or Armagnacs are much less numerous. A few of them, especially women, experience a return of pity for Joan Darc, whose abjuration incensed all those who believed her inspired. With some this indignation still is uppermost and in full force. As these sentiments are indicative of sympathy, they are not uttered aloud but whispered out of fear of the English.

"Well, though the Maid's strength once failed her, it will not fail her to-day."

"It would seem that she had not lied to us. She will now maintain until death that she is inspired of God. Poor child."

"And yet she abjured!"

"Whoever lied once may lie again."

"If she abjured it was out of fear of the flames—that can be easily understood."

"She proved herself a coward! And she was thought so brave!"

"Well, in the face of the pyre one may well tremble! Just look at those fagots soaked in pitch."

"When one thinks that the whole pile will be in flames all around Joan like so much straw on fire, singeing and consuming her flesh!"

"My hair stands on end at the bare thought."

"Poor child! What a torture!"

"What else can you expect? Our seigneurs and the doctors of canon law condemn her. She must be guilty!"

"Such learned men could not be mistaken. We must believe them."

"When the Church has uttered herself we must bow down in silence. A body has religion, or has none."

"Well, I have no suspicions. I am an Armagnac and a royalist, and I detest the English rule. I looked upon Joan as upon a saint before her condemnation. Now I cannot even take pity upon her. It would be throwing discredit upon her judges. My religion as a good Catholic shuts my mouth. We must believe without reasoning."

"Did not the ecclesiastical tribunal show how merciful the Church is by accepting Joan's repentance?"

"But why did she relapse!"

"So much the worse for her if she is now burned. It will be her own doing."

"You must admit that by voluntarily going to the pyre she proves her courage. She is an intrepid girl!"

"She is simply displaying her rebellion and idolatrous boastfulness."

"Did not Joan Darc defeat the English in a score of battles? Did she not have the King consecrated at Rheims? Answer!"

"What you say is true. But our seigneurs the bishops judge such matters differently, and better than we could. This is the way I reason, and it is as simple as correct: The Church is infallible; the Church condemns Joan; consequently Joan is guilty."

This method of reasoning, which sways the minds of the more orthodox, prevails over the timid and rare utterances that betoken interest in and sympathy for Joan; she is destined to behold even those who had remained French under English rule led astray by the recent Pharisees, and impassibly assist at her execution, the same as her master Jesus, who, sentenced to a malefactor's death, saw the poor and suffering people whom he loved so well, look gapingly on at the execution of a sentence of death that was also pronounced by the holy doctors of the law and by the priests of his time.

Suddenly a deep commotion is seen swaying the mob. It announces the approach of the condemned woman.

Standing on a cart drawn by a horse, Joan Darc is clad in a "san benito," a long black gown painted over with tongues of flame, and bearing on her head a pasteboard mitre on which are printed the words: "Idolatress," "Heretic," "Relapsed Sinner." The monk Isambard of La Pierre, one of her judges, stands near her on the wagon and imparts to her the last consolations. She seems to listen to him, but his tokens of compassion reach her ear only as a confused sound. She no longer expects aught from man. Her face, raised to heaven, looks into infinite space. She feels detached from earth, she has shaken off her last human terrors. For a moment she is overcome with fear. "Oh!" cries she, sobbing, "must my body, so clean of all stain, be destroyed by fire! I would prefer to be beheaded!" But after this last cry, drawn from her by the dread of bodily pain, her soul resumes its mastery, and the virgin of Gaul proceeds resolutely to the pyre. The wagon stops at the foot of the platform on which the Cardinal of Winchester, the two Bishops and the captains are enthroned, in their mitres and their casques.

The monk Isambard of La Pierre alights from the cart and motions Joan Darc to follow him. He assists her with his arm, seeing that the length of her robe impedes her movements. The unhappy girl walks with difficulty. Arrived before the main platform, the monk addresses the victim:

"Joan, kneel down, to receive in a humble posture the excommunication and sentence that Monseigneur the Bishop of Beauvais is to pronounce upon you."

Joan Darc kneels down in the dust at the foot of the platform that is covered with purple. Bishop Peter Cauchon rises, bows to the Cardinal of Winchester, and advances to the edge of the platform.

From the ranks of the English soldiers the cries are heard:

"The devil take any further prayers!"

"On with the execution!"

"Is it a new scheme to keep the strumpet from roasting? We have had enough dilly-dallying!"

"Look out, Bishop! You shall not cheat us this time!"

"To the pyre, without further ado! To the pyre with the sorceress! Death to the girl or to the Bishop!"

Bishop Cauchon silences the growing tumult with a significant gesture and says in a sonorous voice: "My very dear brothers, if a member suffers, the apostle said to the Corinthians, the whole body suffers. Thus when heresy infects one member of our holy Church, it is urgent to separate it from all others, lest its rottenness contaminate the mystical body of our Lord. The sacred institutions have decided, my very dear brothers, that, in order to free the faithful from the poison of the heretics, these vipers may not be allowed to devour the bosom of our mother the Church. Wherefore we, Bishop of Beauvais, by divine grace, assisted by the learned and very reverend John Lemaitre and John Graverant, Inquisitors of the faith, say to you Joan, commonly styled the Maid:—We justly pronounced you idolatrous, a soothsayer, an invoker of devils, bloodthirsty, dissolute, schismatic and heretic. You abjured your crimes and voluntarily signed this abjuration with your own hand. But you quickly returned to your damnable errors, like the dog returns to his vomit. On account of this do we now excommunicate you and pronounce you a relapsed heretic. We sentence you to be extirpated from the midst of the faithful like a rotten, leprous member, and we deliver you, and abandon you, and cast you off into the hands of secular justice, and request it that, apart from your death and the mutilation of your members, it treat you with moderation!"

The sentence is received with an explosion of shouts of ferocious joy. The English soldiers signify their satisfaction. The mob looks at Joan Darc with horror. One of the assessors descends from the platform and speaks to Isambard in a low voice, whereupon the latter turns to Joan:

"You have heard your sentence, rise, my daughter."

Joan Darc rises, and pointing to heaven as if taking the spheres for her witness, says in a loud voice and with an accent of crushing reproach to Bishop Cauchon, who remains standing near the edge of the platform above her:

"Bishop! Bishop! I die at your hands!"

Despite his audacity, Peter Cauchon trembles, grows pale, bows his head before the girl's anathema, and hastens to resume his seat near the Cardinal.

Two executioners draw near at the words of the prelate consigning Joan Darc to the secular powers. Each seizes her by an arm and they lead her to the pyre, Isambard following.

"Father," says Joan to the latter, "I wish to have a cross, so as to die contemplating it."

The request being overheard by several English soldiers, they answer:

"You need no cross, relapsed sinner!"

"Witch! To the fagots with you!"

"You only want to gain time!"

"We have had enough delays—death to the heretic!"

"To the fagots! To the fagots!"

The monk Isambard says a few words in the ear of the assessor; the latter leaves hurriedly in the direction of a neighboring church. One of the two executioners, a fellow with a blood-stained apron and a hardened face, who also overhears Joan's request, feels deeply affected. Tears are seen to gather in his eyes. He pulls his knife from his belt, and cuts in two a stick that he holds in his hand; in his hurry he drops his knife to the ground, takes a string from his pocket, ties the two pieces of wood in the shape of a rude cross, roughly thrusts aside two English soldiers who stand in his way, and then, handing the cross to the monk, falls back a few steps, contemplating the victim with something akin to adoration.

The monk passes the cross to Joan Darc, who, seizing it with transport and taking it to her lips, says: "Thank you, Father!"

"I have sent to the Church of St. Ouen for a large crucifix bearing the image of our Savior. It will be held at a distance before your eyes as long as possible. Address your prayers to Jesus Christ," the monk answered in a low voice.

"Tell them to hold it high so that I may see the image of the Savior to the very end."

Again cries break out from the ranks of the English soldiers:

"Will there ever be an end of this?"

"What is the tonsured fellow whispering to the witch?"

"Let him travel to the devil in her company!"

"To the fagots with the witch, and quickly, too!"

"To the flames, both the monk and the Maid!"

Led to the foot of the pyre, Joan Darc measures its height with her eyes and is unable to suppress a shudder; the executioners wave their torches in the air in order to enliven their flames; two of them precede the victim to the masonry platform within the pile of fagots; they cover it up with straw and twigs, the top layer of the heaped-up combustibles; they then hold up the iron clamps that are fastened to the stake.

"Climb up this way," says one of the executioners to Joan Darc, pointing to the stairs, "you will not come down again, witch!"

"I shall accompany you, my dear daughter, to the top of the pyre," says the monk.

Joan Darc slowly ascends the steps, greatly embarrassed in her movements by the folds of her gown, and reaches the top of the pyre. A tremendous shout breaks forth from the mob. When the noise subsides, Joan cries out aloud: "God alone inspired my actions!"

Hisses and furious imprecations drown her voice. The Cardinal of Winchester, the Bishops, judges, and captains rise simultaneously so as to obtain a better view of the execution. After placing Joan standing with her back against the stake, one of the executioners fastens her to it by the waist and neck with iron carcans; a chain holds her feet; only her hands remain free, and with them she clasps the rough wooden cross that one of the English executioners has just fashioned for her, and that she holds close to her lips. A priest in a surplice, carrying one of those large silver crucifixes usually borne at the head of processions, arrives in a hurry; he places himself at a distance opposite the pyre and holds up the crucifix as high as his arms allow him. It is the crucifix that the monk Isambard has sent for. He points it out to Joan Darc. She turns her head towards it and keeps her eyes fastened upon the image of Christ.

"Come, reverend Father," says one of the executioners to the monk Isambard, "do not stay here. The flames are about to shoot up."

"In a moment," answers the monk; "I shall follow you. I only wish to finish the prayer that I began."

"I shall make you come down faster than you would like, my reverend mumbler of prayers," observes the executioner in a low voice.

The two executioners descend from the platform of the pyre; the monk administers to Joan Darc the supreme consolations.

Suddenly a dry and lively crackling is heard from the base of the pyre, followed by puffs of smoke and thin tongues of flame.

"Father!" cries Joan Darc anxiously, "descend! Descend quickly! The pyre is on fire!"

Such is the sublime adieu of the victim to one of her judges!

The monk descends precipitately, casting an angry look at the executioners. These light the pyre at several places. Volumes of black smoke rise upward, and envelop Joan Darc from the public gaze. The fire glistens; it runs and twines itself through the lower layers of the fagots; presently the pile is all on fire; the flames rise; they are fanned by the breeze that blows away the cloud of smoke, and Joan Darc is again exposed to view. The fire reaches the straw and twigs on top of the platform on which her feet rest. Her gown begins to smoke. Firmly held by the triple iron bands that clasp her neck, waist and feet, she writhes and utters a piercing cry:

"WATER! WATER!"

A second later, as if regretting the vain appeal for mercy that pain drew from her, she exclaims:

"IT IS GOD WHO INSPIRED ME!"

At that moment Joan Darc's gown takes fire and the flames that flare up from it join the hundred other lambent tongues that shoot upward. From the midst of the tall furnace a voice in a weird accent is heard to exclaim:

"JESUS!"

The virgin of Gaul has expiated her immortal glory.

The flames subside, and finally go out. A smoldering brasier surrounds the base of the masonry pile that served as the center for the pyre. At its top, and held fast by the iron clamps fastened to the charred and smoking stake, is seen a blackened, shapeless, nameless something—all that is left of the Maid.

The two executioners place a ladder on the side of the stone pile; they climb up, strike down with their axes the members of her who was Joan Darc, and with the help of long iron forks hurl them all down into the brasier. Other executioners lay fresh fagots on the heap. Tall flames re-rise. When the second fire is wholly extinguished nothing remains but reddish ashes interspersed with charred human bones, a skull among them. The ashes and bones are gathered by the executioners and thrown into a wooden box, which they lay on a hand-barrow, and, followed by a large and howling mob, the executioners proceed to the banks of the Seine, into which they throw the remains of the redeeming angel of France.

Finally, the Cardinal, the Bishops, the captains and the ecclesiastical judges leave the market place of Rouen in procession, in the same order that they had entered. They have gloated over the death of Joan Darc. The justice of the courtiers, of the warriors and of the infallible clergy is satisfied.

EPILOGUE.

I, Jocelyn the Champion, now a centennarian as was my ancestor Amael who fought under Charles Martel and who later knew Charlemagne, wrote the above narrative, a part of which, the tragedy of Joan Darc's execution, I witnessed with my own eyes.

On the eve of her execution I arrived in Rouen from Vaucouleurs. Communication was difficult in those days between distantly located provinces. It thus happened that the tidings of Joan's captivity at Rouen and her trial did not for some time reach her family. Finally apprized thereof by public rumor, her family was anxious to learn of her fate, but, despite their desolation, they neither were able nor did they dare to undertake the long journey. I called upon Denis Laxart, the worthy relative of Joan whom I had long known intimately, and offered him to go to Rouen myself. My fervent admiration for the plebeian heroine inspired me with the resolution. Despite my advanced age, I was not frightened by the perils of the journey. But I was poor. This difficulty was overcome by Denis Laxart and several good people of Vaucouleurs. The necessary funds were scraped together, a horse was bought, and I started with my grandson at the crupper.

Arrived at Rouen on May 29, 1431, after encountering no end of difficulties, I learned of the solemn abjuration of Joan Darc and saw how her enemies pronounced her a fraud and her former friends, a coward. I was not then aware of the black plot that had brought about the apostasy; nevertheless, my own instinct and reasoning, the recollection of my frequent conversations with Denis Laxart, who had often recounted to me the details of Joan's childhood, and finally the reports of her glorious deeds that penetrated as far as Lorraine—everything combined to point out to me that an abjuration that so utterly belied the courage and loyalty of the martial maid concealed some sinister mystery.

The following day I appeared early at the market place, taking my grandson with me. We managed to stand in the front ranks of the mass that witnessed the execution and that crowded us forward. We were pushed so far forward that we stood near the benign executioner who volunteered to fashion a cross for the unhappy victim, and who in his haste dropped his knife. It fell at my grandson's feet. I took it up and shall preserve it as the emblem that is to accompany this narrative.

Immediately after the execution of Joan Darc I was the witness of a strange incident. Near myself and my grandson was a priest wrapped up in his gown and cowl. He mumbled to himself. He had watched with seeming indifference the preparations for Joan Darc's execution, until when, writhing with pain, she cried out: "Water! Water!" At these words the priest trembled.

He raised his hands to heaven and murmured: "Mercy! Oh, mercy!" Finally, when with her last breath Joan Darc made the supreme invocation—"Jesus!" the priest cried out in a suffocated voice:

"I am damned!"

He immediately dropped to the ground, a prey to violent convulsions. He still lay there in a tremor when the mob left the market place to follow the executioners who were to throw the remains of Joan Darc into the Seine. Moved with pity for the man whom all others took no notice of, or considered possessed of an evil spirit, my grandson and myself raised him and took him to our inn that faced the market place. We carried him to our room and tended him. By degrees he came to himself and looked upon us with distracted eyes that seemed to reveal deep repentance and also terror, as he cried: "I am damned! I am the accomplice and instrument of the Bishop of Beauvais in the killing of Joan! God will punish me!"

That priest was the Canon Loyseleur.[117] The gowned monster did taste repentance—strange, incredible revulsion, that I never would have believed had I not myself witnessed its unquestionable evidence. The wretch was devoured with remorse; he admitted his guilt to us, and when he noticed the horror that his admissions filled us with he cried: "A curse upon the help I rendered to you, Bishop of Beauvais, assassin!" With quavering voice he asked me whether I pitied Joan. My tears answered him. He then wished to know who I was, and learning of my passionate admiration for the virgin of Gaul and my desire for the sake of her desolate family, to be informed upon what had happened, Canon Loyseleur seemed struck by a sudden thought, and asked me to wait for him at the inn that very evening. "Never," said he, "shall I be able to make amends for or expiate my crime; but I wish to place in your hands the means to smite the butchers of the victim."

That same evening Canon Loyseleur brought to me a bundle of parchments. It contained:

1.—The general confession of Joan Darc transcribed by himself on the very day when he received it, and when that great soul unveiled itself to him in all its heroic simplicity.

2.—Notes which he had taken and preserved after his interviews with the emissary of George of La Tremouille, and which revealed the plot that was concocted against Joan by the people of the Court, the captains and the ecclesiastics, before the first meeting of the heroine and Charles VII.

3.—A copy of a contemporaneous chronicle entitled "Journal of the Siege of Orleans," and another memoir written by Percival of Cagny, equerry to the Duke of Alençon, who did not leave Joan's side from the time of the raising of the siege of Orleans down to the siege of Paris. These two manuscripts were a part of the documents that Bishop Peter Cauchon had gathered to draw up the indictment.

4.—One of the minutes of the process, containing the questions put to Joan, and her answers.

5.—A complete admission and detailed account of the machinations of Loyseleur and Bishop Cauchon to capture Joan's confidence in her prison, as also of the plans they had laid during a long conversation before the trial.

These materials were given to me by the canon in the hope of enabling me some day to rehabilitate the memory of Joan Darc. As to himself, he realized that, pursued by inexorable remorse, he would soon die, or lose his senses. On that very morning he did not dare to take his seat on the platform among Joan's judges, fearing she might recognize him. The spectacle of her martyrdom and agony finally overthrew him. After depositing these manuscripts in my hands, the canon left me precipitately and with a wild look. I know not what became of him.

The next morning I left Rouen with my grandson, and once again in Vaucouleurs I proceeded to write the story of Joan Darc. Thanks to the information I received from Denis Laxart and the documents of Canon Loyseleur, I have been able to draw up the above truthful narrative. To it I have attached the executioner's knife, as an additional relic of our family.

Until now and in this country of Lorraine, the cradle of the virgin of Gaul, I have vainly sought to rehabilitate Joan in the eyes of her friends and even of her parents. All have given me the same answer that I received so often in Rouen and so many other towns:

"Despite her glory, despite her immense services rendered to France, Joan is guilty, Joan is criminal, Joan will burn in the everlasting flames of hell— THE INFALLIBLE CHURCH CONDEMNED HER!"

But the judgment of men passes—true glory is imperishable. Some day the Maid will be exalted and her murderers spat upon.

THE END.

FOOTNOTES:

[1] *Trial and Condemnation, and Proceedings of the Rehabilitation of Joan of Arc, known as The Maid*, by Jules Quicherat, after the manuscripts in the Royal Library; vol. I, p. 39.

[2] The same.

[3] *Trial of Joan of Arc*, vol. I, p. 40.

[4] *Trial of Joan of Arc*, vol. I, p. 74.

[5] *Song of Merlin the Enchanter*, in Villemarqué, *Popular Songs of Brittany*, vol. I, p. 219.

[6] Villemarqué, *Popular Songs of Brittany*, vol. I, p. 219.

[7] The citation is literal. Denis Laxart, uncle to Jeannette, testified to having heard her say: "Has it not been long prophesied that France, desolated by a woman, would be restored by a woman?" (*Proceedings of the Rehabilitation of Joan of Arc*, edited by Jules Quicherat, vol. II, p. 444.) The wife of Henry Rolhaire also deposed and said: "Jeannette asked: 'Have you not heard it said that France, lost by a woman, would be saved by a virgin of the marches (borders) of Lorraine, born near an oak forest?'" (The same, p. 447.)

[8] "*Descendet virgo dorsum sagitarii*. Among other writings was found a prophecy of Merlin, speaking in this manner."—Testimony of Matthew Thomassin, given by Quicherat in the *Rehabilitation*, vol. III, p. 15.

[9] See "The Iron Arrow Head," the tenth of this series.

[10] Volume one of this series, "The Gold Sickle."

[11] *Trial and Condemnation of Joan of Arc*, vol. I, p. 67.

[12] *Trial and Condemnation of Joan of Arc*, vol. I, p. 87.

[13] *Trial and Condemnation of Joan of Arc*, vol. I, p. 88.

[14] *Trial and Condemnation of Joan of Arc*, vol. I, p. 88.

[15] The same, p. 89.

[16] The same, p. 89.

[17] *Trial and Condemnation of Joan of Arc*, vol. I, p. 77.

[18] The same, p. 77.

[19] The same, pp. 79, 80.

[20] *Trial and Condemnation of Joan of Arc*, vol. I, p. 79.

[21] *Trial and Condemnation of Joan of Arc*, vol. I, p. 80.

[22] The same, p. 80.

[23] *Trial and Condemnation*, vol. I, p. 80.

[24] *Trial and Condemnation*, vol. I, p. 80.

[25] *Trial and Condemnation*, vol. I, p. 88.

[26] *Trial and Condemnation*, vol. I, p. 29.

[27] *"Mammae ejas erant pulcherimas"*—Testimony of the Duke of Alençon (*Proceedings of the Rehabilitation of Joan of Arc*, vol. III, p. 220).

[28] *Trial and Condemnation of Joan of Arc*, vol. I, p. 127.

[29] *Trial and Condemnation*, vol. I, p. 67.

[30] *Proceedings of the Rehabilitation*, vol. II, p. 79.

[31] *Proceedings of the Rehabilitation*, vol. II, p. 435.

[32] This, and the succeeding answers of Joan in this interview which are authenticated by references to the *Proceedings of the Rehabilitation*, are all, with the exception of two otherwise designated, taken from that portion of vol. II between pp. 436 and 439.

[33] *Proceedings of the Rehabilitation*.

[34] The same.

[35] The same.

[36] The same.

[37] *Proceedings of the Rehabilitation*.

[38] The same, vol. II, p. 459.

[39] *Proceedings of the Rehabilitation*.

[40] The same, vol. II, p. 80.

[41] *Proceedings of the Rehabilitation*, vol. II, p. 401.

[42] *Proceedings of the Rehabilitation*, vol. II, p. 657.

[43] *Proceedings of the Rehabilitation*, vol. II, p. 657.

[44] *Proceedings of the Rehabilitation*, vol. II, p. 567.

[45] See the preceding volume of this series, "The Iron Trevet."

[46] *Proceedings of the Rehabilitation*, vol. II, p. 450.

[47] Godefroid, *Chronicle of the Maid*, p. 500; Godefroid, *Chronicle of Berry*, p. 376; *Memoirs of Argus and Richemont*.

[48] Godefroid, p. 754. quoted by Jules Quicherat, in the introduction to the *Trial and Condemnation of Joan of Arc*, p. 27.

[49] *Chronicle of Percival of Cagny*, vol. IV. p. 19.

[50] *Chronicle of Percival of Cagny*, vol. IV. p. 19.

[51] *Chronicle of Percival of Cagny*, vol. IV. p. 19.

[52] It is useless to cite the chroniclers severally on the subject of this shameless and abominable examination. They are all agreed on the fact.

[53] *Chronicle of Percival of Cagny*, cited by Quicherat, vol. III, p. 71.

[54] The interrogations and the replies thereto by Joan are here taken in the main literally from *The Chronicle of the Maid*, a manuscript now in the possession of the Institute at Paris, No. 245, cited by Quicherat in his *Trial and Condemnation of Joan of Arc*, vol. IV, p. 209; also in the *Proceedings of the Rehabilitation*, vol. III, pp. 204-206.

[55] *Proceedings of the Rehabilitation*, vol. II, p. 75. This remarkable reply is quoted literally, like the rest of the inquisition.

[56] *Trial and Condemnation of Joan of Arc*, vol. I, p. 87. Even English authors have been wont to quote with praise this virile letter of the Maid.

[57] *Proceedings of the Rehabilitation*, vol. III, p. 84.

[58] *Proceedings of the Rehabilitation*, vol. III, p. 80.

[59] *Journal of the Siege of Orleans*, vol. IV, p. 105.

[60] *Trial and Condemnation of Joan of Arc*, Vol. III, p. 74.

[60a] *Trial and Condemnation of Joan of Arc*, vol. III, p. 72, the testimony of Louis Leconte.

[61] *Trial and Condemnation of Joan of Arc*, vol. III, p. 72, the testimony of Louis Leconte.

[62] *Proceedings of the Rehabilitation*, vol. III, p. 87.

[63] *Proceedings of the Rehabilitation*, vol. III, p. 124.

[64] *Proceedings of the Rehabilitation*, vol. III, p. 110.

[65] *Proceedings of the Rehabilitation*, vol. III, pp. 108-109.

[66] The same.

[67] The same.

[68] The same, p. 179.

[69] *Proceedings of the Rehabilitation*, vol. III, pp. 69-70.

[70] *Trial and Condemnation*, vol. I, p. 29.

[71] *Proceedings of the Rehabilitation*, vol. III, pp. 69-70.

[72] The same.

[73] *Proceedings of the Rehabilitation*, vol. III, p. 70.

[74] The same.

[75] The same.

[76] *Journal of the Siege of Orleans*, vol. III, p. 171.

[77] *Journal of the Siege of Orleans*, vol. III, p. 171.

[78] *Trial and Condemnation*, vol. I, p. 49.

[79] *Chronicle of the Maid*, pp. 220-224, cited by Quicherat, vol. IV. Also the *Journal of the Siege of Orleans*.

[80] *Chronicle of the Maid*, p. 224.

[81] *Chronicle of the Maid*, p. 225.

[82] The same.

[83] John Chartier, vol. IV, p. 57. Given by Quicherat.

[84] John Chartier, vol. IV, p. 58, cited by Quicherat. The decision of the council is here given literally from the records. There can be no doubt on this abominable attempt at treason.

[85] John Chartier, vol. IV, p. 58.

[86] John Chartier, vol. IV, p. 59.

[87] John Chartier, vol. IV, p, 60.

[88] The same.

[89] Deposition of Simon Charles, Master of Petitions. *Proceedings of the Rehabilitation*, vol. III, p. 117; *Chronicle of the Maid*, p. 227; John Chartier, vol. IV, p. 50. All the chronicles are in accord on this so capital fact.

[90] Testimony of Simon Charles.

[91] *Chronicle of Percival of Cagny*, vol. IV, p. 171.

[92] *Journal of the Siege of Orleans*, vol. IV, p. 179.

[93] Literally the testimony of John Pasquerel, Joan's confessor, who confessed her that very day. (*Proceedings of the Rehabilitation*, vol. III, pp. 108-109.)

[94] *Trial and Condemnation*, vol. I, p. 79.

[95] Testimony of Colette, wife of Millet, *Proceedings of the Rehabilitation*, vol. III, p. 124.

[96] *Journal of the Siege of Orleans*, vol. IV, p. 160.

[97] *Journal of the Siege of Orleans*, vol. IV, p. 160.

[98] *Journal of the Siege of Orleans*, vol. IV, p. 166.

[99] The same.

[100] *Journal of the Siege of Orleans*, vol. IV, p. 166.

[101] *Proceedings of the Rehabilitation*, vol. II, p. 180.

[102] Testimony of the Duke of Alençon, *Proceedings of the Rehabilitation*, vol. II, p. 79.

[103] *Chronicle of the Maid*, vol. III, p. 129.

[104] Testimony of Gerardin of Epinal, *Proceedings of the Rehabilitation*, vol. II, p. 421.

[105] This letter is taken literally from the Archives of Lille. See also Quicherat, vol. V, p. 126.

[106] With some abridgment, the text of this chronicle is cited almost literally.

[107] Latin, *from the egg*, i.e., the beginning.

[108] Rymer, cited by Quicherat, vol. X, p. 459.

[109] The same.

[110] Rymer, cited by Quicherat, vol. X, p. 459.

[111] Rogier, cited by Quicherat, vol. V, pp. 168-169.

[112] Fowler, bird-catcher.

[113] *Tractatus de haersi pauperum de Lugduno*, cited by Marten in his *Thesaurus of Anecdotes*, vol. V, collected 1787.

[114] This answer of Joan, together with all the others, and all the questions and decrees of the judges throughout the trial, are taken literally from the records.

[115] "*Medicina animae dictae Joannae*", literally, *Trial and Condemnation*, vol. I, p. 297.

[116] These inscriptions are all recorded by an eye-witness, Clement of Franquenberg; see Quicherat, vol. IV, p. 460.

[117] For the repentance of Canon Loyseleur, see *The Proceedings of the Rehabilitation of Joan of Arc*, vol. II, p. 178.

Lightning Source UK Ltd.
Milton Keynes UK
UKHW011822040123
414830UK00005B/392